CAN'T EVEN

Can't Even

How Millennials Became
the Burnout Generation

ANNE HELEN
PETERSEN

Chatto & Windus
LONDON

13 5 7 9 10 8 6 4 2

Chatto & Windus, an imprint of Vintage,
20 Vauxhall Bridge Road,
London SW1V 2SA

Chatto & Windus is part of the Penguin Random House group of companies
whose addresses can be found at global.penguinrandomhouse.com.

Penguin
Random House
UK

First published in the US by Houghton Mifflin Harcourt in 2020
First published in the UK by Chatto & Windus in 2021

penguin.co.uk/vintage

A CIP catalogue record for this book is available from the British Library

ISBN 9781784743345

Printed and bound in Great Britain by Clays Ltd, Elcograf S.p.A.

Penguin Random House is committed to a sustainable future
for our business, our readers and our planet. This book is made
from Forest Stewardship Council® certified paper.

MIX
Paper from
responsible sources
FSC® C018179

CONTENTS

AUTHOR'S NOTE

"MILLENNIALS DON'T STAND A CHANCE." THAT'S HOW Annie Lowrey titled her piece, several weeks into widespread quarantine amidst the spread of COVID-19, detailing the myriad ways the millennials generation is indeed screwed. "The Millennials entered the workforce during the worst downturn since the Great Depression," she writes. "Saddled with debt, unable to accumulate wealth, and stuck in low-benefit, dead-end jobs, they never gained the financial security that their parents, grandparents, or even older siblings enjoyed." And now, right when we should be reaching our "peak earning years," we're faced with "an economic cataclysm more severe than the Great Recession, near guaranteeing that they will be the first generation in modern American history to end up poorer than their parents."[1]

For many millennials, articles like Lowrey's feel less like a revelation than a confirmation: Yes, we're screwed, but we've known we're screwed for years. Even as the stock market rose and official unemployment numbers fell in the supposedly halcyon economy of the late 2010s, very few of us felt anything close to *secure*. In truth, we were just waiting for the other shoe to drop, for the bottom to fall out, for whatever metaphor you want to choose to describe the feeling of just barely arriving at something like financial or job security, while also feeling certain that it could and would all disappear. It wouldn't matter how hard you worked or for how long, how much you devoted yourself to your job, how much you *cared*. You'd find yourself back in that lonely, panicky place, wondering all over again how the road map set out for you — promising that if you do this, and you'll arrive at *this* — could've proven so very wrong.

But again: Few millennials are surprised. We don't expect jobs, or the companies that provide them, to last. So many of us live under storms of debt threatening to swallow us up at any moment. We're exhausted by the labor of trying to maintain some sort of equilibrium: for our kids, in our relationships, in our financial lives. We've been conditioned to precarity.

For millions of people and communities in the United States and across the world, precarity has been a way of life for decades. To live in poverty, or to live as a refugee, is to be conditioned to it. The difference, then, is that this was not the narrative that millennials — particularly white, middle-class millennials — were sold about themselves. Like the generations before us, we were raised on a diet of meritocracy and exceptionalism: that each of us was overflowing with potential and all we needed to activate it was hard work and dedication. If we worked hard, no matter our current station in life, we would find stability.

Long before the spread of COVID-19, millennials had begun to come to terms with just how hollow, how deeply and depressingly fantastical, that story really was. We understood that people keep telling it, to their kids and their peers, in *New York Times* editorials and in how-to books, because to stop would be tantamount to admitting that it's not just the American Dream that's broken; it's America. That the refrains we return to—that we're a land of opportunity, that we're a benevolent world super-power—are false. That's a deeply discombobulating realization, but it's one that people who haven't navigated our world with the privileges of whiteness, middle-class-ness, or citizenship have understood for some time. Some people are just now realizing the extent of the brokenness. Others have understood it, and mourned it, their entire lives.

Writing this from the middle of the pandemic, it's become apparent that COVID-19 is the great clarifier. It clarifies what and who in your life matters, what things are needs and what are wants, who is thinking of others and who is thinking only of themselves. It has clarified that the workers dubbed "essential" are, in truth, treated as expendable, and it has made decades of systemic racism—and resultant vulnerability to the disease— indelible. It has highlighted the ineptitude of our current federal leadership, the dangers of long-term, cultivated mistrust of science, and the ramifications of allowing the production of medical equipment to be run like a business where profits matter above all else. Our medical system is broken. Our relief program is broken. Our testing capability is broken. America is broken, and we, too, along with it.

When COVID-19 first began its spread in China, I was finishing the final edits to this book. When cities began shutting down, my editor and I began wondering how we could address the seismic emotional and economic and physical changes that have accompanied the spread of the disease. But I didn't want to wedge commentary into each chapter, pretending each section had been written with these new shifts just slightly out of mind. That would be harder, but it would also feel weirder, falser.

Instead, I want to invite readers to think of every argument in this book, every anecdote, every hope for change, as amplified and emboldened. Work was shitty and precarious before; now it's *more* shitty and precarious. Parenting felt exhausting and impossible; now it's *more* exhausting and impossible. Same for the feeling that work never ends, that the news cycle suffocates our inner lives, and that we're too tired to access anything resembling true leisure or rest. The fallout of the next few years won't change millennials' relationship to burnout and the precarity that fuels it. If anything, it will become even more ingrained in our generational identity.

But it doesn't have to be this way. That's the refrain of this book, and that, too, remains true. Maybe all we need to act on that feeling is an irrefutable pivot point: an opportunity not just for reflection, but to build a different design, a different way of life, from the rubble and clarity brought forth by this pandemic. I'm not talking about utopia, per se. I'm talking about a different way of thinking about work, and personal value, and profit incentives — and the radical idea that each of us matter, and are *actually* essential and worthy of care and protection. Not because of our capacity to work, but simply because we are. If you think that's too radical of an idea, I don't know how to make you care about other people.

It's true, as Lowrey puts it, that millennials don't stand a chance. At least not in this current system. But the same dire prediction holds true for large swaths of Gen X and boomers, and will only get worse for Gen Z. The overarching clarity offered by this pandemic is that it's not any single generation that's broken, or fucked, or failed. It's the system itself.

INTRODUCTION

"I THINK YOU'RE DEALING WITH SOME BURNOUT," MY editor at BuzzFeed very kindly suggested over Skype. "You could use a few days off."

It was November 2018, and frankly, I was insulted by the idea. "I'm not burnt out," I replied. "I'm just trying to figure out what I want to write about next."

For as long as I could remember, I'd been working pretty much nonstop: first as a grad student, then as a professor, now as a journalist. Throughout 2016 and 2017, I had been following political candidates around the country, chasing stories, often writing thousands of words a day. One week in November, I went straight from interviewing the survivors of a mass shooting in Texas to spending a week in a tiny Utah town, hearing the stories of dozens of women who'd fled a polygamous sect. The work was vital and exhilarating — which was exactly why it felt so hard to stop. Plus, I'd had rest after the election. I was supposed to be refreshed. The fact that I'd found myself fighting tears every time I talked to my editors? Totally unrelated.

Still, I agreed to take a few days off, right before Thanksgiving. And do you know what I did with them? Tried to write a book proposal. Not for this book, but a far worse, more forced one. Obviously, that didn't make me feel better, because I was just working even *more*. But by that point, I wasn't really feeling anything at all. Sleep didn't help; neither did exercise. I got a massage and a facial and they were nice, but the effects were incredibly temporary. Reading sort of helped, but the reading that interested me most was politics-related, which just circled me back to the issues that had exhausted me.

What I was feeling in November wasn't anything new, either. For months, whenever I thought about going to bed, I felt overwhelmed by the steps I'd have to take to responsibly get from the couch to the bed. I felt underwhelmed by vacations — or, more precisely, like vacation was just another thing to get through on my to-do list. I at once resented and craved time with friends, but after I relocated from New York to Montana, I refused to devote time to actually make new ones. I felt numb, impervious, just totally . . . flat.

In hindsight, I was absolutely, ridiculously, 100 percent burnt out — but I didn't recognize it as such, because the way I felt didn't match the way burnout had ever been depicted or described to me. There was no dramatic flameout, no collapse, no recovery on a beach or in an isolated cabin. I thought burnout was like a cold you catch and recover from — which is why I missed the diagnosis altogether. I had been a pile of embers, smoldering for months.

When my editor suggested I was burning out, I balked: Like

other type-A overachievers, I didn't hit walls, I worked around them. Burning out ran counter to everything that I had thus far understood about my ability to work, and my identity as a journalist. Yet even as I refused to call it burnout, there was evidence that something inside me was, well, broken: My to-do list, specifically the bottom half of it, just kept recycling itself from one week to the next, a neat little stack of shame.

None of these tasks was essential, not really. They were just the humdrum maintenance of everyday life. But no matter what I did, I couldn't bring myself to take the knives to get sharpened, or drop off my favorite boots to get resoled, or complete the paperwork and make the phone call and find the stamp so that my dog could be properly registered. There was a box in the corner of my room with a gift for a friend I'd been meaning to send for months, and a contact lens rebate for a not-insignificant amount of money sitting on my counter. All of these high-effort, low-gratification tasks seemed equally impossible.

And I knew I wasn't the only one with this sort of to-do list resistance: The internet overflowed with stories of people who couldn't bring themselves to figure out how to register to vote, or submit insurance claims, or return an online clothes order. If I couldn't figure out what I wanted to write for my job, at least I could write about what I jokingly termed "errand paralysis." I started by sorting through a vast array of articles, mostly written by millennials, and mostly published on millennial-oriented websites, on the everyday stresses of "adulting"—a word adopted to describe the fear of doing or pride in completing tasks associated with our parents. As one piece put it, "The modern Millennial, for the most part, views adulthood as a series of actions, as opposed to a state of being. Adulting therefore becomes a verb." And part of adulting is getting the things done on the bottom half of your to-do list, even if they're hard.

As I read, it became clear that there are actually three types of adulting tasks: 1) the kind that are annoying because you've never done them before (taxes, making friends outside the framework of school); 2) the kind that are annoying because they underline that being an adult means spending money on things that are no fun at all (vacuums, lawnmowers, razors); 3) the kind that are more than just annoying—they're time-consuming and unnecessarily labyrinthian (finding a therapist, submitting medical reimbursement bills, canceling cable service, quitting your gym, consolidating your student loans, figuring out if and how to access state support programs).

Adulting—and, by extension, completing your to-do list— is hard, then, because living in the modern world is somehow both easier than it's ever been and yet *unfathomably* complicated. Within this framework, it was clear why I was avoiding each task loitering on my to-do list. Every day, we all have a list of things that need to get done, places where our mental energy must be allocated first. But that energy is finite, and when you keep trying to pretend that it isn't—that's when burnout arrives.

But my burnout was more than the accumulation of undone errands. If I was honest with myself—actually honest, in the sort of way that makes you feel uncomfortable—the errands were just the most tangible indication of a much larger affliction. Something wasn't just wrong in my day-to-day. Something had been increasingly wrong for most of my adult life.

The truth was, all of those tasks would take away from what had become my ultimate task, and the task of so many other millennials: working all the time. Where had I learned to work all the time? School. Why did I work all the time? Because I was terrified of not getting a job. Why have I worked all the time since actually finding one? Because I'm terrified of losing it, and because my value as a worker and my value as a person have become intractably intertwined. I couldn't shake the feeling of *precariousness* — that all that I'd worked for could just disappear — or reconcile it with an idea that had surrounded me since I was a child: that if I just worked hard enough, everything would pan out.

So I made a reading list. I read about how poverty and economic instability affects our decision-making abilities. I explored specific trends in student debt and home ownership. I saw how "concerted cultivation" parenting trends in the '80s and '90s connected to the shift from free, unstructured play to organized activities and sports leagues. A framework started to emerge — and I put that framework squarely on top of my own life, forcing me to reconsider my own history, and the way I've narrativized it. I went on a long walk with my partner, who, unlike my "old millennial" self, grew up right in the peak of millennial-ness, in an even more academically and financially competitive environment. We compared notes: What changed in the handful of years between my childhood and his? How did our parents model and promote an idea of work as wholly devouring? What did we internalize as the purpose of "leisure"? What happened in grad school that exacerbated my workaholic tendencies? Why did I feel great about writing my dissertation on Christmas?

I started writing, trying to answer these questions, and couldn't stop. The draft ballooned: 3,000 words, 7,000, 11,000. I wrote 4,000 words in one day and felt like I'd written nothing at all. I was giving shape to the condition that had become so familiar, so omnipresent, that I'd ceased to recognize it as a condition. It was just my life. But now I was amassing language to describe it.

This wasn't just about my individual experience of work or errand paralysis or burnout. It was about a work ethic and anxiety and exhaustion particular to the world I grew up in, the context in which I applied to college and tried to get a job, the reality of living through the biggest economic collapse since the Great Depression, and the rapid spread and ubiquity of digital technologies and social media. In short: It was about being a millennial.

*   *   *

"Burnout" was first recognized as a psychological diagnosis in 1974, applied by the psychologist Herbert Freudenberger to cases of physical or mental collapse as the result of overwork.[1] Burnout is of a substantively different category than "exhaustion," although the two conditions are related. Exhaustion means going to the point where you can't go any further; burnout means reaching that point and pushing yourself to keep going, whether for days or weeks or years.

When you're in the midst of burnout, the feeling of accomplishment that follows an exhausting task—passing the final! finishing the massive work project!—never comes. "The exhaustion experienced in burnout combines an intense yearning for this state of completion with the tormenting sense that it cannot be attained, that there is always some demand or anxiety or distraction which can't be silenced," Josh Cohen, a psychoanalyst specializing in burnout, writes. "You feel burnout when you've exhausted all your internal resources, yet cannot free yourself of the nervous compulsion to go on regardless."[2] It's the sensation of dull exhaustion that, even with sleep and vacation, never really leaves. It's the knowledge that you're just barely keeping your head above water, and even the slightest shift—a sickness, a busted car, a broken water heater—could sink you and your family. It's the flattening of life into one never-ending to-do list, and the feeling that you've optimized yourself into a work robot that happens to have bodily functions, which you do your very best to ignore. It's the feeling that your mind, as Cohen puts it, has turned to ash.

In his writing about burnout, Cohen is careful to note its antecedents: "melancholic world-weariness," as he puts it, is noted in the book of Ecclesiastes, diagnosed by Hippocrates, and endemic to the Renaissance, a symptom of bewilderment with the feeling of "relentless change." In the late 1800s, "neurasthenia," or nervous exhaustion, afflicted patients run down by the "pace and strain of modern industrial life." Burnout as a generalized condition is nothing (entirely) new.

But contemporary burnout differs in its intensity and its prevalence. People patching together a retail job with unpredictable scheduling while driving Uber and arranging childcare have burnout. Startup workers with fancy catered lunches, free laundry service, and seventy-minute commutes have burnout. Academics teaching four adjunct classes and surviving on food stamps while trying to publish research to snag a tenure-track job have burnout. Freelance graphic artists operating on their own schedule without healthcare or paid time off have burnout. Burnout has become so pervasive that in May 2019, the World Health Organization officially recognized it as an "occupational phenomenon," resulting from "chronic workplace stress that has not been successfully managed."[3] Increasingly—and increasingly among millennials—burnout isn't just a temporary affliction. It's our contemporary condition.

In a way, it makes sense that millennials are feeling this phenomenon most acutely: Despite the fact that this generation is often portrayed as a bunch of underachieving college students, in actuality, we are currently living through some of the most erratic, anxiety-filled years of adulthood. According to Pew Research Center, the youngest millennials, born in 1996, will turn twenty-four in 2020. The oldest, born in 1981, will turn thirty-nine. And population projections suggest there are now more of us in the United States — 73 million — than any other generation.[4] We're not seeking our first jobs, but trying to take the next steps, and confronting pay ceilings in the ones we have. We're not just paying off our own student debt, but figuring out how to start saving for our young children. We're balancing skyrocketing housing prices *and* childcare costs *and* health insurance premiums. And the promised security of adulthood never seems to arrive, no matter how hard we try to organize our lives, or tighten our already tight budgets.

Until the term "millennial" coalesced around our generation, there were other names vying to label the millions of people born after Generation X. Each gives you a sense of how we were defined in the popular imagination: There was "Generation Me," which put a fine point on our perceived self-centeredness, and "Echo Boomers," a reference to the fact that the vast majority of our parents are members of the single largest (and most influential) generation in American history.

The name "millennial" — and much of the anxiety that still surrounds it — emerged in the mid-2000s, when the first wave of us were entering the workforce. Our expectations were too high, we were scolded, and our work ethic too low. We were sheltered and naive, unschooled in the ways of the world — understandings that have ossified around our generation, with little regard to the ways we confronted and weathered the Great Recession, how much student debt we're shouldering, and how inaccessible so many milestones of adulthood have become.

Ironically, the most famous characterization of millennials is that we believe that everyone should get a medal, no matter how poorly they did in the race. And while we do, as a generation, struggle to shed the idea that we're each unique and worthy in some way, talk to most millennials and the thing they'll tell you about growing up isn't that they conceived of themselves as special, but that "success," broadly defined, was the most important thing in their world. You work hard to get into college, you work hard in college, you work hard in your job, and you'll be a success. It's a different sort of work ethic than "work the fields from dawn to dusk," but that doesn't mean it's not work ethic.

Still, the millennial reputation lingers. Part of its resilience, as will soon become clear, can be attributed to long germinating anxieties about '80s and '90s parenting practices, as boomers translated residual anxieties about the way they raised us into critiques of the generation at large. But part of it, too, stems from the fact that many of us did have high expectations and incongruous ideas about how the world works—expectations and ideas we'd internalized from a complicated, self-reinforcing nexus of parents, teachers, friends, and the media that surrounded us. For millennials, the predominant message of our upbringing was deceptively simple: All roads should lead to college, and from there, with more work, we'd find the American Dream, which might no longer include a picket fence, but certainly had a family, and financial security, and something like happiness as a result.

We were raised to believe that if we worked hard enough, we could win the system—of American capitalism and meritocracy—or at least live comfortably within it. But something happened in the late 2010s. We looked up from our work and realized, there's no winning the system when the system itself is broken. We're the first generation since the Great Depression where many of us will find ourselves worse off than our parents. The overarching trend of upward mobility has finally reversed itself, smack dab into the prime earning years of our lives. We're drowning in student debt—an estimated $37,000 per debtor—

that's permanently stunted our financial lives. We're moving in greater numbers to some of the most expensive zip codes in the country, in search of the intense, high-profile job of our dreams. We're saving far less and devoting far more of our monthly income to paying for childcare, rent or, if we're lucky enough to somehow get the money for a down payment, a mortgage. The poorest among us are getting poorer, and those in the middle class are struggling to remain there.

And that's just the financial baseline. We're also more anxious and more depressed. Most of us would rather read a book than stare at our phones, but we're so tired that mindless scrolling is all we have energy to do. We're more likely to have bad insurance, if we have it all, and little by means of a retirement plan. Our parents are inching toward the age at which they're going to need more and more of our help, financial and otherwise.

The only way to make it all work is to employ relentless focus — to never, ever stop moving. But at some point, something's going to give. It's the student debt, but it's more. It's the economic downturn, but it's more. It's the lack of good jobs, but it's more. It's the overarching feeling that you're trying to build a solid foundation on quicksand. It's the feeling, as the sociologist Eric Klinenberg puts it, that "vulnerability is in the air."[5] Millennials live with the reality that we're going to work forever, die before we pay off our student loans, potentially bankrupt our children with our care, or get wiped out in a global apocalypse. That might sound like hyperbole — but that's the new normal, and the weight of living amidst that sort of emotional, physical, and financial precarity is staggering, especially when so many of the societal institutions that have previously provided guidance and stability, from the church to democracy, seem to be failing us.

It feels like it's harder than ever to keep our lives — and our family's lives — in order, financially solvent, and prepared for the future, especially as we're asked to adhere to exacting, and often contradictory expectations. We should work hard but exude "work/life balance." We should be incredibly attentive mothers, but not helicopter ones. We should engage in equal partnerships with our wives, but still maintain our masculinity. We should build our brands on social media, but live our lives authentically. We should be current, conversant, and opinionated about the breakneck news cycle, but somehow not let the reality of it affect our ability to do any of the above tasks.

Trying to do all of that at once, with little support or safety net—that's what makes millennials the burnout generation. People from other generations have been burnt out; that's not a question. Burnout, after all, is a symptom of living in our modern capitalist society. And in many ways, our hardships pale in comparison. We did not weather a Great Depression, or the catastrophic loss of life that accompanied a world war. Scientific advances and modern medicine have increased our standard of living in many meaningful ways, but our financial calamity has nonetheless changed the economic trajectory of our lives; our wars are not "great" ones, but they are deeply unpopular forever wars that drain our trust in government, fought by those in economic situations where the military is the only route to stability. And then there's climate change, which requires a global effort and systemic rewiring so massive that no generation or even nation can address it alone.

There's a pervasive feeling that despite some of the legitimate wonders of modern society, our potential has been capped. And yet we strive, because we know nothing else. For millennials, burnout is foundational: the best way to describe who we've been raised to be, how we interact with and think about the world, and our everyday experience thereof. And it isn't an isolated experience. It's our base temperature.

* * *

The millennial burnout piece that finally made its way online, attracting more than seven million readers, was a personal essay stretched to try to encompass the experience of a generation. The response suggested that, in some crucial ways, it had. One woman told me she'd worn herself so thin in her prestigious grad school program that she had to quit, then spent the last year working at a dog kennel, scooping poop and cleaning. An elementary school teacher in Alabama kept getting told that she was a "saint" for the work that she was doing, even though she has fewer and fewer resources to do her job. She quit this spring. A mother of two wrote me: "I recently described myself to my therapist as a 'walking to-do list' who 'only exists from the neck up.'" There were thousands of impassioned emails, many several pages long, and more come in every day. It gradually became clear to me that I'd simply articulated what to that point had been largely unspeakable. We didn't have a common vocabulary across our generation — and thus struggled to articulate the specifics of what was happening to those outside our generation.

But that was just the beginning. What you'll find over the next couple hundred pages is an attempt to expand and elaborate on that original piece, drawing on extensive academic and historical research, over three thousand responses to surveys I created, and countless interviews and conversations. You can't understand the way we live now without looking deeply at the economic and cultural forces that shaped our childhoods — and the pressures our parents faced as they raised us. So we'll examine them. We'll look at the massive, macro-level shifts in the way that labor is organized and valued, as well as the way "risk" — on the job, in finances — is distributed between companies and those who make them run. We explore what it is about social media that's so exhausting, how leisure disappeared, why parenting has become "all joy and no fun," and how work got so shitty—and has stayed that way—for so many of us.

This is still a book informed by my own experience of burnout, but I've attempted to expand the understanding of what burnout feels like beyond the presumed bourgeois experience. Because the way that the word *millennial* has typically been deployed—to talk about our high expectations, laziness, and tendency to "destroy" entire industries, like napkins or wedding rings—has been to describe the stereotypical behaviors of a particular subset of the millennial population: one that is almost always middle class, and often white.

And that's simply not the reality for millions of millennials. Of the 73 million millennials living in the US in 2018, 21 percent, over a fifth of the population, identify as Hispanic. Twenty-five percent speak a language other than English at home. Only 39 percent of millennials have a college degree.[6] Just because burnout has become a defining millennial experience doesn't mean that every millennial experience of it is the same. If a white middle-class person feels exhausted reading the news, what does an undocumented person navigating the world endure? If it's tedious to deal with implicit sexism in the workplace, how about adding in some not-so-implicit racism? How does burnout work differently when you don't have access to generational wealth? How does student debt sting more when you're the first in your family to go to college?

Decentering the white middle-class millennial experience as *the* millennial experience is an ongoing and essential aspect of this project. I find myself returning to the words of Tiana Clark, who wrote a piece on the specifics of Black burnout in response to my own: "No matter the movement or era," she wrote, "being burned out has been the steady state of black people in this country for hundreds of years."[7] And while many white Americans are attempting to reclaim economic security, that sort of security has *always* been elusive for Black Americans. As the sociologist Tressie McMillan Cottom makes clear, in today's economy, "achieving upward mobility, even in thriving cities that compete for tech jobs, private capital, and national recognition, is as complicated as it was in 1962," during the March on Washington. "In that economy," Cottom explains, "black Americans hustled in the face of legal racial segregation and social stigma that cordoned us off from opportunities reserved for white Americans. In 2020, Black Americans can legally access the major on-ramps to opportunity — college, workplaces, public schools, neighborhoods, transportation, electoral politics — but despite hustling like everyone else, they do not have much to show for it."[8]

I remember the first-generation Chinese immigrant who messaged me after the piece, telling me that she never heard the words "anxiety" or "depression" in her home growing up. "I heard the terms 吃苦 ('eating bitterness') and 性情 ('heart feeling') as both my parents felt the depression that is common for newcomers to Canada, struggling to find stable work in a society that places white folks above all others," she explained. "Accepting the fact that I, too, can be burned out, depressed, and anxious while still being a Chinese person has been a tough process."

And I think of a report from the Pew Research Center, examining the difference in student debt and home ownership between generations. That's useful, but using stats for the entire generation leaves another story untold: how millennial student debt as a whole has ballooned, but for Black Americans, especially those who attended predatory for-profit colleges, it has skyrocketed. A recent study examining the fate of loans taken out by students in 2004 found that by 2015, 48.7 percent of Black borrowers had defaulted, compared to 21.4 percent of white borrowers.[9] That's not just a significant statistical difference; that's another version of the millennial narrative altogether.

Different types of millennials have experienced the road to burnout, well, *differently,* whether in terms of class, parental expectations, location, or cultural community. After all, so much of generational identity has to do with your age/place within the generation at the time of massive cultural, technological, and geopolitical events. For example: I spent my college years taking pictures on my Vivitar and getting them developed weeks later. But so many millennials had to figure out college and adulthood at the same time they began to navigate Facebook and what it meant to represent themselves online. Some millennials experienced the attacks on 9/11 as an abstract event, inconceivable to their elementary school minds; others endured years of harassment and suspicion because of their religious or ethnic identity.

And then there's the Great Recession. As an old millennial, I was already in grad school by the time the bank bailouts and the foreclosures started happening. But others finished high school or college and stepped right into the financial crisis, giving them little option than to do the thing for which our generation would later be roundly ridiculed: move back home. At the same time, tens of thousands of millennials watched their parents lose jobs, the homes they grew up in, their retirement savings—making it harder, if not impossible, to move back home. Some millennials' experience of the recession was realizing how fortunate they were to have a safety net; others' was realizing how far you can fall without one.

What we talk about when we talk about millennials, then, depends on who's doing the talking. These events, and their aftermaths, have made us who we are—but they've made us differently. This book cannot fully cover any version of the millennial experience, including the white middle-class one. That's not an abdication of responsibility, but an acknowledgment: This is the start of the conversation, and an invitation to talk more. There's no burnout Olympics. The most generous thing we can do for others is to attempt to not just see, but really and truly *understand,* the parameters of someone else's experience. In short, acknowledging someone else's burnout does not diminish your own.

In writing that article, and this book, I haven't cured anyone's burnout, including my own. But one thing did become incredibly clear: This isn't a personal problem. It's a societal one — and it will not be cured by productivity apps, or a bullet journal, or face mask skin treatments, or overnight fucking oats. We gravitate toward those personal cures because they seem tenable, and promise that our lives can be recentered, and regrounded, with just a bit more discipline, a new app, a better email organization strategy, or a new approach to meal planning. But these are all merely Band-Aids on an open wound. They might temporarily stop the bleeding, but when they fall off, and we fail at our new-found discipline, we just feel worse.

Before we can start fighting what is very much a structural battle, we first need to understand it as such. That might seem intimidating, but any easily implementable life hack or book promising to unfuck your life is just prolonging the problem. The only way to move forward is to create a vocabulary and a framework that allows us to see ourselves — and the systems that have contributed to our burnout — clearly.

That might not seem like much. But it is an essential beginning, an acknowledgment, and a declaration: *It doesn't have to be this way.*

CAN'T EVEN

1

Our Burnt-Out Parents

"YOU THINK YOU'RE BURNT OUT? TRY SURVIVING THE Great Depression and World War II!" In the wake of the millennial burnout piece, that was the most common critique in my inbox. The sentiment usually came from boomers, who, somewhat ironically, had endured neither the Great Depression nor World War II. Other greatest hits: "Buck up, life is hard" and "I worked my tail off in the '80s, and you don't see me complaining about being burnt out." These statements are variations of what I've come to understand as the boomer refrain: *Stop whining, millennials—you don't know what hard work is.*

The thing is, whether they realize it or not, boomers were the ones who taught us not only to expect more from our careers, but to consider our thoughts on the state of work, and our exhaustion, important: worth expressing (especially in therapy, which was slowly becoming normalized) and worth addressing. If we're as special, and unique, and important as we were told we were throughout childhood, it's no surprise we refuse to shut up when our lives don't make us feel that way. And that can often-times sound like *complaining*, especially to boomers.

In truth, millennials are boomers' worst nightmare because, in many cases, we were once their most well-intentioned dream. And in conversations about boomers and millennials, that's the connection that's often left out: the fact that boomers are, in many ways, responsible for us, both literally (as our parents, teachers, and coaches) and figuratively (creating the ideologies and economic environment that would shape us).

For years, millennials and Gen-Xers have chafed at critiques from boomers but couldn't do much about it. Boomers had us outnumbered and surrounded: Our parents were boomers, but so were so many of our bosses, and professors, and superiors in the workplace. What we could do was roast them online using memes. "Old Economy Steve" first appeared on Reddit in 2012, pairing a 1970s high school portrait with a caption suggesting he's now your market-loving dad who won't shut up about how you should really start putting money into your 401k. Subsequent iterations narrativized his economic privilege: DRIVES UP FEDERAL DEFICIT FOR 30 YEARS / HANDS THE BILL TO HIS KIDS, one version of the meme exclaims; "WHEN I WAS IN COLLEGE MY SUMMER JOB PAID THE TUITION" / TUITION WAS $400 says another.[1]

More recently, on TikTok, Gen Z popularized the phrase "OK Boomer" as a reaction to someone with an outdated, intractable, and/or bigoted point of view. It could be directed, as Taylor Lorenz pointed out in the *New York Times,* toward "basically any person over 30 who says something condescending about young people — and the issues they care about." But the contemporary connotation of "boomer" as condescending and single-minded is worth noting.[2]

It's not just that boomers are old or uncool; every generation gets old and uncool. Boomers are increasingly positioned as hypocritical, unempathetic, completely unaware of just how easy they had it — the generational equivalent of being born on third base and thinking you hit a triple. This criticism emerged forcefully in 2019: the year boomers were projected to cede their status as the largest generation to millennials. To be fair, Gen-Xers have a long and glorious history of boomer antagonism. Yet this particular argument was popularized, particularly online, as the tangible differences between boomers' and millennials' financial situations have become more pronounced.

Whether or not someone is familiar with the stats — that, say, the net worth of millennials, according to a 2018 study commissioned by the Federal Reserve, is 20 percent lower than that of boomers at the same point in their lives, or that boomers' family income was 14 percent higher when they were millennials' current age — they can still intuit boomers' role in our current generational divide. As the comedian Dan Sheehan put it in 2019, in a tweet that's been liked more than 200,000 times, "Baby Boomers did that thing where you leave a single square of toilet paper on the roll and pretend it's not your turn to change it, but with a whole society."

I shared that animosity — and reading all those emails from boomers only stoked my anger. But as I began reading more and more about the currents that contributed to the massive expansion of the American middle class, it became clear that while boomers, as a generation, *grew up* in a period of unprecedented economic stability, their adulthoods were marked with many of the same pressures of our own: generalized scorn from their parents' generation, particularly around their perceived entitlement and aimlessness, and panic over the ability to maintain (or obtain) a spot in the middle class.

Boomers were anxious and overworked and deeply resentful of the critiques levied at them. The problem, and why it's often hard to think of them charitably, is their inability to tap that experience in order to empathize with their own children's generation. But that doesn't mean that their anxiety, or attitude toward work, didn't influence us. The boomer ethos of the '80s and '90s was the backdrop of our childhood, the foundation for so many of our ideas about what our future could look like, and the roadmap to achieve it. To understand millennial burnout, then, we have to understand what shaped — and, in many cases, burnt out — the boomers that made us.

*   *   *

Boomers were born between 1946 and 1964, the eighteen-year "baby boom" that began with the economic recovery of World War II and accelerated as soldiers returned home. They became the biggest, and most influential, generation the United States had ever seen. Today, there are 73 million boomers in America, and 72 percent of them are white. Donald Trump is a boomer — so is Elizabeth Warren. They're now in their sixties and seventies, parents, grandparents, and in some cases great-grandparents, retiring and grappling with the aging process. But back in the 1970s, they were in the position that many millennials find themselves now: entering the workplace for the first time, getting married, and figuring out what raising a family might look like.

The cliched understanding of the '70s is that society was, as a whole, in retreat: still recovering from the hangover of the '60s, backing away from activism, and embracing a newfound focus on the self. In *New York Magazine,* the author Tom Wolfe famously dubbed the '70s "The Me Decade," describing, in hypnotic detail, boomers' obsession with self-improvement through threesomes, spiritualism, Scientology, or organic co-ops.[3] "The old alchemical dream was changing base metal into gold," Wolfe wrote. "The new alchemical dream is: changing one's personality—remaking, remodeling, elevating, and polishing one's very *self*... and observing, studying, and doting on it. (Me!)" Self-care, but with a very '70s hue.

It will surprise no one that the tendencies Wolfe described and softly lampooned in his article were actually those of the professional middle class: people with the means, financial and temporal, to pay more for groceries or spend their weekends attending deep-breathing seminars in hotel ballrooms. But beneath that supposedly self-obsessed turn was a shared anxiety, spreading across the nation: a creeping realization that after decades of prosperity, things in America seemed to be getting markedly worse.

More specifically: the train ride of growth and progress that had marked boomers' entire lives had significantly slowed. There were multiple, interlocking reasons for this deceleration, and they all come back to versions of the same narrative, which begins something like this: Amidst the Depression, one of the most significant bills signed into law by President Franklin D. Roosevelt was the National Labor Relations Act of 1935, which granted legal protections to many employees in the private sector if and when they attempted to organize or join a union. The Labor Relations Act also gave that union "teeth": from that point forward, business owners were *legally required* to participate in collective bargaining, in which union representatives negotiate with business owners to establish a pay and benefits structure that applies to all union members. If an agreement could not be reached, union members could go on strike — and be legally protected from losing their jobs — until one was. With considerable risk, you could organize or join a union before 1935. But after 1935, you could organize or join a union with the law on your side.

A single employee could never stand up to the whims of management, but when every union employee did, it made them all the more powerful. And between 1934 and 1950, unions leveraged that power toward favorable working conditions. Depending on the workplace, "favorable" could mean a few things, all related to the general health and well-being of the worker: increased safety on the assembly line, say, or recourse for mistreatment, and regular breaks. It could mean an hourly wage high enough to support a middle-class lifestyle, what was colloquially known as the "family wage." Or, as stipulated by the Fair Labor Standards Act of 1938, getting paid overtime if your workweek exceeded forty-four hours, which helped prevent overwork, simply because it was more expensive for the company. "Favorable" could also mean healthcare, so you wouldn't go bankrupt paying medical bills or devote significant mental energy to worrying what would happen if you did, and a pension, which would keep you out of poverty as you aged. (It did not mean Ping-Pong tables at work, or free cab rides home after nine p.m., or catered lunches on Monday and Wednesday, or any of the other employee "perks" so often sold to millennials today as a means to paper over the fact that the employer is paying barely enough to afford rent in the city where it's located.)

Favorable work conditions were the result of robust unions, but they would've been impossible without what the labor scholar Jake Rosenfeld calls "an active state": a government invested in growing the middle class, working with big, healthy employers across the economic sector. Which is part of why this postwar period has become known as a time of "economic miracles," where unprecedented growth meant "average people everywhere had reason to feel good."[4] As you aged and grew weary, you could retire with a pension and/or Social Security, easing the burden on your children. Some call it the "Great Compression," a reference to the ways rich people became less rich and poor people became less poor as income distribution "compressed" into the middle class.

During this period, the Greatest Generation achieved the closest to equitable distribution of wealth that this country has ever seen. Companies were allocating more money to paying wages and benefits; CEOs were paid relatively little, especially compared with today, and in proportion to the rest of the employees of the company. (In 1950, CEOs made about 20 times more than the regular employee; by 2013, they made more than 204 times more.)[5] Corporations enjoyed "unrivaled economic progress," generated steady profits, invested in their employees, and experimented and innovated — in part because they were far less beholden to shareholders, who didn't yet expect the endless, exponential growth of today. "The jobs might have been repetitive, but so were the paychecks," the labor historian Louis Hyman writes. "Capitalism worked for nearly everyone."[6]

To be clear, the benefits of the Great Compression were not equally distributed. The protections fought for by unions, and granted by the US government, did not extend to the millions of workers in the home and in the field. When Social Security was first signed into law, it excluded federal and state employees; agricultural workers; and domestic, hotel, and laundry workers until 1954. As Hyman points out, the reforms of the 1930s may have been a "turning point" for white men, but not for the Black men and women who, in many parts of the country, were still governed by the restrictive Jim Crow laws. There were still deep pockets of poverty across the United States; employees, union or not, were periodically subject to layoffs during mini-recessions; the "family wage" was still a pipe dream to anyone working outside of a major corporation.

* * *

The 1950s and '60s weren't some immaculate golden age. But general volatility for companies — and for those on the job — was significantly lower than it is today. Following the economic and societal catastrophe of the Great Depression, the political scientist Jacob Hacker argues, "political and business leaders put in place new institutions designed to spread broadly the burden of key economic risks, including the risk of poverty in retirement, the risk of unemployment and disability, and the risk of widowhood due to the premature death of a breadwinner."[7] Some of these programs, like Social Security, would be "paid into" with every paycheck; others, like pensions, would be part of the employment contract. But the idea was the same: Some risks are just too great for the individual, on their own, to bear; instead, the risk should be spread across a much broader pool of people, thus blunting the effect when and if individual catastrophe does arrive.

When people talk about the growth of the middle class after World War II, then, they're talking about some sort of economic utopia — a massive growth in the number of people (largely, but not exclusively, white men) across the country, with or without college degrees, who were able to find economic security and relative equality for themselves and their families.[8] And as Hacker explains, it briefly expanded the "fundamental expectations" of the American Dream to millions.

This was the environment in which middle-class boomers grew up. Which was also why when some of them reached college age, they felt increasingly comfortable pushing back on the status quo. As Levinson explains, this era of economic stability "arguably engender[ed] the confidence that brought vocal challenges to injustices — gender discrimination, environmental degradation, repression of homosexuals — that had long existed with little public outrage."⁹ But when these boomers began to protest segregation, or patriarchal norms, or American engagement in Vietnam, or even just the perceived conformity of the suburban existence, they were labeled as ungrateful and spoiled. The renowned neoconservative sociologist Edward Shils called student protesters of this era "a uniquely indulged generation"; in a passage that should sound familiar to any millennial, another sociologist, Robert Nisbet, placed the blame on "massive doses of affection, adulation, devotion, permissiveness, incessant and infant recognition of youthful 'brightness' by parents."¹⁰

To these critics, whose generation had weathered the deprivations of the Great Depression and World War II, these boomers were simply ungrateful. They'd been given the keys to the American Dream but failed to cultivate any sort of work ethic, or the sort of deferred gratification that would allow them to pass their middle-class status down to the next generation. Instead, boomers "dropped out" of society in their early twenties. They opted for "occupations," like cabdriver or house painter, instead of white-collar work. They ignored social mores, and stayed in seemingly endless graduate programs instead of pursuing honorable *careers*.

Or at least that was one way of looking at it, codified in books like Midge Decter's *Liberal Parents, Radical Children*, released in 1975. Dector detailed the various archetypes of disappointment: There was the new graduate who "once made his parents the envy of all the rest, handsome, healthy, gifted, well-mannered, winner of a scholarship to Harvard," who "languishes now in a hospital where the therapists feel that in another few months he might attempt a few tasks and ultimately—for the prognosis is good—even hold down a job," and another son who "lately sent a postcard to his sister announcing that he had taken up photography and that as soon as he gets some work he plans to buy himself a piece of land and build himself a house on it." There was a daughter living with a divorced older man, and the other daughter on her "third—or is it her fourth?—postgraduate degree."[11]

This discourse—articulating the fear that white bourgeois boomers had gone "soft" in some way—was like so many conversations about child-rearing and generational expectations: moralizing in tone, but deeply rooted in class anxiety. The unique thing about the middle class, after all, is that middle-class-ness must be reproduced, re*claimed,* with each generation. "In other classes, membership is transmitted by simple inheritance," Barbara Ehrenreich writes in *Fear of Falling: The Inner Life of the Middle Class.* "If you are born into the upper class, you can expect to remain there for life. Sadly, too, most of those born into the lower classes can expect to remain where they started out."[12] But the middle class is different. Its form of capital "must be renewed in each individual through fresh effort and commitment. In this class, no one escapes the requirements of self-discipline and self-directed labor; they are visited, in each generation, upon the young as they were upon the parents."[13] The son of a lawyer must work just as many years as his father did, for example, to sustain the same position in society.

The middle-class boomers who refused that path were perceived as neglecting that lifelong slog to stay in the middle class. Or at least that was the view of a handful of jaundiced conservative critics writing the 1970s equivalent of a David Brooks or Bret Stephens op-ed bemoaning the state of kids these days. But that sentiment was just part of a much larger, creeping societal anxiety, one that boomers would internalize as they came of age. The postwar expansion and solidification of the American middle class—which had lasted just long enough for people to believe that it could last forever—was over.

Consider the psychological impact of this downturn on the American worker: Thanks to wage stagnation, the amount of money you receive every month stays the same, or even goes up, but its actual *worth,* along with the rest of your savings, goes down. Unemployment hit 8.5 percent in 1975, as American jobs began their slow migration overseas, where corporations could pay less (and avoid unions) to manufacture similar products. But that wasn't all. In the wake of the civil rights and women's movements, more people of color and women were competing for jobs, from manufacturing to medicine, that had been formerly limited to (white) men. And all of this took place against the backdrop of the Vietnam War, Watergate, the resignation of Nixon, and generalized disillusionment with the government at large. Major demographic change, declining trust in public institutions, financial precarity—all of this should sound familiar.

And so, after years of post-Depression, post–World War II collectivism, many in the middle class began to turn inward. Culturally, and somewhat superficially, that looked a lot like what Wolfe described as "The Me Decade." But it also manifested as a rightward shift in their politics: the embrace of Reaganism and "market-oriented thinking," also known as the idea that the market should be allowed to work things out without government intervention, as well as union busting and massive cuts to public programs that accompanied it.

In *The Great Risk Shift,* Hacker maps the concurrent development of the "Personal Responsibility Crusade," or the increasingly popular idea, articulated in various forms across culture and society, evident in the tax code and reigning economic thought, that "government should get out of the way and let people succeed or fail on their own."[14]

Central to this framework, Hacker argues, was the notion that "Americans are better off dealing with economic risks on their own, without the overweening interference or expense of wider systems of risk sharing." In other words, risk sharing, be it in the form of robust funding for higher education or company-run pensions, was presumptuous, and indulgent, and unnecessary. And then there was the argument, now so familiar to conservative thought as to feel mundane, that safety nets make people lazy, or ungrateful, or self-indulgent—and are thus, at their heart, un-American. "By protecting us from the full consequences of our choices," Hacker explains, insurance was thought to "take away our incentive to be productive and prudent."[15]

The risk shift also took the form of transferring the responsibility for training to the individual, rather than the employer. In the past, many companies would hire workers with or without college degrees and pay them as they trained them for a specific job. In a factory, someone hired as a packager could get trained up to inspector; a receptionist at an accounting firm could eventually get her CPA. A mining company, for example, would help fund engineering programs at local colleges, and create scholarships for students to attend them. They might not be doing the training themselves, but they were effectively paying for it —with the "risk" (e.g., the cost) falling on the company, not the worker.

These days, the vast majority of employers require applicants to shoulder the burden of their training. We pay for undergraduate degrees, certificates, and graduate degrees, but we also foot the bill for internships and externships, in which a person "self-finance[s] their own training in the workplace," either in the form of paying for college credits (to provide free labor in an internship that doubles as a "class") or just providing un-compensated labor.[16] Some companies still train workers out of necessity (highly specific trades, like solar panel work) and some white-collar employers foot the bill for employee MBAs. And there's always, of course, the military. But the responsibility for the vast majority of training now falls on the worker—and even then is no assurance of a job. This shift happened so gradually that it's hard to see how profound a change it is, and how much student debt has resulted from it, but it started, however quietly, as boomers came of age.

The most obvious by-product of the risk shift is the fate of the pension, which has become so rare in today's economy, so wholly outside what we can imagine, that for many, it feels glut-tonous to even think about, let alone expect such a thing. When I think of my Granddad's pension—which he began receiving when he retired, at age fifty-nine, from his job at 3M—my im-mediate reaction is that it was *preposterous*. But the idea of a pen-sion was not, and is not, extravagant. It's premised on the idea that some of the profits you help produce for a company should go not to stockholders, or the CEO, but back to longtime work-ers, who would continue to receive a portion of their salary even after they retire. In essence, the worker committed years of their life to making the company profitable; the company then com-mits some extra years of its profits to the employee.

Combined with Social Security—which every worker pays into for their entire working life—most unionized and profes-sional workers during the postwar period were able to retire in comfort. They weren't sent to the literal poorhouse, as many el-ders were before the Depression and the passage of the Social Security Act; nor were they forced to depend on their children. But as the economy shifted in the 1970s, companies began to see the pension as a liability. Starting in 1981, some companies exchanged pensions for 401k programs, which allow workers to save pre-tax dollars for retirement. A portion of those companies also provided "matching" dollars up to a certain point: If you put one dollar in, they'll put in anywhere from five to fifty cents.

But more and more companies began to offer nothing at all. In 1980, 46 percent of private-sector workers were covered by a pension plan. In 2019, that number had fallen to 16 percent.[17] A Pew Charitable Trusts analysis of data from the 2012 Survey of Income and Program Participation found that 53 percent of private sector employees had access to a "defined contribution" plan, like a 401k or a Roth 401k IRA. And while many celebrate the ability to move from job to job instead of sticking with an employer simply to maximize pension benefits, that flexibility creates significant 401k "leakage": employees forget to roll over a 401k, or withdraw it to cover "hardship" expenses, from college tuition to medical emergencies.[18] And access to a plan is different from participation: Only 38 percent of private sector workers actually enrolled in offered defined contribution plans. It's difficult, after all, to force yourself to save for future security when your present feels so incredibly insecure.

When my other set of grandparents retired in the late '80s, they were able to live — not luxuriously, but live — on their Social Security benefits. Today, to survive on Social Security alone often means barely covering basic expenses. And yet the idea of personal responsibility has persisted: If you plan well and start saving when you first started working, *theoretically* you should be fine. But you might also end up living Social Security check to Social Security check, even after a lifetime of hard work. Before the Great Depression, that was the American way: abject insecurity for the vast majority of the country. That's what the Greatest Generation lived through; those are the stories that were passed down, with reverence rivaling any war story, to their boomer chil-

dren. Which is why it can feel so mind-boggling that either generation would willingly return to that American way again.

But like so many contradictory ideological turns, it's mind-
boggling and yet readily understandable. Americans, after all,
love the idea of the self-made, bootstrapping American whose
success could be linked to dogged perseverance no matter the
barriers. But the myth of the wholly self-made American, like all
myths, relies on some sort of sustained willful ignorance — often
perpetuated by those who've already benefited from them.

The endurance of the "pull yourself up by your bootstraps"
narrative, for example, has always relied on people ignoring who's
allowed boots and who's given the straps with which to pull them
up. The cult of the individual elides all the ways in which the individual's hard work was able to take root and flourish because of
federally implemented programs and policies, from the Home-
stead Act to the G.I. Bill — programs that often excluded people
who were not white or male.

But it's easier — and more heroic — if the story of middle-
class ascendency is all about individual hard work. And no one
wants to lose any of the hard-won benefits of that work. Which
helps explain the popularity of the Personal Responsibility Crusade amongst both boomers and their parents: Members of the
middle class were so freaked out by seeping economic instability
that they started pulling the ladder up behind them. They helped
elect leaders, like President Ronald Reagan, who promised to
"protect" the middle class through tax cuts, even though Reagan's policies, once put in practice, worked to defund many of the
programs that had allowed the middle class to achieve that status
in the first place. On the state level, they elected lawmakers who
passed "right to work" legislation to defang unions, which were
increasingly depicted as greedy, corrupt, and destroying American competitiveness in the global market.

Pulling up the ladder also meant justifying the elimination of social services by demonizing "welfare queens," and signing on to the newly accepted wisdom that programs intended to alleviate poverty actually kept people in it. It meant deep cuts to departments that disproportionately affected Black communities, like Housing and Development. As Maurice A. St. Pierre, writing in the *Journal of Black Studies,* explained in 1993, "The policies of the Reagan administration — based on the philosophy of hard work, independence, thrift, minimum government intervention in the lives of citizens, and making America strong again — affected the poor, many of whom are Black, more negatively than the economically better-off."[19]

The best way to the collective good, according to Reaganism, was through eagle-eyed focus on cultivation of me and mine, with little thought of how the reverberations of those actions would affect their children and grandchildren in the years to come. This notion developed into the only-kinda-joking argument that (white, middle-class) boomers are, at their heart, sociopaths: lacking in empathy, egotistical, with a high disregard for others. In his book *A Generation of Sociopaths: How Baby Boomers Betrayed America,* published in 2017, Bruce Gibney argues that boomers are also antisocial: not in the "doesn't want to go to the party" connotation of the term, but in the "lacks consideration for others" way.

It's not a scientifically rigorous hypothesis, but today, Gibney's overarching thesis feels more and more credible. All the way back in 1989, Barbara Ehrenreich had articulated a similar idea. Tracing the development of the student protest movement, the backlash against it, and the anxiety over the newly expanded and newly threatened stability of the middle class, she argues that boomers retreated from the liberalism of the '60s into "a meaner, more selfish outlook, hostile to the aspirations of those less fortunate."[20] They broke the "social contract" that, according to the economists Matthias Doepke and Fabrizio Zilibotti, had defined the postwar period, "and decided to look out for themselves: they invested more in their education and individual success, while deeming social protection less important."[21]

Critics and scholars of this time are careful to note, however, that this was largely the trajectory of the rich and the "professional" middle class, the mix of managers and college graduates and professors and doctors and writers and consultants whose class status was "confirmed" through the production of organization and knowledge. They were mostly but not exclusively white; they were most likely suburban, but scattered throughout the United States, endemic to college and factory towns alike. They were salaried, as opposed to paid by the hour, and unlikely to be part of a union.

While these professional middle-class boomers were by no means the majority—making up just 20 percent of the population—their proximity to levers of power and cultural visibility gave them, and the ideologies they embraced and propagated, outsize force. They were "the elite," and as Ehrenreich argues, "an elite that is conscious of its status will defend that status, even if this means abandoning, in all but rhetoric, such stated values as democracy and fairness."[22]

Such hostility toward others was motivated, at least in part, by their fear of falling from their class perch, and the social humiliation that would follow.[23] In order to avoid that fate, some of those young boomers—graduating into the late '70s and early '80s—began to adopt a different understanding of the purpose of education and consumption. Like millennials graduating into and after the Great Recession, they finished high school or college and the long-assumed jobs were nowhere to be found. They were the first boomers to enter into the workplace *after* the "miracle economy," and understood, in some way, that they'd have to chart a different route than their parents toward middle-class security.

Ehrenreich calls that new mindset "the Yuppie Strategy." Like the hipsters of the late 2000s, yuppies (or young urban professionals) were a social category to which few willingly admitted membership, mercilessly satirized in texts like *The Yuppie Handbook*. But their popularity — as the subject of media trend stories, as a cultural punching bag — suggested a new societal direction, at once disconcerting and aspirational.

The most stereotypical yuppies were college educated, lived in New York, and worked in finance or consulting or law. They consumed in a way that rejected the thrift of their parents, spending lavishly on gadgets (the Cuisinart) and specialty food items (sun-dried tomatoes, sushi) and status-oriented vacations (the Bahamas) and purchases (Rolexes). They got into wine, house plants, and the newly cool hobby of "jogging." They bought up real estate in gentrifying neighborhoods, making prices unaffordable for everyone except other yuppies. (If all of this sounds like a slightly dated version of our current consumer culture, that's because it is.)

Most important, they were unembarrassed about loving *money*. As an iconic *Newsweek* cover story put it, the yuppies had "marched through the '60s, then dispersed into a million solitary joggers, riding the crests of their own alpha waves, and now there they go again, barely looking up from the massed gray columns of the *Wall Street Journal,* they speed toward the airport, advancing on the 1980s in the back seat of a limousine." They weren't necessarily Gordon Gekko in *Wall Street,* a movie released in 1987, but Gekko was a distillation of their worst traits. Unlike earlier boomers, "they did not waste time 'finding themselves' or joining radical movements," Ehrenreich writes. "They plunged directly into the economic mainstream, earning and spending with equal zest." That "yuppy" was a play on Yippie — the name for one of the radical protest groups of the 1960s — was part of the point. The hippies had gone corporate.

The first step of the yuppie strategy, according to Ehrenreich, was a sort of "premature pragmatism": choosing a major based on which one that would land them in a position to make a lot of money very quickly. Between the early 1970s and the early 1980s, the number of English majors declined by nearly 50 percent, as did those majoring in social sciences. During the same period, business majors *doubled.*[24]

This "pragmatism" should be familiar to millennials. Yuppies wanted what they'd been trained to want, which is the same thing that middle-class millennials were trained to want: a middle-class lifestyle like their parents', if not membership in an even higher socioeconomic bracket. But because of the shifting economy, a college degree was no longer enough to assure that lifestyle. They had to choose the *right* major, and get the *right* job to shore up that elite status — and start treading water fast enough to keep afloat.

Yet the "right job" was often one that exacerbated the conditions that made yuppies so frantic in the first place. As the historian Dylan Gottlieb points out, yuppies were "the beneficiaries of the unequal social order they helped to create."[25] For yuppies to keep treading water, others had to sink below the surface — economic casualties of yuppies' on-the-job actions as stockbrokers, consultants, and corporate lawyers.

This is why yuppies became such a flash point in conversations about the '80s and boomers in general: "Talking about yuppies was a means to make sense of the eclipse of manufacturing and the rise of the financial, professional, and service industries," Gottlieb explains. "Yuppies were a way to signify the growing inequality between the college-educated upper middle class and those who were being left behind."

Not all boomers were yuppies—not even close—but thinking through the actions of the yuppies gives us a window into the larger anxieties of the boomer middle class. They took form over the course of the '70s, metastasized in the '80s, and became the base temperature of the '90s. Sometimes the blame for the end of prosperity is placed on "big government," sometimes on vague understandings of global competition. It became more acute during small economic recessions, but the "recoveries" offered only slight relief. Some boomers managed to cling to their parents' class status, while others became part of what became known as the "disappearing middle class," a.k.a. the working middle class, whose jobs and class security had been jeopardized and then, in many cases, completely destroyed. But the animating, enervating question for this generation remained the same: Where did our security go, and why can't we get it back?

Navigating a baseline nervousness about your class position, and struggling to find a job that will allow you to try and maintain it—that was the boomer's iteration of what we now know as burnout. They didn't have cell phones or massive piles of student debt to exacerbate it, but they did have the fundamental unease, the psychological toll of dealing with everyday precarity.

Examining boomers through the lens of economic history helps explain so much: about their voting habits, and their turn inward. But if you're still wondering what this has to do with millennial burnout, think about it. Surrounded by perceived threats and growing uncertainty, middle-class boomers doubled down on what they could try to control: their children.

2

Growing Mini-Adults

"I STARTED TO FEEL BUSY AT AGE SEVEN." THAT'S WHAT Caitlin, who identifies as biracial and grew up in the suburbs of Washington, DC, in the 1980s, told me. At first, there were all sorts of activities — swimming, T-ball, art class — at least one every day after school. By the time she got to middle school, she had more say in her extracurriculars, and dedicated herself to dance and theater. Both of her parents worked full-time, and her dad was often traveling, so an au pair would bring her to and from her activities and supervise homework time after school. Her mom cared a lot about grades — As and Bs only — and wanted to make sure she was always hanging out with the "right" crowd.

"As an adult, I've realized I get stressed when I'm not doing something," Caitlin says. "I feel guilty just relaxing. Even in college, I found myself needing to take eighteen to nineteen units a semester, have a campus job, join clubs, volunteer, work on the plays and musicals, and I'd still feel like I wasn't doing enough."

Stefanie, who is white, was born in 1982 and grew up in North Idaho, just miles from the Canadian border. Her father was a logger, working from three a.m. until dark; her mother stayed home with her and her four siblings. All of her grandparents and several aunts and uncles lived nearby, and she was close with all of them. Even as a young child, she and her siblings were given wide range to roam on their bikes; during the summer, they'd go to a nearby elementary school and play unsupervised for hours. Along with her cousins, they'd play kick the can, capture the flag, cops and robbers — again, unsupervised — outside, late into the night.

In middle school, Stefanie's family moved out of town onto a five-acre spread of land. "We built a lot of forts, started fires, and basically had free run," she told me. Her mom helped teach her to read, but after that was pretty hands-off when it came to school and homework. There was no family "schedule" to speak of, save church on Sundays, and, once a month, a big family get-together at her grandparents' house to celebrate whoever had a birthday.

Caitlin's and Stefanie's childhoods took place thousands of miles away from each other, against different socioeconomic backgrounds, and at different ends of the millennial age span. They represent two paradigms of parenting, and ideas of what "preparation" for adulthood should look like — one of which, over the course of our millennial childhoods, increasingly superseded the other. People knew this shift was happening, but it had hardly been studied, at length, with any sort of nuance. At least not until Annette Lareau.

Between 1990 and 1995, Lareau, a sociologist at the University of Pennsylvania, followed eighty-eight children, beginning in the third grade. Like Caitlin and Stefanie, these children came from different economic and racial backgrounds; they attended different schools and had very different expectations of what they should be doing outside of school hours.

For the study, Lareau and her research assistants spent long hours with the children and their families, in and around their homes, blending in as much as possible. The goal: observe, in granular detail, how parenting, and the expectations of childhood that attend it, changed across the socioeconomic spectrum. They met "Little Billy" Yanelli, a white boy who lived in a small, neat home with his parents, both of whom had dropped out of high school. His mother worked as a house cleaner for rich families in the suburbs; his father painted houses. He managed Bs in school but regularly acted out; his teacher called him a "goofball." Apart from one organized sport, Little Billy spent most of his out-of-school time playing with neighborhood kids, or with relatives, the vast majority of whom lived nearby.

Then there was Stacy Marshall, a Black girl who lived in a middle-class suburban neighborhood with her sister and her parents, who both moved from the South to attend college in the area. Her father was a civil servant; their mother worked in what we'd now call "tech." Stacey took piano lessons and was a skilled gymnast, and spent her summers attending a variety of camps. When she barely missed the cutoff for the Gifted and Talented program at their school, her mother arranged for her to retake it. Even though the Marshalls made good salaries—enough to buy the girls' the latest in new clothes and toys—they were always worried about money, and fearful of industry downsizing.

And there was Garrett Talinger, one of three brothers growing up in a nearly all-white upper-middle-class neighborhood in the suburbs. His parents graduated from Ivy League schools and worked hard to juggle the necessary travel for their jobs as consultants. They had a pool, regular house cleaners, and membership to an elite private country club. But the parents rarely talked about money—even when Garrett's mother stepped down from her job to spend more time with the family and finances became tighter.

The Talinger family's lives rotated around "the calendar," which overflowed with times for tryouts, practices, and games, many of which required travel. Garrett participated in special leagues and tournaments for three different sports, and took lessons for the piano and the saxophone. He was a good student, and behaved well in class, but he was also often exhausted, "competitive with and hostile towards" his siblings, and resentful that his parents didn't make enough money to send him back to the expensive private school he used to attend. In many ways, Garrett's life feels like a bad stereotype of the millennial existence: overscheduled, overprivileged, and, one can easily imagine in the years to come, deeply burnt out.

Lareau discerned a divide between parents who practiced what she called "concerted cultivation" and those, generally of lower-class status, who refused or didn't have time to orient their lives entirely around children's activities and future resume-building. It's not as if these lower-class parents were "bad" parents—it's just that the skills they cultivated in their children, including independence and imagination, are not the ones valued by the bourgeois workplace. To be valued there, you need plans, lengthy resumes, ease and confidence interacting with authority figures, and innate understandings of how the job ladder works. You need connections, and a willingness to multitask, and an eagerness to overschedule.

Some millennials were raised this way, alternately resisting and reconciling themselves to their parents' best intentions. Others have struggled their entire lives to adopt and approximate behaviors they were never taught. So much depends on when and where and how you were raised: whether your parents were married or divorced, whether you lived in the city or amidst wide-open spaces, and what "activities" were even available, let alone affordable. But the common denominator between experiences remains the same: to "succeed," as a millennial kid, at least according to middle-class societal standards, was to build yourself for burnout.

*   *   *

The tenets of concerted cultivation will sound familiar, because they're what have been represented, and tacitly agreed upon, as "good" parenting for the last three decades. The child's schedule — beginning with naptimes and continuing through competitive dance, or music, or sports — takes precedence over the parent's; the child's well-being, and, more importantly, their future capacity for success, is paramount. Baby food should be homemade; toddler play should be enriching; private tutors should be enlisted if necessary.

Within the framework of concerted cultivation, a child should develop a large vocabulary, feel capable of questioning people in authority and advocating for their own needs, and learn how to negotiate and plan for the demands of their schedule at a young age. They should be trained to become good networkers, good employees, good multitaskers. Every part of a child's life, in other words, can be optimized to better prepare them for their eventual entry into the working world. They become mini-adults, with the attendant anxiety and expectations, years before adulthood hits.

Concerted cultivation is, at its heart, a middle-class practice. But over the last thirty years, its ideals have transcended class lines, becoming the foundation of "good parenting," especially for those who'd fallen, or were anxious about falling, out of the middle class. And while no one outside of academia called it "concerted cultivation," boomers from across the United States told me about aspiring to whatever iteration of the ideal they could make work.

When Sue and her husband were raising their millennial children in the Philadelphia area, for example, they were both blue-collar workers, living paycheck to paycheck. Her version of concerted cultivation was scrimping every month to cover tuition at the local Catholic school. From 1983 to 1987, Rita found herself a single parent to two kids, moving to various cities across the United States. She knew that volunteering at her children's school was important, but her work schedule made it difficult, even though the school was just a block away. And while the family lived below the poverty line, she still put aside ten dollars a month in order to provide the sort of "enrichment" she could afford: a camping trip every summer.

For Cindi, a Hispanic mother from South Texas, money was always tight, especially after both she and her husband were laid off. The experience brought them closer together as a family, she told me, and made them stronger in their faith. Despite financial pressures, the children remained central. She helped their teachers with laborious tasks, chaperoned field trips and events, and fundraised. "We lived and sacrificed for our children," she said. "Children first, marriage second."

Because of my age (old millennial) and location (like Stefanie, a small town in North Idaho), my parents either missed, felt less pressure to embrace, rejected, or just didn't have access to many of the tenets of concerted cultivation. But that didn't mean my mom, as the primary caregiver, didn't end up incorporating elements of it in my childhood, purposefully or not.

Most of my mom's parenting philosophy, she told me, was

largely derived from what she had learned in her teacher ed classes, especially developmental psychology. "I sought experiences that would shape your thinking from a very early age," she told me, like reading two books every night, "both to begin a love of reading but also to establish a routine that made clear when you were supposed to sleep," and making three healthy meals a day with limited snacking.

I went to preschool, which I remember loving, in the basement of our church, for three hours a day. Because my mom didn't work outside of the home, she was able to pick me up, drop me off, and supervise me for the rest of the time. There was no competition for my preschool, not even a waiting list. When I started elementary school, I walked the five minutes to the bus stop and rode the bus thirty minutes in either direction. Starting around fourth grade, when my mom had returned to work, I was allowed to be home alone after school—a time I cherished, and filled with Bagel Bites and episodes of *Star Trek: The Next Generation*.

Unlike many middle-class millennials, I didn't start organized activities of any kind until I was in the second grade, when I began taking piano lessons. My mother had played, and thought learning to read music and knowing "what it takes to make music" was important. "I didn't think about the other benefits, such as the discipline to remember to practice, or the importance of learning to play in public," she told me recently.

Because my mom had left behind a teaching job at an elite private school in Minnesota when she moved to Idaho, she felt strongly that she "owed something" to me and brother:

She became president of the PTA (Parent Teacher Association) and was elected to the school board. There weren't a lot of "enrichment" activities in town, but she enrolled me in what was available, usually with my enthusiastic consent: I was a Girl Scout, I continued to play piano. I loved writing, which she encouraged by having me do free-writes with one of her adult friends who taught high school English. I loved reading, but the agreement was that I had to alternate each Baby-Sitter's Club book (easy, comforting reads) with a non–Baby-Sitter's Club book.

"I wanted you to be educated," my mother told me. What's interesting, then, is all the ways, some of them highly camouflaged, that education took shape *outside* of the classroom. She was preparing me for adult life, but specifically preparing me for *middle class,* professional, cultured adult life. My brother and I accompanied our parents to sit-down restaurants, where we learned manners, and were exposed to "different" types of foods (one of my most vivid sensory memories of childhood is tasting escargot, an incredibly '80s version of "sophisticated" food). We received a "fancy" good grades dinner to reward, in my mom's words "an accomplishment that took a long time to achieve." My parents also brought us to places outside of our small town — to Seattle, or Spokane — and took us to museums to learn about how to behave in public.

And yet all of my parents' concerted cultivation took place against a backdrop of extended, almost entirely unsupervised play. We lived on a cul-de-sac in a relatively new development. There were no parks within walking distance, but there was a massive swath of undeveloped land behind our house, known colloquially as "the weeds," which gave my childhood a feeling, if not reality, of unrestricted wildness.

The neighborhood was filled with kids, and I played with them — in my backyard, in their backyards and then, as we grew older, in the streets and in "the weeds" — for large expanses of time. My first childhood friend lived next door, and the boundaries between his house and mine felt fluid. We rode bikes together, made forts out of fallen locust trees, caught grasshoppers for hours. Summers always felt like a wild, endless expanse, dotted with swimming lessons, camping trips, and a week of Vacation Bible School. Mostly, though, it was just endless hours of trying to entertain myself: outside, biking on my own, at the pool, in my room.

My brother and I enjoyed a largely unstructured childhood that, like many millennials, we periodically haul out to contrast ourselves with what feels like the overly supervised lives of kids today. Other older millennials recall similar freedoms: Ryan, who grew up in a middle-class suburb of Kansas City, Missouri, remembers endless afternoons at home with his brothers while his parents were at work in the '80s and early '90s. "We mostly stuck around our home, often terrorizing each other," he said. "I would climb the tree in our backyard to escape my brothers and they would get the hose and spray me until I came down. When at least one of my parents was home, we had more range to play in our entire neighborhood, unsupervised."

Mary, who was born in 1985, grew up "almost totally unsupervised" in rural Virginia—her father was the priest of a wealthy congregation, but they were almost always broke. "I would play and read alone in the acres of woods behind our house," she recalled, "wander alone around the church campus across the street, teach myself to cook weird stuff in the kitchen, and go for long, solo walks around the neighborhood." Emily grew up on a farm in Illinois, five miles from the closest small town. "I could hop on a horse bareback whenever I wanted," she said, "and swing on ropes into the hay piles and go look for crawfish under the bridge and build our fake town out in the woods."

But most of the millennials I talked to who had such freedoms were either older or grew up in rural areas where crime was not a concern. As the ideals of concerted cultivation continued to spread, they consolidated into behaviors we now think of as "helicopter parenting," which could also just be described as *more* parenting, and particularly more time spent with children, especially during the afterschool and weekend times when those children were previously on their own.

In "The Overprotected Kid," published in the *Atlantic* in 2014, Hanna Rosin's husband realizes that their own daughter, then ten, had probably experienced no more than ten minutes of unsupervised time *in her entire life.*[1] Rosin traces the shift toward increased supervision—and the concurrent attempt to eliminate risk in children's play—back to two major events in the late '70s. First, in 1978, a toddler seriously injured himself on a twelve-foot-long slide in Chicago. His mother, who'd been right behind him before he fell through a gap at the top of the slide, sued the Chicago Park District and the companies responsible for constructing and installing the slide.

The suit, which was later settled for $9.5 million, was one of several that ushered in a wave of "playground reform" across the United States, as thousands of playgrounds across the United States exchanged fixtures newly conceived of as "dangerous" for ostensibly safer, and almost always standardized, new equipment. (At my elementary school, teeter-totters and a merry-go-rounds were replaced with slides made of that hard, static-producing yellow plastic; if you're an older millennial, you might recall something similar.)

The second event took place in Manhattan in 1979, when a six-year-old named Etan Patz, who'd pleaded with his mother to let him walk to the school bus stop by himself, was finally granted his request—and disappeared. The story became national news and, along with the abduction and murder of a four-year-old Florida boy, Adam Walsh, helped incite a national panic over missing children, "stranger danger," and the omnipresent threat of child molesters. Photos of missing children first began showing up on milk cartons in the early '80s; 38 million people watched a dramatization of Walsh's abduction, simply named *Adam,* when it aired in 1983; Ronald Reagan declared the day of Patz's disappearance National Missing Children's Day.

For all of the anxiety, "crimes against children" did not, in fact, spike in the early '80s, and since the early '90s, they've actually been in decline. "A child from a happy, intact family who walks to the bus stop and never comes home is still a national tragedy," Rosin writes, "not a national epidemic." But the *perception* of increased danger to children, whether on the playground or in public, compelled parents (with the ability and time to do so) to prevent or decrease exposure to those spaces.

The anxiety over "stranger danger" was, in many ways, a displacement of other anxieties about the shifting understanding of family, of the increase in working mothers, of a weakening of community and the cohesion that accompanied it. There was so much that seemed out of a parents' control, but where and how a child played, whether or not they were supervised at all times — *that* could be closely monitored.

As millennials hit high school and college over the course of the 2000s, this type of helicopter parenting became widespread — readily identifiable and derided. But back in 1996, the sociologist Sharon Hays had described the phenomenon in her book *The Cultural Contradictions of Motherhood.* "In sum," she wrote, "the methods of appropriate child rearing are construed as child-centered, expert-guided, emotionally absorbing, labor-intensive, and financially expensive."[2]

The crucial word here is *construed* — just because middle-class parents decided that a certain style of parenting is superior doesn't mean it empirically *is.* For example, as Lareau shows, there are elements of the lower- and working-class parenting that are incredibly valuable and largely absent from concerted cultivation. One of the most important: "natural growth," or the conscious or unconscious allotment of *un*structured time, which allows children to cultivate curiosity, independence, and learn to negotiate peer dynamics on their own.

In practice, this turn to concerted cultivation meant less of the wild, roaming time that Rosin and I remembered so fondly. It meant neighborhood games became adult-coached and supervised competitive league sports. It meant less of a chance to seek and test personal limits, less time spent wholly with other children, developing unsupervised hierarchies, community rules and logic, and the feelings of competence and independence that accompanied completing small tasks (going to the store, walking to the bus stop, coming home to an empty house and making yourself Bagel Bites) on one's own. "Risk management used to be a business practice," Malcolm Harris writes in *Kids These Days: Human Capital and the Making of Millennials.* "Now it's our dominant child-rearing strategy."

There were developmental consequences to that strategy — but sometimes it's easiest to see those consequences when we look at what happened in their absence. Danielle, who's white and grew up in the outskirts of Orlando, remembers her childhood as largely unsupervised, with free rein of the neighborhood. Her family was on the poorer side of her friend group, and periodically on food stamps. The only scheduled activity she recalls was choir, which was free and organized through her school. "My parents never went to college, so I don't think they had a framework for the 'fill up your kids' schedule so their college application looks good' idea," she recalled. "I think their focus was on making sure there was a roof over our heads and food on the table."

In hindsight, she's grateful for that attitude: "I saw from an early age how work can grind you up and spit you back out, as well as the benefits of leisure time," she told me. "I have some friends who are just a little younger than me, who take work much more seriously (and personally), and I can't help but think my semi-feral unscheduled childhood has something to do with it."

Like Danielle, I'm increasingly convinced that one of the reasons I was able to avoid burnout as long as I did can be directly traced to the amount of "natural growth" I experienced. But so many millennial kids never experienced it at all. As Rosin points out, "a common concern of parents these days is that children grow up too fast. But sometimes it seems as if children don't get the space to grow up at all; they just become adept at mimicking the habits of adulthood." Middle class kids become mini-adults earlier and earlier—but as the rise of "adulting" rhetoric makes clear, they're not necessarily prepared for its realities. They've spent a ton of time with adults, and learned the external markings of performing adulthood, but lack the independence and strong sense of self that accompanies a less surveilled and protected childhood.

Take, for example, the story of Maya. She's white, and was born in 1996—the tail end of the millennial generation—and grew up middle class, in the suburbs of Chicago, with both parents working. Her neighborhood was "nice," and filled with kids her age, but she never saw anyone: "There was no sense of closeness, no united feeling that we could play together or meet up," she recalls. All the kids were already siloed into activities away from the neighborhood, including her. "I always felt like I had 'consigned' time more than a 'schedule.' Consigned time at daycare, consigned time at afterschool programs, consigned time after high school activities and my car-less self waited until my parents could pick me up. I felt like I was forced to live at school."

She recalls her parents as focused entirely on grades and extracurriculars "but not as much on teaching me how to make friends" or "how to spend unstructured time." Her mom taught her to give every teacher a gift, she wrote every adult a holiday card, she took notes at every conference or public speaking event. Maya calls those tendencies—which she still practices, in slightly modified form—"insanely anal teacher's pet behaviors," but they could also be called preparation for the upwardly mobile workplace.

Maya's mother was extremely conscientious and knew the language of good parenting, often repeating the refrain of "You can tell me anything." But when Maya wanted to talk about body issues, or negative thoughts, or obsessive fears, her mother quickly became frustrated. She took Maya to a therapist, but seemed unwilling to directly engage with the messiness of parenting. Today, Maya draws a straight line between the cultivated busyness of her childhood to her feelings of exhaustion, shame, and burnout. "I look back on my five hours of sleep, my roster of activities I cared about, the thesis I poured my soul into, and I know there's no way I could have stretched myself further without hurting myself and hating what I was doing," she told me. "But then my practical brain is like, *You should have hurt yourself. You're playing catch-up now.*"

The stereotype of the oversurveilled, overprotected kid is that they grow up to be weak and lazy. But in my experience, the millennial trait of "laziness" has a lot more to do with economic security—either the family's actual security, or total insulation from precarity as a child or in adulthood. The laziest millennials I know are the ones who've been saved from the consequences, economic or otherwise, of every mistake they've made. But that's still just a small sliver of the actual millennial population. Most who grew up middle class and overprotected also grew up to be hypervigilant about maintaining or obtaining class status: hustling harder, as Maya puts it, networking more aggressively, interning more, sleeping less. So many millennials end up defining themselves *exclusively* by their ability to work hard, and succeed, and play it safe—instead of their actual personal tastes, or their willingness to take risks, or experiment and even fail.

Amanda, who grew up in a suburb of Detroit, still struggles with unstructured free time. When she arrived at college in the early 2000s, she no longer had a chock-full schedule of activities around which to orient her life. "Any down time began to feel like I was being lazy and unproductive," she recalls, "which in turn made me question my self-worth." Today, if she's not doing something, she feels like she's wasting time. She started going to therapy after an anxiety attack landed her in the ER, but finds it difficult to heed her therapist's suggestion that she shouldn't feel guilty about taking a day to do whatever she wants—even if that is a day of Netflix bingeing, or a day of rest—because she doesn't really know what she might *want* to do if it's not work.

For some millennials, helicopter parenting wasn't an over-reaction to class anxiety. It was the appropriate, measured reaction to real, not perceived, threat—and systemic racism. Rhiann, who spent her early childhood in Gary, Indiana, recalls a childhood of locks and forbidden areas. There were iron bars on her windows, and her backyard was enclosed with cinderblocks. Her garage had been broken in to several times, and there had been attempts to do the same to her home. "I grew up knowing that the world is a scary place and people sometimes did terrible things and there was no such thing as being 'too careful,'" she told me. "We went nowhere alone. We could not play outside without immediate supervision."

That changed, somewhat, when she moved out of Gary and into a suburban subdivision outside the city, where they were the only Black family in the neighborhood. There was less threat in the form of break-ins and recognized crime, but her family had to deal with constant harassment, especially from the golfers who passed through the course that shared a border with her back-yard. "There were loud, tipsy white men who asked my brother and I if my parents were hired help," she recalled, "and would interrogate us about our parents' jobs and incomes."

Before the move, Rhiann and her brother mostly played indoors, or in the backyard, and were isolated from other kids and always, always supervised. Afterward, they could bike and roller-skate in the far more open space, so long as they stayed within the reception area of the walkie-talkies their dad had purchased for them.

As they grew up, Rhiann took pleasure in studying, and her mother, who was a teacher, was "exceptionally attentive" to her schoolwork. But her parents' priority was safety, then education. For white parents, that might seem like helicopter parenting; for a Black family, it was just common sense. She internalized the idea that the world was a fickle place, and nothing, certainly not their class stability, was guaranteed. "We often talked about how the overall systems that people rely on really weren't made to work for everyone," Rhiann recalled. "My parents were also clear about how there will likely always be someone who is offended by who we were, and the spaces we were in. They taught us that education was the way to freedom, and we had to work doggedly hard to get there."

In sixth grade, Rhiann began attending a school that was predominantly white. She found herself continually underestimated by her teachers and her peers. "The adage 'You will have to work twice as hard for half of the results' really resonated with me," she told me, "and I haven't slowed down since then." She was top of her class, in every club, on every committee. "Being busy used to feel like 'home' because that 'hustle' attitude was prominent in my home," she explained. "Always moving, always improving, always learning something. In a way, it was like the darkness in the world can't win so long as you don't stop running." Rhiann's parents practiced concerted cultivation—but with a very conscious modification for what it takes to succeed as a Black woman in a white world.

That strategy—well, it worked. Today, Rhiann is almost thirty. She has multiple degrees and a family of her own. "I have high career aspirations and my heart still beats to the rhythm of productivity," she told me. "But I am also so very tired."

* * *

Boomer parents were worried about all the things parents are always worried about. But they were also deeply anxious about creating, sustaining, or "passing down" middle-class status amidst a period of widespread downward mobility—priming a generation of children to work, no matter the cost, until they achieved it. That anxiety consolidated into a new set of parenting ideals, behaviors, and standards regarded as the building blocks of "good," aspirational parenting.[3] Whether or not you agree with the actual effectiveness of those practices matters far less than the pressure many boomer parents felt to perform them.

And as parents worked hard to be "good" parents, the children in these households internalized ideas about what work itself could and could not provide. As Katherine S. Newman puts it in *Falling from Grace,* one of the primary messages gleaned from a family's downward mobility was that "one can play by the rules, pay one's dues, and still be evicted from the American Dream. There is no guarantee that one's best efforts will be rewarded in the end."[4]

For Brenna, who grew up in Marin County, California, in the '80s and '90s, the message of her childhood was that her status as a "smart kid" was the only way her family would regain financial security. Her parents had fallen out of the middle class when her father, a television executive, was diagnosed with brain tumors. Her mother, who had stayed home with the family, was forced to go back to work. They still maintained their "identity" as middle class, finagling a way for Brenna to attend an exclusive private school, even though their finances were never stable.

As a teen, Brenna took on an increasingly demanding schedule, mostly focused on grades — she thought, and her parents reinforced the belief, that grades would help restore the family's middle-class stability. "I didn't realize until after college," she admitted, "that these things weren't what actually made people rich." By then, her posture toward work was already in place, modeled after her mom, who supported the family on her own after Brenna's father passed away when she was sixteen. "My mom works from home these days, and I have a hard time convincing her to leave the house, or take vacations," Brenna told me. "I see myself repeating these behaviors, and have to make an effort to make time for things like seeing a movie with my husband, or cooking dinner."

Amy spent her childhood in the Midwest and told me that when her dad got laid off from his factory job in the early '80s, "it changed the whole trajectory" of her family. Her mom went to work full-time; her dad didn't find full-time "good" work for years. She went on reduced lunch at school, and her parents simply could not pay for many of the activities and experiences that they wanted for her — going to camp, traveling. "The words 'We can't afford it' should have been on a monogrammed pillow in our house," she said.

"It absolutely changed me," Amy explained. "I knew early on that employment was not guaranteed." When she started thinking about career paths, she only considered those that would offer complete financial security. She was the first person in her family to go to college, and the only things she understood as financially secure were law and medicine. "I just knew that lawyers and doctors had a lot of money," she said.

And then there's Pam, who grew up in Flint, Michigan. Her parents were teachers, so she wasn't directly affected by GM plant closures that in some years would scatter half of her class. They'd go "from Michigan to Tennessee, to follow the factories," she explained, "from houses to trailers, from trailers to apartments." Because of the fluctuation in population, her parents and other teachers were regularly pink-slipped—laid off at the end of the school year, then rehired, contingent on population, for the new school year. Their teachers' union went on strike, adding further insecurity; both of her older sisters had to leave the state to find work when their husbands were laid off from their manufacturing jobs.

"I internalized the insecurity," Pam said. "And when I found out what tenure was, it sounded like the only secure job in the world, so I decided to become a college professor." What she didn't understand: how entering the job market in 2008 would torpedo her job prospects. As we'll see, the disconnect between the seemingly "most secure jobs in the world," whether in academia, medicine, or the law, and the reality of the post-recession economy, is a major contributing factor to millennial burnout: If working hard to achieve those jobs can't offer security, what can?

Growing up, I knew that if your parent was a doctor your family got nice things, and that there were other children whose parents were different kinds of doctors, who got nicer things. But that's often the extent of the upper-class hierarchy in a small town: slight variations on upper-middle-class professionals, who practiced a diluted version of the "yuppie strategy." One of the reasons my dad went into medicine was because he knew it was a means to achieve the middle-class lifestyle his parents were always hovering just above and below.

As a child, I had little sense that my family had financial struggles, that my dad was barely making enough to cover his student loans and the mortgage in those early years, or that my mom felt out of place at events where every other doctor's wife was wearing a Nordstrom dress and she was wearing something she'd sewn herself the year before. But that's the thing about the upper middle class: They rarely talk about money, at least not the precariousness of money. Not with each other, and rarely with their children. One of the behaviors of middle-class-ness, after all, is avoiding talking about the crude specifics of how it's maintained — or masking them in the simple rhetoric of "hard work."

As a result, until I reached tenth grade, I had sensed little, if any, class precariousness — even as my town underwent seismic changes, first with the state's passage of right-to-work laws, which gutted the power of the unions that helped maintain the blue-collar middle class, and then with litigation over forest management, which gradually eliminated high-wage logging and sawmill jobs across the area. I have memories of homes all over town with THIS HOUSEHOLD SUPPORTED BY TIMBER DOLLARS signs in their window, but because kids are taught not to talk with each other about financial matters, and my family wasn't experiencing it directly, I thought of it as a community crisis, not a financial one.

In my town, most of the parents I knew were the middle-class workers with "good jobs" who over the course of the '80s and '90s, experienced bouts of joblessness, as the timber industry collapsed, or general precarity, after right-to-work legislation passed in 1986 and the unions began to disappear. Some were farmers, who increasingly had to find additional work to supplement the unpredictable income from the land. And then there were the people who never had "good" jobs or fell from those good jobs into double shifts or two jobs. People who worked in retail, people pulling double shifts to support a family as a single mom. People whose parents didn't speak English. People who worked as house cleaners, hairdressers, bartenders, nurses' aides, or any number of other jobs that weren't unionized. People who remained largely invisible. Some weren't working; some were what's come to be known as the working poor: barely, barely making ends meet.

As millennials grew up in towns like mine all over America, our families were experiencing—or cognizant and scared of—downward mobility. Divorced women were some of the most affected—if understudied—by this trend. Pre-divorce, the men in these families had been the primary or only breadwinner. Post-divorce, mothers "made do" with 29 to 39 percent of the income they had before.[5] Lenore Weitzman, author of *The Divorce Revolution,* points out that while men's standard of living often improves following divorce (with an average increase of 42 percent in the first year), the standard of living for women and their minor children declines sharply (an average decline of 73 percent). If you've been through a divorce, either your own or your family's, you likely understand this math on a visceral level.

For those who haven't been intimate to a divorce, or only to an incredibly copacetic one, it might be hard to understand these metrics: Wouldn't the father still be contributing the same financial support to the family as before? Of course not: Child support payments may only cover the basic expenses of caring for a child; they are very rarely enough to bring the "household income" back to the same level as before the divorce. (What's more, in the 1980s, the average child support award was also in decline—and fewer than half were able to collect the child support owed them.)

Ironically, part of the reason for this type of downward mobility was the rise of "no fault divorce," first adopted by the state of

California in 1969, which allowed both parties to file for divorce without evidence of wrongdoing on either part. This made it easier for women in unhappy and/or abusive marriages to leave their husbands, but there was little societal attention to what would happen to those women once divorced.

For most divorced women, it was incredibly difficult, if not impossible, to make the sort of money that would render them financially independent. It's not that these women weren't hard workers—but many had quit their jobs in order to raise children. When the marriage ended, they often found it difficult or impossible to reestablish themselves on the career track or even find work. Their ex-husbands, by contrast, still had the same job or career they had before the divorce, as well as what Newman calls "job mobility"—the ability, if laid off, to chase job opportunities or find employment at the same level.

The psychological impact of post-divorce downward mobility, and the feeling of precarity that accompanies it, is multilayered: Children are not only confronted with the dissolution of the family unit, but of their understanding of their family's financial situation, their class position, what they can and cannot afford. In previously middle-class families, it also often sets up a dynamic in which children are put in the position to ask, beg, or negotiate with one parent for "extras" not explicitly covered by child support: car repairs, glasses, camp tuition, or assistance with college.

This is precisely what happened when my parents divorced when I was sixteen. My mom, working as a teacher, had helped put my dad through medical school—and then had quit her job to take care of my brother and me, largely in deference to my father's much higher earning potential. When my parents divorced, my mom hired a good lawyer to advocate for financial acknowledgment of what she'd lose in the divorce, otherwise known as alimony.

In this, my mom's situation—and, by extension, my family's—was unique. She was able to complete her master's degree, which she had opted not to pursue back when my dad was in medical school. Payment for many of the activities that were part of my larger "education" were stipulated as a part of the divorce decree. But there were other financial realities—quite small, in the grand scheme of economic deprivation, that nevertheless deeply destabilized me. That's what downward mobility does, whether the cause is divorce or a lost job: It moves the ground beneath your feet. For the first time in my life, I was acutely aware of money—not my own, but how much each parent had at their disposal on a monthly basis. I knew we couldn't afford the mortgage on the home we'd lived in as a family, and, as we looked for new homes, exactly what kind of house, in what kind of neighborhood, we could afford. I knew what it felt like to ask, plead, and harass a parent for repairs on the car I drove to school, even as I did my best to avoid any indicators of class instability to my friends and the rest of the world.

To be clear, even after the divorce, my family was still able to maintain a middle-class lifestyle. But to do so—and to try to decrease reliance on my father, especially when the alimony ended—my mom adopted a rigorous posture toward work that I'd later adopt. Specifically, a mentality of working all the time. I don't begrudge her this—she was scared, and mad, and desperate for a modicum of economic security. But I watched her work spread, like a spilled glass of water, into all corners of our lives. She graded while we watched television; she wrote in the evenings after we'd gone to bed. In an attempt to make extra money to supplement the small amount she was paid to adjunct at the local college, she started writing math textbooks, which took up more of her time on weekends and during the summer.

I've had conversations with my mom about this time—and

what it took, many years later, for her to develop a different, far less militaristic attitude toward work. It wasn't her fault I reacted to our family's economic anxiety in a way that would harden my resolve to avoid a similar situation in my own life. For example, I would not, and have still not, put myself in a situation where my career and financial well-being could be jeopardized through a breakup. I attended grad school when I wanted to attend grad school; I was skeptical and remain so of the need for marriage. And I internalized that working all the time was the surest way to make yourself feel less panicked about the things you couldn't control. This might feel like a logical coping mechanism, but as so many of the millennial generation can attest, it is rarely a healthy or manageable one.

In the conclusion to *Falling from Grace,* Newman's take on the effects of widespread downward mobility is bleak—but also, in some ways, revolutionary: "Downward mobility is not merely a matter of accepting a menial job, enduring the loss of stability, or witnessing with dismay the evaporation of one's hold on material comfort; it is also a broken covenant," she writes. "It is so profound a reversal of middle-class expectations that it calls into question the assumptions on which their lives have been predicated."

Most burnt-out millennials I know have arrived at that point of calling those expectations into question, but it didn't happen right away. Instead, it's taken *decades*: Even after watching our parents get shut out, fall from, or simply struggle anxiously to maintain the American Dream, we didn't reject it. We tried to work *harder,* and *better,* more efficiently, with more credentials, to achieve it. And everyone, including our parents, seemed to agree on the first and most necessary stop on that journey: college, the best one possible, no matter the cost.

3

College at Any Cost

BY HIS JUNIOR YEAR IN HIGH SCHOOL, A STUDENT known around campus as "AP Frank" had a course schedule so jam-packed that he couldn't take a lunch break. All of his classes were AP—hence the nickname—all taken in an effort to gain Frank attendance to Harvard: "The Xanadu of his mother's dream, the ticket to a life free of failure." Frank eventually got into Harvard, but before he left for school in the mid-2000s, he wrote a post on his blog:

Weighted GPA: 4.83
SAT: 1570, 1600
SAT II Physics: 790, 800
SAT II Writing: 800
SAT II Math IIc: 800

Number of APs taken: 17
Number of 5s received: 16
Number of times I wish that my parents would see me as a
person, not as a resume: 4 years = 365 days + 1 day for the leap
year = 1461

The rest of the post outlines the other, non-resume-build-
ing activities Frank missed out on: He'd never been drunk, he'd
never "hooked up" with a girl, he'd only slept over at a friend's
house twice in his entire school-age life.

Reading Frank's blog post today feels deeply, disturbingly sad.
But to many teen readers of that time, the trajectory of his life,
as included in Alexandra Robbins's *The Overachievers: The Secret
Lives of Driven Kids,* was aspirational. Published in 2006, *The
Overachievers* is compulsively readable—Robbins, who's embed-
ded herself in over half a dozen other "subcultures," paints each
of her subjects as complicated, compelling characters as they go
through the heady process of applying for college. But it also
reads like a burnout prequel: "When teenagers inevitably look at
themselves through the prism of our overachiever culture," Robbins writes, "they often come to the conclusion that no matter
how much they achieve, it will never be enough."[1]

The first chapter of the book is filled with similar warnings
about the psychological toll of this type of behavior—and the
wages of thinking of oneself as a resume. But multiple people
told me they read it as a sort of instruction manual. Sure, these
kids were unhappy, stressed, sleep-deprived, and ambivalent. But
they still got into good schools, right?

Depending on where a millennial lands on the generational
age span, where they grew up, and what their high school was
like, that attitude might be incredibly familiar. In the late '90s, I
experienced what felt like a prototype of it—College Stress 1.0

—in which I was convinced that my choice of college would determine the trajectory of my life. But there wasn't a culture of college competition at my high school: I had to drive thirty miles to take the SAT, which I did, once; my college guidance counselor actually questioned why I was interested in applying for out-of-state schools.

But six hours away, in Seattle, students at competitive prep and public schools were having a very difference experience. At the magnet school one of my soon-to-be best friends attended, students posted their college acceptance and rejection letters on a public bulletin board in the newsroom of their school paper. And that was in 1998.

Over the next fifteen years, the college application process continued to evolve, as millennials began flooding schools with applications. As more and more students were vying for (only slightly more) spots at the elite schools, overflow applicants pooled around other forms of elite schools: elite liberal arts colleges, elite public universities, schools that accumulated elite connotations through sports recognition, "schools that change lives." The Ivies were the pinnacle. But the Ivy *promise*—that getting into an elite college could quell economic anxiety and buy a ticket to "a life free of failure"—trickled down to virtually every type of secondary education.

Millennials became the first generation to fully conceptualize themselves as walking college resumes. With assistance from our parents, society, and educators, we came to understand ourselves, consciously or not, as "human capital": subjects to be optimized for better performance in the economy.

That pressure to achieve wouldn't have existed without the notion that college, no matter the cost, would provide a path to middle-class prosperity and stability. But as millions of overeducated, underemployed, and student-debt-laden millennials will tell you, just because everyone around you believes in the gospel doesn't mean it's necessarily true.

College didn't alleviate the economic anxiety of our parents. It didn't even guarantee our position in the middle class, or, in many cases, actually prepare us for the job market. But the preparation for college taught us a valuable, lingering lesson: how to orient our entire lives around the idea that hard work brings success and fulfillment, no matter how many times we're confronted with proof to the contrary.

*   *   *

Up until World War II, college education was a rarified experience, available to those who were white and male and born into money. Most people learned their trades through apprenticeships or on-the-job training; even doctors and lawyers were somewhat self-taught (they studied on their own, or with a mentor) until the formalization of graduate school in the late nineteenth century. In 1940, just 4 percent of American women aged twenty-five or older had bachelor's degrees, and just 5.9 percent of men.[2] Only 14 percent of the population had completed high school. (In 2018, 90.2 percent of the population over age twenty-five had completed high school, while 45.4 percent has an associate's or bachelor's degree.)[3]

After the end of the war — and amidst growing concern over the United States' place in the global world order — a commission appointed by President Truman issued a six-volume report entitled "Higher Education for American Democracy." Amongst its recommendations: doubling the number of students enrolling in college by 1960, thereby tapping the potential of millions of Americans who'd been excluded from higher ed.

Central to increasing college attendance would be providing

government assistance, whether in the form of loans or grants. "There must be developed in this country the widespread realization that money expended for education is the wisest and soundest investments in the national interest," the report declared. "The democratic community cannot tolerate a society upon education for the well-to-do alone. If college opportunities are restricted to those in the higher income brackets, the way is open to the creation and perpetuation of a class society which has no place in the American way of life."

The idea that schooling would make society more democratic and equitable, more fundamentally American, was foundational to the development of what W. Norton Grubb and Marvin Laverson call "the education gospel," which includes the idea that school, and the credentials that come with it, are the only way to keep up as the economy shifts from industrial production to the "Knowledge Revolution," and the information-based jobs many feared it would create.

Grubb and Laverson chose the word *gospel* to evoke just how ideologically integrated—how naturalized—the idea had become. *Of course* more education is better than less education, *of course* you should go to college by any means necessary—even when the costs of that college outweigh the benefits—despite increasing evidence that college is not "worth" its cost for those who drop out, or for those who come from lower-class backgrounds.[4] They point to the National Commission on the High School Senior Year, released in 2001: "In the agricultural age, post-secondary education was a pipe dream for most Americans," it declared. "In the industrial age, it was the birthright of only a few. By the space age it became common for many. Today, it is just common sense for all."[5]

Lily, who went to a prep school in New York, told me that she never even considered not going to college: "My oldest sister almost didn't, and the narrative in the family was that she was in danger of failing at life and dooming herself." That's a common refrain amongst many millennials—especially amongst the middle class, or anyone who wanted to escape their town, or find something better than what their parents had. "It never occurred to me that college was optional," Caroline, who graduated in 2000 from a high school near La Jolla, California, said, "or that my life would be worth living without a college degree."

*   *   *

Human capital is, in Malcolm Harris's words, "the present value of a person's future earnings, or a person's imagined price at sale, if you could buy and sell free laborers—minus upkeep."[6] Crass as that might sound, it's a clear-eyed look at what capitalism does to the humans who work within it. Like the machines we work with, our worth is measured in our ability to *create value* for those who employ us. Think about any hiring process, or salary negotiation. The employer asks themselves: "What is this person worth?" and "Is this person a good investment?" An employer can get in "low" (get a good deal by offering less than a worker's true value), or make a bet that a worker's ostensibly low value will appreciate with time.

If you're a physical laborer, your primary value is rooted in your healthy, able body. If you're a service worker, it's your ability to perform a task with skill, precision, and efficiency. If you work in a creative field, it's what your mind can produce—and how regularly it can produce it. If any of those qualities diminish or disappear, you become less valuable: your human capital, at least in that industry, decreases.

You can see how this conceptualization, mapped onto the whole of society, creates problems. When one's value depends on the capacity to work, people who are disabled or elderly, people who cannot labor full-time or who provide care in ways that aren't paid at all or valued as highly—all become "less than" in the larger societal equation. And as much as we like to believe in a society where a person's value is found in the strength of their character, or the magnitude of their service and kindness to others, it's difficult to even type that sentence without being confronted with how little it reflects our current reality.

To be valuable in American society is to be able to work. Historically, more work, more toil, more commitment, more loyalty, more grit—all of that could make you *more* valuable. That's the very foundation of the American Dream. But in our current economic moment—often referred to as "late capitalism," to evoke how much of the economy is predicated on the buying and selling and leveraging of things that aren't, well, *things*—hard work only becomes truly valuable when accompanied by existing connections (a.k.a. class status and privilege) or credentials (diplomas, recommendations, resumes).

Which explains our current "best practices" for achieving middle-class success: Build your resume, get into college, build your resume, get an internship, build your resume, make connections on LinkedIn, build your resume, pay your dues in a soul-sucking low-level position you're told to be grateful for, build your resume, keep pushing, and eventually you'll end up finding the perfect, stable, fulfilling, well-paying job that'll guarantee a place in the middle class. Of course, any millennial will tell you that this path is arduous, difficult to find without connections and cultural knowledge, and the stable job at the end isn't guaranteed.

And yet it's easy to see how parents of all classes would become fanatical about college prep: If you can just get on the path, that good, stable job is in sight! To make things better for the next generation, you don't need revolution, or regime change, or raised taxes. All that's necessary, at least to start, was your kid's college acceptance letter.

That idea, of course, isn't entirely novel. Millions of Gen-Xers and boomers also grew up believing a college education was a ticket to the middle class. But as the economists Matthias Doepke and Fabrizio Zilibotti point out, the rise in economic inequality and the fear of class instability have significantly shifted parents' attitudes and behaviors, particularly when it comes to educational achievement. "In a world of high stakes, the appeal of permissive parenting faded," they write. "Middle-class parents started pushing their children to adopt adult-style, success-oriented behavior." Instead of raising kids, so many parents, consciously and subconsciously, began raising *resumes*.

In *Kids These Days,* Harris points out how the obsession with building value — that is, building resumes — intersected with the tenets of concerted cultivation. Pickup games, for example, became organized, year-round league sports — a potential line, somewhere down the road, on a resume. Playing an instrument for fun became playing an instrument for public, judged performance — another resume line.

The value-adding process starts with grades, which, depending on location and class, means that it begins with preschool. "The idea that underlies contemporary school is that grades, eventually, turn into money, or if not money, into choice, or what social scientists sometimes call 'better life outcomes,'" Harris writes.[7] "When students are working, what they're working on is their own ability to work."

Put differently: What you're doing when practicing your times tables or taking a standardized test or writing an essay isn't learning, but *preparing yourself to work*. This is an incredibly utilitarian view of education, implying that the ultimate goal of the system is to mold us into efficient workers, as opposed to preparing us to think, or to be good citizens. And this utilitarian view matches how our current educational system operates, in which success hinges on a student's ability to adhere to a narrow understanding of "successful" behaviors: getting good grades, performing well on standardized testing, behaving "appropriately" and deferentially toward teachers, establishing "normal" social bonds with peers, and being willing to participate in physical education.

And none of these "successful behaviors" actually reflects a student's intelligence. I'm reminded often of what I was told while studying for the GRE, which holds true for so many types of standardized testing: It's not a test of your intelligence, but a test of your ability to take this particular test. And what each particular test is testing for, over and over again throughout our childhoods, is our capacity to perform work in its rawest form: to be presented with a series of problems and a rigid set of constraints in which to solve them, and to accomplish the task uncritically, with as much speed and efficiency as possible. But the curious thing about these tests, at least in America, is that a student's results can always—with the right amount of money, and connections—be supplemented.

*　*　*

Having talked to hundreds of millennials who experienced or rejected the pressure around college, I've found that there are three overarching categories of students: 1) those whose parents oriented their children's lives entirely around college acceptance, like AP Frank's; 2) those whose parents didn't really have an understanding of the realities of the college application process, thus forcing the student to take the burden of self-development onto themselves; 3) those who found themselves somewhere between those two extremes, with their college desires and self-development supported by their parents, but not enforced, systematized, or militarized.

Again, a lot of the variance had to do with location, experience, and parental history with college and/or downward mobility. My parents graduated from a small Lutheran college in Minnesota, and there was never a question of whether or not my brother and I would go to college, but it was simply *where* we would attend— and what opportunities, most of them social and cultural, that college experience would offer us that our small-town Idaho upbringing had not. (My primary interest in college, if I'm being honest, was finding boys who would think that smart girls were hot.)

I had a similar experience, in many ways, to Daria, who grew up in a white middle-class home in Sonoma County, where she attended a magnet high school with an IB (international baccalaureate) program in the late 1990s and early 2000s. "I don't remember *not* thinking about college," she told me. "I got focused on the idea that I was going to be a professor in about eighth grade, and so I always imagined getting my PhD."

Her parents were both first-generation college students who'd had little information or choice when it came to college. "They wanted my sister and me to go to the kinds of great schools they never knew existed," Daria said. "My dad in particular was enamored with small liberal arts schools. A copy of *Colleges That Change Lives* showed up in our house very early in high school."

To make that dream happen, her parents prioritized activities from a young age: She started taking ballet at five, for example, but they remained open to letting her "organically" find her passion, which turned out to be theater. They then focused on clearing the way for her to become the "very best": Her high school

career was filled with play practice in nearby towns, summer in-
tensives, and participation in every theater camp available.

Daria was focused on school, but not overly stressed; she
fondly remembers her and her boyfriend alternating between
studying for their IB diplomas (a sort of finishing exam) with
making out. She worked a part-time job and fulfilled her school's
volunteering component, but mostly focused on theater. She
scored an 800 on her verbal SAT and in the low 600s on her math,
which her parents hired a tutor to help raise. But apart from the
SAT tutor, the building of human capital was not overt, or even
conscious. "Never once do I remember them saying something
out loud like 'You should do this for your college applications.'"

Across the country, Elliott grew up working class in rural
Pennsylvania, on the edge of Appalachia, and attended a high
school that ranked in the bottom tenth percentile in the state.
His mother had a master's degree in nineteenth-century material culture, but worked as a substitute teacher; his father worked
as the local sewage plant operator. College, to Elliott, was the
"ticket out"—to "do something more freeing, to get paid to do
those things you love." And he started thinking about how to
make it happen when he was very young.

Few people around him had gone to college, though, so his intel was poor. All he knew was that he needed to stick out from his
peers. He enrolled in academic programs every summer, starting in seventh grade. He took the SATs for the first time the year
after, through a program supported by the Johns Hopkins Center for Talented Youth. He filled his resume with extracurriculars he "didn't really enjoy." When he spent his summers at academic college programs, his friends resented him. He avoided
any scenario that could get him into trouble, for fear that anything on his permanent record could prevent him from entrance
into the very best college possible. Elliott's mother helped with

applications, but the impetus to develop his resume was all self-imposed.

The tendency toward self-imposed resume-building became widespread in the '90s, when millennials first hit high school, but it intensified over the course of the 2000s. One reason: technology that facilitated visualizing (and tracking) that competition in unprecedented ways. Danielle, a Korean American from a suburban magnet school in Southern California, recalled constant, looming stress, exacerbated by "the advent of portals like 'school loop,' where we could log in and check our grades and see how they fluctuated as test/essay/assignment scores were uploaded by teachers."

At the same time, websites like College Confidential, Collegewise, College Prowler, as well as communities on *LiveJournal* and Tumblr, provided an online apparatus to compare, contrast, and obsessively check to see when others across the country received acceptances. On College Confidential, the most sprawling of the forums, "basically every anxiety you could imagine about any topic had a massive thread," someone who went through the college application process in the mid-2000s told me. On Parchment, you could ask members to "chance" you—i.e., guess at how likely you were to be accepted to a given college—based on your resume, location, and test scores.

The overarching goal was to make yourself the most interesting, marketable version of yourself—even if just on paper. Conrad, who attended a Catholic high school in Texas in the mid-2000s, internalized the idea that in order to get into college he had to "emphasize a Hispanic identity that [he] didn't really feel at all connected to," and started joining clubs with impressive names his freshman year. Most didn't even meet.

Gina, a Chinese American immigrant from outside of Detroit, recalls crying in the fourth grade after receiving a B+ in Science, because an older kid had told her that all letter grades were reviewed by Harvard admissions. In high school, she knew that her stellar grades wouldn't be "that interesting of an angle" for an Asian applicant, and so she became desperate for a sport, any sport, to fill her resume, before eventually settling on synchronized swimming. It exhausted her so much that she developed trichotillomania, or chronic hair-pulling. She still has a small bald patch from that time.

Many people who talked to me about their high school college prep stress also reported physical and psychological ailments: forms of trichotillomania, insomnia, anxiety attacks —symptoms that for some, still linger today. So much of their worry stemmed from being put in a position with so few options: for most, it seemed like the only outcomes were total success or abject failure. One woman, diagnosed with the learning disability dyscalculia, felt enormous pressure to pursue college with the same tenacity as her peers. Every year during finals, she stressed herself out so severely that she skipped her period. Another woman, who started taking practice SATs in fifth grade, developed IBS and insomnia.

"When As are expected, there's no way to exceed expectations," Meghan, who grew up in the Portland suburbs, told me. "Physically, the pressure felt like a burning pain around my sternum. I once had a chest x-ray because of it. Now I know I have panic attacks, and I imagine that's what it was . . . I threw up so much I inflamed the cartilage between my ribs." It's easy to see the message internalized during this process: The only route to success involves working to the point of—and then *through*— physical pain.

Some people reported yearning for even the possibility of opting out of college. "I found school exhausting," Marie, who is white and attended a public high school for gifted students in

Florida, told me. "But I never considered not going, because I knew it was unlikely I'd find financial security with just a high school education. It also would have just disappointed my family." Instead, she spent her high school years on an "unbearably intensive" minimal-sleep schedule. "I learned how to sleep anywhere for any amount of time, including sitting up on sidewalks," she said. "I maintain to this day that high school was the hardest thing I did in my life."

David, a first-generation Chinese immigrant, graduated from an elite all-boys prep school in New York during the same period. The most important messages about college came from his mother, who wanted to him to go to Harvard, "which holds a singular status as a college for immigrant Chinese Americans," and study medicine, a career she'd left behind when she came to America.

David recalls the importance of getting into the right schools, but it wasn't until his sophomore year of high school that he became, in his words, "self-motivated." While his high school was fancy, he had grown up in poverty, and quickly realized what would be necessary "in order to jump class strata." He maxed out his academic schedule, with no free periods and avoided all social activity, save sporadic dating, which, because it did not explicitly contribute to resume-building, he did in secret. "All of my objectives were cast in terms of college," he said.

Depending on the high school, there are as many stories of people who escaped or rejected this compunction—or just flamed out. But the overarching narrative, internalized amongst these middle-class and middle-class–aspirational teens, was the same: Optimize yourself into a college-application robot.

*   *   *

For many millennials, the college preparation process felt pre-programmed—but also severe, cold, and out of their control. If your friends are an impediment to success, you cut them off. If an activity can't be spun into a line on a resume, it disappears. If a situation presents a potential "risk" to overall resume value—drinking, having too many sleepovers, reporting a teacher for inappropriate behavior, even having sex—it should be avoided at all costs.

"I remember my dad saying, regarding boys, 'Pregnancy means PCC,' e.g., Portland Community College," Meghan, who grew up in a Portland suburb, told me. "I routinely blew off partying, social events, and guys in college, and I have a sneaking suspicion that my general incompetence in relationships has something to do with the absolute priority I gave school over developing social skills."

It's difficult to see those resume-building behaviors as destructive when they're consistently validated. "My high school allowed you to skip lunch to squeeze in more classes," Mary, who went to high school in a Chicago suburb, told me. "I *still* think about how fucked up it is that fourteen-year-old me ate baggies of Cracklin' Oat Bran instead of meals for years." At Antonia's school in Washington, DC, students were allowed to apply to "only" nine schools; their parents were given a limit on how many times they could meet with counselors. "Years later, I asked my guidance counselor why my school had such strict rules about apps," Antonia told me. "She laughed and just said 'To stop your parents.'"

And then there's the creeping disillusionment that none of it *really* mattered, not then, and not now. Peter, who grew in a white upper-middle-class suburb of Boise, Idaho, developed severe anxiety and depression from "forced perfectionism" in high school. His parents had little idea of the extent to which he'd tied his self-worth to his GPA. "Honestly, I think if I failed to keep my GPA over a 4.0, I might've killed myself," he told me.

The effects of Peter's perfectionism still linger, but so does another realization: "One common refrain I've heard from Gifted and Talented kids is how none of us really learned how to think," he said. "We could just retain information so much easier, and most importantly, we had great reading comprehension, which is 90 percent of school assignments. Once I got to college, I realized how little I really know about studying and effectively *learning* and *thinking* rather than just *reading* and *knowing*."

Others told me that because of their manic activity schedule and homework load, they never got to read the classic books assigned to them, or spend time with creative projects. "I was embarrassingly proud of reading the first and last fifty pages of *A Tale of Two Cities* and getting a 100 percent on the test just from context," Tyler, who went to a magnet school in Louisville, Kentucky, explained. "Every once in a while, when something really connected, like when I fell in love with *The Great Gatsby*, I'd feel like I wasted my time by not skimming it and moving on to the next thing."

And then there was the "resume padding," as Tyler put it —which involved a lot of volunteering in the community. "We got so much credit from counselors for things like 'Paint an old person's house!' or 'Rake up leaves!' when it was essentially me and my friends dicking off for a few hours on a Saturday morning," Tyler explained. "I guess it just made me much more cynical once I realized that everyone, including adults, were pretty much bullshitting to make themselves look better. I didn't really feel like I was making people's lives better. I just felt like a teenager trying to pad his resume to get into college."

If you need a good resume to get into college, and the resume is filled with accomplishments that are largely hollow — then what, ultimately, is college for? And why do so many people pretend that it's about education when it's actually about "jumping class strata," as David, the Chinese American student from New York, put it, or maintaining your parents' current class? So-called Tiger Moms have often been demonized in the press, framed as crass, domineering, and *un-American* for their single-mindedness in preparing their children for college. Yet "good" Americans — which is to say, upper-middle-class white Americans — do the same thing. They simply cloak conversations about college in the rhetoric of "happiness" and "fit" and "fulfilling one's potential." It's less crass. But it's still bullshit.

*   *   *

Ideas become commonly accepted for a reason — and in this case, higher education was framed as the "commonsense" solution to a much more complicated set of economic problems: automation, competition from Russia (and then Japan, and then China), and downward mobility and "the disappearance of the middle class," which, as Ehrenreich reminds us, was mostly the disappearance of the blue-collar middle class.

It's easy to see how college became the easy — if imprecise — solution to those massive, daunting, ever-compounding issues. There were and remain multiple flaws with this framework. First, there are still many high-paying jobs that *don't* require a traditional four-year degree: HVAC installers, pipe fitters, electricians, and other construction trades, especially union ones, offer relatively stable middle-class standards of living. But many millennials have internalized the idea that any job that does not require college is somehow inferior — and ended up overeducated, paying off loans for credentials they didn't necessarily need. I've heard this argument countered with the idea that there's no such thing as "overeducation": Everyone should be able to go to college. Take away the crippling student debt, and I'd agree. Of course a plumber should have the opportunity to get an English degree. But we should also be honest that if you want to be a licensed plumber, you don't *need* to have an English degree, or a four-year degree in any form.

Oftentimes — especially in "college prep–oriented" high schools — that idea can feel like blasphemy. One woman told me that her husband, who attended a high school similar to the ones previously described, rejected the process altogether — and received tremendous pushback from his teachers and peers. "He nearly ended up in the military because of the lack of resources on how to pursue trade schools or apprenticeships," she said. "He had to find his own way."

The second problem is one of distinction. In the past, many "knowledge jobs" used a college degree as a filtering mechanism: If you have one, you can stay in the applicant pool; if not, you're automatically excluded. But as a college education became more and more standardized through the '80s and '90s, employers needed new means of differentiation and distinction. In practice, this means even more reliance on the perceived prestige of a college — but also a newfound demand for graduate degrees. It's a classic case of a time-worn phenomenon: Once an elite experience is opened to many, it's no longer elite, and *another* cordoned area is created to redraw the lines of distinction.

While students internalized the idea that they must to go to college, they and their parents often had little idea of how to make it a reality. In *The Ambitious Generation: America's Teenagers, Motivated but Directionless,* Barbara Schneider and David Stevenson examined longitudinal studies of students in high school in the mid and late '90s, now known as old millennials. What they found was profound: By the end of the decade, more than 90 percent of high school seniors expected to attend college, and more than 70 percent expected to work in "professional" jobs: as doctors, lawyers, professors, business managers.

But many were confronted by what Schneider and Stevenson call "misaligned" ambitions: those with "limited knowledge about their chosen occupations, about educational requirements, or about future demand for these occupations." About the fact, for example, that six times more students wanted to be doctors than the number of doctor positions projected to be open when they hit the job market.

All that young ambition comes from somewhere—and if it's not from parents, or pop culture, or friends, it's often from schools themselves. Liz, who graduated from high school in 2002, was part of a small Latinx population at her public school in Orange County, California. Her sister, who was two years older, had been accepted into a college-prep track, and Liz followed her. But her parents "did not believe in college as a reality," Liz told me. "They never even finished high school in Mexico. It was this amorphous blob of an ambition, something to strive for without a map."

Liz wanted to get out of California, preferably to NYU or somewhere "intellectually interesting," and started building toward that goal during her freshman year in high school. "I made sure I was in clubs that emphasized how smart I was, and that would look good to colleges," she said. She was stressed all the time, but not, as she recalls, from school so much as her home life, which was "awful and cagey." There were activities that she wanted to participate in but avoided because they required parental participation. She wanted to be a part of the upper choir, but it would've cost five hundred dollars that her family couldn't afford.

Her college-prep program required that she apply to a number of California schools, which she did, with waivers for the application fees because of her family's income. She had to veer off her school's set course, though, to do what felt right for her: Instead of attending any of the UCs or CSUs where she was accepted, she opted for community college, tuition-free, and transferred to UC Berkeley two years later.

For other students, the reality of the misalignment didn't hit until they arrived at school. Ann, who is white, grew up on Long Island in a family where no one had gone to college or even really pushed her—save to use a different family member's address to enroll her in the rich-kid college-prep public school. At that school, the percentage of students who went to college was extremely high—and there was pressure, Ann recalls, to keep that percentage up. When she told her guidance counselor that she couldn't afford college, they countered that it was "what you did," and she could take out loans. "I was told that if I went to college, I would get a big fancy job and a nice paycheck," she said. "That appealed to me because of my parents, who are divorced and never had very steady employment."

Ann was never at the very top of her class, but she made honor roll and took every available AP class. Her memories of high school are of crying all the time and being so stressed while taking tests that she would give up near the end. At the encouragement of her counselors, she applied to twelve different New York schools. She picked the one with the best aid package, even though she'd never been to the campus because her family couldn't afford a college tour. Ann's mom had always told her that they'd "make college work," but she was so financially unstable that she couldn't cosign her student loans. Instead, a woman Ann babysat for cosigned her loan application.

"I had no idea what I was doing," Ann told me. "No one in my family did. High school, which had pushed us to go to college so hard, did no real prep whatsoever. I showed up at college, started classes, and was rushed to the ER my first week when I thought I was having a heart attack." It was a panic attack — the first diagnosis of anxiety issues that have never gone away, especially after she graduated with $56,000 in loans "right before the economy went to shit."

Today, Ann works at a nonprofit in New York, and is trying to throw as much money at her loans as possible. She's never missed a payment, and has an 800 credit score — about as close to perfect as you can get. But when she thinks of burnout, she thinks about that student loan payment — over $500 a month, which means *maybe* they'll be paid off by the time she's forty-two — and how exhausted she is with paying for a mistake that was sold to her as a solution.

"I should've never gone to college," Ann says, and I believe her. What she wanted was stability, and a life that was different than her parents. She got some of that. But she also got a life pocked with a different sort of fear and stress, made all the more potent by regret.

There are so many reasons for millennial burnout. But one of the hardest to acknowledge is the one that Ann faces down every day: that the thing you worked so hard for, the thing you sacrificed for and physically suffered for, isn't happiness, or passion, or freedom. Maybe college provided choices, or got you out of your small town or a bad situation. But for the vast majority of millennials, getting a degree hasn't yielded the middle-class stability that was promised to both us and our parents. It's just the same thing it always was, even when it gets dressed up in the fancy robes of the education gospel: more work.

4

Do What You Love and You'll Still Work Every Day for the Rest of Your Life

BACK WHEN I WAS A PROFESSOR, I ONCE TOLD A STU-dent, whose dozens of internship and fellowship applications had yielded no results, that she should move somewhere fun, get any job, and figure out what interested her and what kind of work she didn't want to do. She burst into tears. "But what'll I tell my parents?" she said. "I want a cool job I'm passionate about!"

Those expectations are an unexpected by-product of the "concerted cultivation" that imbued so many millennial child-hoods. If a child is reared as capital, with the implicit goal of cre-ating a "valuable" asset that will make enough money to obtain or sustain the parents' middle class status, it would make sense that they have internalized that a high salary is the only thing that ac-tually matters about a job. There are some students who achieve just that: some doctors, most types of lawyers, maybe all consultants.

Still, we often look at anyone who articulates hope for a "well-paying" job as somehow crude, even though that understanding of work is most similar to our ancestors', who relationship to labor was, above all else, utilitarian. A miner might have taken pride in his hard work, but mining—or farming, or ranching—was not a vocation he chose because it was cool, or because he felt "passionate" about the trade. He did it because it was what his father did, or because it was the most viable option, or because he'd been trained all his life, in one way or another, to do it.

Millennials, by contrast, have internalized the need to find employment that reflects well on their parents (steady, decently paying, recognizable as a "good job") that's also impressive to their peers (at a "cool" company) and fulfills what they've been told has been the end goal of all that childhood optimization: doing work you're passionate about, which will naturally lead to other "better life outcomes."

The desire for the cool job that you're passionate about is a particularly modern and bourgeois phenomenon—and, as we'll see, a means of elevating a certain type of labor to the point of desirability that workers will tolerate all forms of exploitation for the "honor" of performing it. The rhetoric of "Do you what you love, and you'll never work another day in your life" is a burnout trap. By cloaking the labor in the language of "passion," we're prevented from thinking of what we do as what it is: a job, not the entirety of our lives.

The harsh reality of the job search lays bare the contradictions, half-truths, and poorly constructed myths that motivated millennials through childhood and college. Jobs don't magically appear with a college education. The student loans taken out to pay for that college education can limit job choices—particularly when an entry-level salary in a field is too low to offset the minimum monthly payment and the cost of living. Health insurance is crappy or unavailable. Gig work, even doing something you love, barely pays the bills. Your high school and college resume, no matter how robust, can still be a nearly valueless currency. Most of the time, all that passion will get you is permission to be paid very little.

*   *   *

In 2005, Steve Jobs delivered the commencement address at Stanford University—and reaffirmed an idea the university's millennial graduates had spent much of their lives internalizing. "Your work is going to fill a larger part of your life, and the only way to be truly satisfied is to do what you believe is great work," Jobs said. "And the only way to do great work is to love what you do. If you haven't found it yet, keep looking. Don't settle."

Miya Tokumitsu, author of *Do What You Love and Other Lies About Success and Happiness,* sees Jobs's speech as a crystallization of the narrative of "lovable" work: that when you love what you do, not only does the "labor" behind it disappear, but your skill, your success, your happiness, and your wealth all grow exponentially because of it.

This equation is, in itself, premised on a work-life integration poised for burnout: What you love becomes your work; your work becomes what you love. There is little delineation of the day (on the clock and off) or the self (work self versus "actual" self). There is just one long Möbius strip of a person pouring their entire self into a "lovable" job, with the expectation that doing so will bring both happiness and financial stability. As the artist Adam J. Kurtz rewrote the DWYL maxim on Twitter: "Do what you love and you'll ~~never work a day in your life~~ work super fucking hard all the time with no separation and no boundaries and also take everything extremely personally."

Within the framework of "do what you love," any job can theoretically be lovable, so long as it's what you, personally, love. But "lovable" jobs, at least in this moment, are *visible* jobs, jobs that add social and cultural cache, jobs where you work for yourself or with little direct supervision. They can be jobs that are viewed as societally altruistic (teachers, doctors, public defenders, social workers, firefighters) or jobs that are framed as cool in some way (park ranger, microbrewer, yoga instructor, museum curator) or where you have total autonomy over what you do, and when you get to do it.

They're jobs that kids dream about, that people *talk* about, that earn a "Wow, what a cool job" when you bring it up in conversation. Waitressing can be a cool job if you're doing it for the right restaurant; menial backstage work can be a cool if it's for the right theater company. Michael, who is white and grew up middle class in Kansas City, had only the vaguest notions of what his ideal job would be: "Something where I was 'being creative' all day." Rooney, who is Black and working class, conceived of a good job as "meaningful," that she was "passionate about" and "called to." Greta, who's white and grew up middle class, said her favorite media texts—from *Legally Blonde* to *Gilmore Girls* —taught her that a "cool" job is one where you doggedly pursue your passion.

The desirability of "lovable" jobs is part of what makes them so unsustainable: So many people are competing for so few positions that compensation standards can be continuously lowered with little effect. There's *always* someone just as passionate to take your place. Benefits packages can be slashed or nonexistent; freelance rates can be lowered to the point of bare sustenance, especially in the arts. In many cases, instead of offering a writer money for content that goes on a website, the writer essentially pays the website in free labor for the opportunity for a byline. At the same time, employers can raise the minimum qualifications for the job, necessitating more school, another degree, more training—even if that training may or may not be necessary—in order to even be considered.

In this way, "cool" jobs and internships become case studies in supply-and-demand: Even if the job itself isn't ultimately fulfilling, or demands so much work at so little pay so as to extinguish whatever passion might exist, the challenge of being the one in a thousand who "makes it work" renders the job all the more desirable.

For many companies, that's a perfect scenario: a position that costs them little to nothing to fill, with a seemingly endless number of overqualified, incredibly motivated applicants. Which explains why, in the ostensibly robust job market of the late 2010s, companies have found themselves increasingly desperate to fill unlovable, lowly compensated jobs—especially given that many of them, no matter how basic, now require a college degree. As Amanda Mull pointed out in the *Atlantic*, that desperation took the form of the cool job ad, and spending more and more money on perfecting that ad (instead of, say, offering candidates better money, benefits, or flexibility[1]).

According to Indeed.com, between 2006 and 2013 there was a 2505 percent increase in jobs described using the words "ninja"; a 810 percent increase in "rock star," and a 67 percent increase in "Jedi."[2] At the time of this writing, you can apply for a position as a "Customer Support Hero" at Autodesk, a "Nib Ninja" at a Pennsylvania chocolate factory, a "Wellness Warrior" at a clinic in Utah, and a "Rockstar Repair Man" for an Orlando, Florida, rental group. Most of these job ads are for entry-level positions with pay at or just above minimum wage, with few or no benefits.

Some are simply freelance gigs marketed as "earning opportunities." The shittier the work, the higher the chances it gets affixed with a "cool" job title and ad—a means of convincing the applicant that an uncool job is indeed desirable and thus worth accepting the barely livable wage.

That's the logic of "Do what you love" in action. Of course, no worker asks their employer to value them less, but the rhetoric of "Do what you love" makes asking to be valued seem like the equivalent of unsportsmanlike conduct. Doing what you love "exposes its adherents to exploitation, justifying unpaid or underpaid work by throwing workers' motivations back at them," Tokumitsu argues, "when *passion* becomes the socially accepted motivation for working, talk of wages or responsible scheduling becomes crass."[3]

Take the example of Elizabeth, who identifies as a white Latina and grew up middle class in Florida. As an undergrad, she attended the Disney College Program, which provides a hybrid internship and "study abroad" experience, only instead of a foreign country, it's at . . . Disney. Afterward, she was desperate to find a job, any job, with the company—even one at its call center. The position was a total dead end, with no means of advancement, just the expectation that you should be grateful to have a Disney job in the first place. "At Disney, they bank on your love of the company," she said. "I did love the company and their products, but that didn't make the barely-above-minimum-wage pay okay."

When a group of "passionate" workers do advocate for better pay and working conditions—by, say, joining a union—their devotion to their vocation is often called into question. (The exception are occupations that have been unionized for decades, like many firefighters and police officers.) Advocating for a union means identifying oneself first and foremost as a laborer, in solidarity with other laborers. It promotes a sort of class consciousness that so many employers have worked to negate, instead re-framing "jobs" as "passions" and "workplaces" as "family." And God forbid you talk about money with family.

*   *   *

It's easy to see how a profound slippage can develop between pursuing "passion" and "overwork": If you love your job, and it's so fulfilling, it makes sense that you'd want to do it *all the time*. Some historians trace the American cult of overwork to the hiring practices of post–World War II defense industries in the Santa Clara Valley of California. During the 1950s, these companies began recruiting scientists who were, as Sara Martin puts it in her 2012 history of overwork, "single-minded, socially awkward, emotionally detached, and blessed (or cursed) with a singular, unique, laser-like focus on some particular area of obsessive interest."[4]

Once hired, these scientists provided the new standard for the "good" worker. "Work wasn't just work; it was their life's passion," Martin explains, "and they devoted every waking hour to it, usually to the exclusion of nonwork relationships, exercise, sleep, food, and sometimes even personal care." Psychologists at Lockheed, one of the preeminent companies in what would become Silicon Valley, dubbed the particularly desirable worker mentality "the sci-tech personality," Martin says, and molded their work cultures around them: Work whatever hours you want, for as long as you want, in whatever clothes you want, and we'll make it happen. At HP, they brought engineers breakfast "so they would remember to eat" — an early iteration of the cafeterias and free meals and snacks that have come to characterize startup culture.

But it took the runaway success of *In Search of Excellence* —

published in 1982 by two McKinsey consultants — for that particular work ethic to be nationalized and standardized. The argument of the book was straightforward: If companies could find employees like the ones working in Silicon Valley (i.e., employees willing to subsume themselves in work) they too could enjoy the newly mythologized success of the tech industry. In this way, overwork became avant-garde, fashionable, forward-thinking — while unionized protections of the forty-hour workweek became not only old fashioned and out of touch, but distinctly *uncool*.

And as unions — and the legislation that protected them — became unpopular, so too did worker solidarity. Instead, the quest to find and win "lovable" work created an atmosphere of ruthless competition; feeling personally passionate and fulfilled by work takes precedence over working conditions for the whole.[5] "Solidarity becomes suspect when each individual views him- or herself as an independent contractor, locked in a zero-sum battle with the rest of society," Tokumitsu explains. "Every moment he or she spends not working means someone else is getting ahead, to his or her detriment."[6]

Trying to find, cultivate, and keep your dream job, then, means eschewing solidarity for *more work*. If a coworker insists on set work hours, or even just taking a vacation, they're not setting healthy boundaries — they're giving you an opportunity to show that you can work harder, better, *more* than them. In my newsroom, for example, reporters are given the option of taking a day or two off after covering a traumatic event, like a mass shooting. But few take that offered day, because in a job like journalism, where thousands are hungry for your job, it's not actually an opportunity for rest — it's a chance to distinguish yourself as someone who *doesn't* require space for mental recovery.

When everyone in the workplace conceives of themselves as individual contractors in continuous competition, it creates conditions prime for burnout. One worker sets the bar for how early they can get into the office and how late they can stay; other workers try to meet or exceed it. Of course, the cumulative result of this atmosphere is rarely positive: In my case, not taking even a single day off after covering the mass shooting in Sutherland Springs, Texas, turned me into a burnout-denying sad sack reporting lump for months. And a culture of overwork does not mean better work, or more productive work—it just means more time at work, which becomes a stand-in for devotion.

Burnout occurs when all that devotion becomes untenable —but also when faith in doing what you love as the path to fulfillment, financial and otherwise, begins to falter. Still, it usually takes years, even decades, to lose a faith you've spent an equal amount of time internalizing. Take the case of Stephanie, who identifies as "mixed" (white and Asian) and grew up middle class in North Carolina. Stephanie admits she never even considered the possibility of not finding a job immediately after graduation. She was one of the top three students in the Literature Department, was part of the Honors Society, wrote for the newspaper, and helped edit the literary magazine. Because she didn't have a car, and worked full-time in the summers, she couldn't get an internship—the sort of thing that could've built her portfolio. That said, she assumed that her good grades and extracurriculars would carry her through.

"I performed so well academically that I sort of assumed that a job would fall into my lap," she said. "After all, that was how everything in academics worked: I put in my end of the work and everything turned out fine. I thought that because I was a motivated, capable person with excellent writing skills, I didn't have to worry much."

Stephanie's ideal job was somewhere with "a notable amount of 'cool capital'—you know, working at *Vice* or another trendy/

edge place. Somewhere that everyone's heard of." When those opportunities didn't manifest, she told people who asked that she wanted to go into "nonprofits," yet looking back, that desire was much more about, as she puts it, "getting social rewards for being 'good.'" She managed to find placement with AmeriCorps — but the job environment was so awful, she quit in two months. She started waiting tables at a pizza place to pay the bills, and began applying for jobs, aiming for ten a week. She used a spreadsheet to keep track of when and where she'd applied. In the end, she submitted applications to more than 150 jobs. Only a handful even responded.

This went on for two years. Still working at the pizza place, she started drinking heavily with her coworkers, and dating a bartender who ended up being abusive. "I was low energy, hungover all the time, and, at points, suicidal," she recalls. The only way she knew how to get out of the pizza job was to write for free in order to build her portfolio. So that's what she started doing — and eventually, four years after graduation, landed a job at a nonprofit — for fifteen dollars an hour, no benefits, and no 401k.

These days, Stephanie's dubious about whether her degree from a public liberal arts college was worth it. "Getting out of the service industry felt like a huge accomplishment to me," she says. "But the more time I spent in the service industry, the more I wondered if I was egotistical or naive for wanting a directed career as badly as I did."

As a result of this experience, she's radically recalibrated her understanding of what a job can and should be to her. "I've always wanted my work to be my whole life, but now I feel like a good job is something that doesn't require me to work more than forty hours on a regular basis, and with duties that feel challenging and interesting while still doable. I don't want a 'cool' job anymore, because I think jobs that are your 'dream' or your 'passion' consume too much of one's identity outside of work hours in a way that can be so toxic. And I don't want to lose my identity if I lose my job, you know?"

*   ·*   *

When so many millennials entered the job market, it was either in complete shambles or in very, very slow recovery. Between December 2007 and October 2009, the unemployment rate doubled: from 5 to 10 percent. Total employment dropped by 8.6 million. And while a major nationwide recession affects nearly everyone, in some way, it especially affects those on the market for the first time. When millions of experienced workers lost their jobs, they went looking for new ones wherever they could: including the lower-paying, entry-level work where first-time job seekers generally find a foothold in the market. For millennials between sixteen and twenty-four, the unemployment rate rose from 10.8 percent in November 2007 to 19.5 percent in April 2010 — a record high.[7]

"Millennials got bodied in the downturn," Annie Lowrey wrote in the *Atlantic*. They "graduated into the worst job market in eighty years. That did not just mean a few years of high unemployment, or a couple of years living in their parents' basements. It meant a full decade of lost wages." The extent of the effects of this timing is only now coming into focus: A 2018 report issued by the Federal Reserve, for example, found that "millennials are less well off than members of earlier generations when they were young, with lower earnings, fewer assets, and less wealth."[8]

No job, after all, means no ability to save — for a home, for retirement — or invest. Some millennials went back to school to weather the storm and emerged, two or six years later, with tens of thousands of dollars in student debt — and job prospects hardly improved. Those forced to move home were also forced to endure anxious discourse, from our own parents and the media, that we'd never leave: aimless and lazy, instead of weathering an economic cataclysm entirely out of our control.

It was, and remains, a bleak reality. But millennials, even those back at home in their childhood bedrooms, weren't raised to resign themselves to market forces. We were raised to work harder to find that promised perfect job, eager to perform what Kathleen Kuehn calls "hope labor": "un- or under-compensated work, often performed in exchange for experience and exposure in hopes that future work will follow."[9] In other words, internships, fellowships, and other quasi jobs, many of which hold dubious value yet feel compulsory for most jobs, especially, as Tokumitsu points out, "lovable" ones.

When I graduated from college in 2003, few of my friends had done internships, or even had known to seek them. Ten years later, as a professor, I fielded far more questions from advisees about how I could connect them with internships than requests to explain, say, their coursework on Lacan's psychoanalytic theory. Because as difficult and impenetrable as Lacan's theoretical concepts are, for most students they're still less difficult than landing an internship.

You can just read more to understand a theory: put in more work, and incomprehension will eventually solve itself. But internships are about connections and, above all else, the willingness and ability to work for little to nothing. And if you can't get a job without a portfolio, and you can't build a portfolio without internships, and you can't afford to work for free to snag those internships — then, in theory, only a certain sort of person (read: a person with means, a person with private funding from their university, a person who can take out even more loans to cover an internship while they're in school) can afford to provide "hope labor."

Some of us were only able to take on internships because we were living at home. Others, to make ends meet, relied on parents, or student loans, or side hustles. Many gave up the dream of finding work in their desired field entirely. But that didn't mean the overarching idea that you should do what you love, no matter the cost, faded away.

Sofia, a white woman who grew up "privileged as fuck," had a string of unpaid internships at small museums and Sotheby's before graduating from a small liberal arts college with a degree in art history. But it was 2009, and a promised job at Sotheby's suddenly evaporated. She applied for hundreds of paid and unpaid internships in New York and Chicago; she finally got a single interview with a theater company and took it, knowing that her parents could help support her, since the internship was unpaid.

She tried to get a waitressing job on the side, going door to door in Astoria, Queens, distributing her resume to every restaurant. She never heard a thing, landing a job only when a position opened up at the restaurant where a friend worked. "If I learned anything in that search, it was that networking, nepotism, and insider connections are largely the only way to get a job," she said. "And even then, that job was an unpaid internship."

And yet, that internship led to a paid internship, which eventually led her to a PhD program. But before she got that far, Sofia helped assist the intern coordinator at one of the museums where she worked—and gained "firsthand knowledge of how nonchalantly they exploited interns (in terms of low/no pay) because they knew how competitive the internships were."

Each internship opportunity attracted thousands of applicants; it was harder, in certain ways, to land the internship than to get into an Ivy League school. "They knew, because they had a prestige brand, that they could do anything they wanted when it came to compensation," Sofia said. "No one gets into the arts world for money anyway, right? You have to be *passionate* about it to pursue it! And they wonder why museums have such bad reputations for hiring diversity."

In truth, there are three options to cover unpaid or underpaid work while in undergrad or graduate school: Take out student loans to cover it, work another job to subsidize it, or rely on parental support (in the form of living/eating at home, or parents footing the bill for living expenses). In a 2019 blog post, Erin Panichkul, the first in her family to go to college, wrote about how she'd taken out loans throughout her undergrad career, not just for tuition, but to cover rent, groceries, utilities, and books: first at Santa Monica Community College, then at UCLA, and finally at law school. When the prospect of the unpaid internship came up at the United Nations, she knew she had to take it—even if it meant taking out student loans (i.e., paying) to do work for free.

"Exposure does not pay bills," Panichkul wrote, in a post entitled "Unpaid Internships Keep Women Like Me Out of the Legal Field." "Experience doesn't cover rent. It doesn't pay for my transportation to get to my internship. It doesn't feed me. But I believed the experience was so important that taking out a loan was worth it." It's an "unwritten rule" that the resume builders obtained through internships are essential to landing a job at a firm. Thus, it's an "unwritten rule" that you must take on internships, no matter how little they pay, in order to get a job. "Getting paid for working should not be a luxury," Panichkul writes. "When I was a law student, I was always so damn grateful for these opportunities that I never questioned the practice until now."

When people follow a "calling," money and compensation are positioned as secondary. The very idea of a "calling" stems from the early precepts of Protestantism, and the notion that every man can and should find a job through which they can best serve God. American Calvinists interpreted dedication to one's calling—and the wealth and success that followed—as evidence of one's status as elect. This interpretation was conducive to capitalism, the cultural theorist Max Weber argues, as it encouraged every worker to see their labor not just as broadly meaningful, but worthwhile, even sacred.

In a seminal study on zookeepers, J. Stuart Bunderson and Jeffrey A. Thompson examined the hardships endured by those who conceived of their work with animals as "a calling." Zookeepers are highly educated but poorly paid, with an average salary of $24,640 in 2002. The majority had to take on a second job in order to make ends meet. There's very little room for advancement, and they spend a not insignificant amount of time each day cleaning up waste and performing other "dirty work." But they also articulated an unwillingness to consider quitting, or finding a new line of work. As Bunderson and Thompson point out, "If one feels hardwired for particular work and that destiny has led one to it, then rejecting that calling would be more than just an occupational choice; it would be a moral failure, a negligent abandonment of those who have need of one's gifts, talents, and efforts."[10]

Alex, who's white and grew up lower-middle class, graduated from college in 2007 and started looking for a job pastoring a church. In the twelve years since he first started looking, he's applied to over a hundred jobs. Sometimes, he works multiple jobs; others, he can't find even one. He currently has a job with a church, but his contract ends this summer, and he doesn't know what's next for his family, who moved in with his parents last year to make ends meet. He's currently looking for any job with a consistent schedule, a reasonable commute, and a clear mission or focus. "Healthcare," he says, "would be a big plus."

But as he continues to seek — and fails to find — work as a pastor, he finds himself cycling between anxiety and shame and depression, and all of it bumping up against the sense of "calling." "There's the idea that we are being led to something larger than ourselves: God, the universe, whatever," he told me. "So when we are burnt out, or put up boundaries, there is a sense that we are somehow betraying our call by not loving every single minute of it."

A "calling," in other words, is often an invitation for exploitation, whether you're a zookeeper or a teacher or a pastor. In *The Job: Work and Its Future in a Time of Radical Change,* Ellen Ruppel Shell points out that employers have even created algorithms that examine an application in order to discern "called" applicants from those simply "applying," based on the understanding that "the former will happily tackle any task without argument or demand."[11] It doesn't matter how many people admit that un- and underpaid internships are exclusionary and exploitative. New graduates still flock to them. A fellowship at BuzzFeed attracts thousands of applicants; a recruiter for various late-night television shows told me that for the summer of 2019, she fielded ten thousand applicants for fifty positions on two shows. The promise of hope labor is that if you can just make it in the door, it doesn't matter how you or other hope laborers are treated. What matters is that there's a *chance* that you'll end up doing what you love, however poorly paid you will be.

Erin, who identifies as white and Middle Eastern, grew up in a rural area of California. She attended a state school, where she received a degree in global studies, and was eager to find a job in education or at a nonprofit, "doing something that would be meaningful or allow [her] to do good, but also allow [her] to travel and live abroad." In the lead-up to graduation, she, like so many others, spent a great deal of time at the career center, attending workshops, trolling the center's website, and checking the boxes that, in addition to a college degree, she assumed would put her on a path to a secure job.

In her first post-college search, Erin applied for "too many jobs to remember," but only got called back for two: as a low-paid canvasser for an environmental nonprofit (think: the people who stop you on the street and ask if you "have a second for the environment today"); and as a junior financial analyst, a position for which she was deeply unqualified. She hated the idea of moving back home, but eventually realized she had no other option: "I couldn't afford anything else without a job," she told me.

Initially, she was ashamed — this was 2008, and, at least in her town, the broad effects of the recession had yet to manifest. But in time, nearly everyone from her class who didn't go into STEM, or find their way to grad school, had also moved home. She spent several months job searching, fighting a growing sense of anxiety and shame, before eventually landing a part-time job at an after-school program at the local YMCA, which "paid nothing."

One day, Erin's first grade teacher showed up and gave her a folder: She'd saved all of her old assignments and a collection of the best work she'd done after, all the way through eighth grade. The teacher had intended the gift as a way of showing Erin how much potential she'd always seen in her, but Erin internalized it as deep disappointment. "I had always been the smart one, and in my hometown was seen as one of those kids with a bright future," she said. "Which is why it was such a crushing blow to move home — I was supposed to go create peace in the Middle East and here I was, back in my small town."

The cultivation of hope — no matter how small the chances

are of actually succeeding — has become a business strategy. Interns and fellows create content and provide labor at a fraction of the price of a salaried employee, but they're just the most obvious example of hope laborers. Freelance writers are hope laborers. So are temps, hoping for that coveted "conversion to full-time." Entire industries thrive on a surfeit of workers willing to ask for less in order to work more — so long as they can tell themselves and others that they have a job they "love."

See especially academia, which has effectively become a hope labor industrial complex. Within that system, tenured professors — ostensibly proof positive that you can, indeed, think about your subject of choice for the rest of your life, complete with job security, if you just work hard enough — encourage their most motivated students to apply for grad school. The grad schools depend on money from full-pay students and/or cheap labor from those students, so they accept far more master's students than there are spots in PhD programs, and far more PhD students than there are tenure-track positions.

Through it all, grad students are told that work will, in essence, save them: If they publish more, if they go to more conferences to present their work, if they get a book contract before graduating, their chances on the job market will go up. For a very limited few, this proves true. But it is no guarantee — and with ever-diminished funding for public universities, many students take on the costs of conference travel themselves (often through student loans), scrambling to make ends meet over the summer while they apply for the already-scarce number of academic jobs available, many of them in remote locations, with little promise of long-term stability.

Some academics exhaust their hope labor supply during grad school. For others, it takes years on the market, often while adjuncting for little pay in demeaning and demanding work conditions, before the dream starts to splinter. But the system it-self is set up to feed itself as long as possible. Most humanities PhD programs still offer little or nothing in terms of training for jobs outside of academia, creating a sort of mandatory tun-nel from grad school to tenure-track aspirant. In the humanities, especially, to obtain a PhD — to become a *doctor* in your field of knowledge — is to adopt the refrain "I don't have any marketable skills." Many academics have no choice but to keep teaching — the only thing they feel equipped to do — even without fair pay or job security.

Academic institutions are incentivized to keep adjuncts "do-ing what they love" — but there's additional pressure from peers and mentors who've become deeply invested in the continued vi-ability of the institution. Many senior academics with little expe-rience of the realities of the contemporary market explicitly and implicitly advise their students that the only good job is a tenure-track academic job. When I failed to get an academic job in 2011, I felt soft but unsubtle dismay from various professors upon tell-ing them that I had chosen to take a high school teaching job to make ends meet.

It didn't matter that I had no other options. What mattered was that I'd fallen off the only acceptable path: staying in aca-demia, no matter what. "We were supposed to accept the sta-tus quo because we were doing good," Erin recalls. "When I quit teaching to work in tech — because I was literally starving! — I felt judged by my former colleagues." If you left teaching, the idea was that you "couldn't cut it" or were neglecting to make the work "about the students." She felt like a traitor for not "not sucking it up."

If and when academics find themselves disillusioned with the system, that disillusionment is often accompanied by a sprawling and stubborn sense of shame. It doesn't matter if they followed every piece of advice on how to mold themselves into an ideal job candidate, or that the system thrived on their seemingly infinite stores of ambition and labor. What matters is that they spent a decade or more of their lives working toward what they loved — and failed to reach the finish line. That's what happens when we don't talk about work as work, but as pursuing a passion. It makes quitting a job that relentlessly exploited you feel like giving up on yourself, instead of what it really is: advocating, for the first time in a long time, for your own needs.

For Hiba, a Pakistani woman and first-generation American, the realities of performing that hope labor, wholly without recognition, proved too much to bear. As an undergrad, she wrote regularly for her campus newspaper and the local Muslim newspaper; when she graduated, her professors told her she'd quickly land a job at a local newspaper and eventually work her way up to something with more clout. But when she started applying for jobs — sometimes up to thirty a day, all over the United States — she heard nothing. Even though writing about Muslim issues was a passion, advisors told her to leave her experience with the Muslim newspaper off her resume to avoid bias. Still: nothing.

Eventually, Hiba landed a job as a research analyst at a technology company. The pay was decent — a salary of $38,000 a year — but the work was stultifying. She sat in a cubicle, inputting data and cold calling, and found herself "desperately bored and depressed." One day she found out that the commencement speaker at her graduation — a guy she was sure would go on to a stellar career in journalism — sat just a few cubicles down.

But Hiba was still driven to find something in journalism: she kept sending applications, and was offered a job as an editorial assistant at a science magazine, but the pay — just $26,000 — was too low to live on. She started taking night classes in Women's Studies, and, in her words, "fell so hard" for it that she eventually completed a master's degree. That's what it took to finally land her much-desired cool job, at a "flashy liberal news magazine" in New York. Even though it was part-time, and she was paid just eight dollars an hour, and she'd have to live on a friend's couch, she jumped at the opportunity.

"A part of me desperately just wanted to be known as a writer," she said. "I wanted to be attached to a news magazines where intellectuals read things. I thought I'd bring an interesting angle, writing about the intersection of being Muslim, and a woman, and having spent three years studying and researching these topics for my graduate degree. Instead, I was exhausted, underpaid, and became extremely depressed." Virtually no one in the office spoke to her.

Hiba had worked long enough in a job that wasn't cool to be able to recognize just how poor the working conditions were when she got to one that was. It might not have been boring, but it wasn't any of the other things she thought it would be. "I thought sticking it out was worth it," she said. "But in the end, the experience was so disheartening, I had to leave."

Do What You Like Just Fine

The fetishization of lovable work means that plain old *jobs* — non-ninja, non-Jedi jobs that might not be "cool" but that nonetheless offer magical powers like "stability" and "benefits" — come to feel undesirable. Within this logic, mailmen and electrician seem like our grandparents' and parents' jobs, the sorts of jobs with a definable start and ending, the sort of jobs that don't subsume the worker's identity. Maybe you don't love it, or feel *passion* for installing air conditioning, but you don't hate it. The hours are fair, the pay is decent, the training is feasible. And yet, these jobs are often coded, at least amongst the educated middle-class, as undesirable.

That's something Samantha, who grew up upper-middle class in Connecticut, and dropped out of college before finishing her degree, still struggles with. After leaving school, she told everyone she knew that she wanted to teach and was just taking time. But what she really wanted was to become the manager at the small grocery store where she worked. Today, she still works at that grocery store, where she makes a good hourly wage and has a flexible schedule. "I still feel like it's not enough, because it's not something I dreamed about doing as a kid," she explained. "But does that mean it's not a good job? Did my grandfather *dream* of being a postman for thirty years? Probably not, but I bet no one begrudged him that good job."

Millennials' growing disillusionment with the "Do what you love" ethos, coupled with continued, steady demand for all of the unsexy services provided by those jobs, has given them a new sort of shine. Amongst my peers, I've noticed a generalized "come to Jesus" moment regarding job requirements and aspirations: They no longer want their dream job — they just want a job that doesn't underpay them, overwork them, and guilt them into not advocating for themselves. After all, doing what they love burnt them to a crisp. Now they're just doing jobs — and fundamentally reorienting their relationship to work.

Consider Erin's new job in tech: It's stable, she can afford to do things like pay for groceries, and unlike with adjuncting, she's able to maintain clear boundaries between her work and non-work life. Growing up, she thought that a good job was something where you could make a lot of money, love what you do, *and* do good deeds; now her definition of a good job is "whatever pays the most and allows me to disconnect after five p.m." It's a trajectory that feels increasingly common amongst millennials: to find a way to do what you *like just fine*.

Millions of millennials, regardless of class, were reared on lofty, romantic, bourgeois ideas of work. Eschewing those ideas means embracing ones that have never disappeared for many working-class employees: A good job is one that doesn't exploit you and that you don't hate. Jess, who's mixed race and identifies as Black, grew up "incredibly poor" with absentee parents. When she graduated from college with a degree in African American literature, she wanted to go into marketing of some sort, but her urgent need for a job in 2009, at the height of the recession, meant working at Starbucks.

Jess would've moved back home with her parents, but that wasn't an option. She took unpaid freelance work, trying to build her portfolio. At first, she just felt great about graduating and had fun as a barista, but she quickly began to feel anxious as younger friends graduated straight into jobs. These days, she does love her job — nonprofit, working for kids in foster care — in part because she never felt the compulsion to find the perfect job, even as friends around her vied for more distinctly aspirational positions. "I have a more realistic view," she said, "because I grew up with a mom that did not have a career. She worked multiple dead-end jobs to raise her four kids alone."

Sofia, who did all those art internships, recently completed her PhD at an Ivy League university. "I thought a good job would be doing work that made me feel like I was creating and learning more about art, at a prestigious institution with name recognition," she admitted. "And the prestige thing didn't go away for a *lonnnnnnng* time. It wasn't until doing my post-PhD job search that I realized that prestige has nothing to do with job satisfaction. Luckily, I had seven years of grad school, plus all those internships, to realize what parts of the work made me happy and fulfilled."

After going on the market, she found her first permanent job with benefits. It's not in academia, per se—but teaching history to middle school students. "It makes me really happy, pays pretty well, and leaves me feeling challenged and fulfilled every day," says. "It's not prestigious, but it's awesome."

*   *   *

One of the pernicious assumptions of "Do what you love" is that everyone who's made it in America is doing what they love—and conversely, everyone who's doing what they love has made it. If you haven't made it, you're doing it wrong: "Central to this myth of work-as-love is the notion that virtue (moral righteousness of character) and capital (money) are two sides of the same coin," Tokumitsu explains. "Where there is wealth, there is hard work, and industriousness, and the individualistic dash of ingenuity that makes it possible."

Where there is not wealth, this logic suggests, there is not hard work, or industriousness, or the individualistic dash of ingenuity. And even though this correlation has been disproven countless times, its persistence in cultural conditioning is the reason people work harder, work for less, work under shitty conditions.

When that cool, lovable job doesn't appear, or appears and is unfeasible to maintain for someone who's not independently wealthy, it's easy to see how the shame accumulates. Over the last ten years, Emma, who's white, has attempted to break in to the information science world—what the rest of us know as librarians. When she graduated with her master's, she was offered a full-time temp job, with the understanding that it would turn permanent "if she worked hard enough."

"It was my dream job," Emma explained. "I thought I was the luckiest person on earth." But the organization went through a "leadership change" and she was strung along on temp contract after temp contract, pushing herself to her psychological and physical limits. "I worked above and beyond, putting every drop of energy I had into being the most enthusiastic, invested employee," she said. "But the new leadership did not like me, no matter how hard I tried."

During her repeated job searches, she experienced depression, low self-worth, intense regret about her investment in education, and a generalized lack of dignity. "I questioned every aspect of my identity," she says. "Is it the way I talk? My hair? My clothes? My weight?"

Part of the problem was misaligned expectations: when she was getting her master's, her professors told her that she would graduate and find a full-time position, with a $45,000 minimum salary, benefits, and the ability to immediately enroll in a public service loan forgiveness program. In practice, after numerous job searches, she's in a job outside her field for which she's overeducated. She's making $32,000. Still, she feels lucky, every day, that she's one of the few in her field who's found full-time employment.

When Emma looks back on the last ten years, she feels cynical but grateful. "It's always been implied that if you fail to succeed, you aren't passionate enough," she said. "But I no longer invest in work emotionally. It isn't worth it. I learned that every single person is expendable. None of it is fair or based on passion or merit. I don't have the bandwidth to play that game."

When I hear stories like Emma's, so similar to thousands of

other millennials', I realize all over again just how aggressively, and tirelessly, so many of us worked toward that dream job. Which is why it's so difficult for millennials to fathom the most enduring criticism of our generation: that we're spoiled, or lazy, or entitled. Millennials did not germinate the idea that 'lovable work' was the ideal, nor did we cultivate it. But we did have to deal with the reality of just how frail that idea became once exposed to the real world.

When someone says millennials are lazy, I want to ask them: Which millennials? When someone says we're entitled, I do ask them: Who taught us we should be able to do work that we love? We were told that college would be the way to a middle-class job. That wasn't true. We were told that *passion* would eventually lead to *profit*, or at least a sustainable job where we were valued. That also wasn't true.

Entering into adulthood has always been about modifying expectations: of what it is and what it can provide. The difference with millennials, then, is that we've spent between five and twenty years doing the painful work of adjusting our expectations: recalibrating our parents' and advisors' very reassuring understanding of what the job market was with the realities of our own experience of it, but also arriving at a wholly utilitarian vision of what a job can and should be. For many of us, it took years in shitty jobs to understand ourselves as laborers, as *workers,* hungry for solidarity.

For decades, millennials have been told that we're special — every one of us filled with potential. All we needed to do was work hard enough to transform that potential into a perfect life absent all the economic worries that defined our parents. But as boomers were cultivating and optimizing their children for work, they were also further disassembling the sort of societal, economic, and workplace protections that could have made that life possible. They didn't spoil us so much as destroy the likelihood of our ever obtaining what they had promised all that hard work was for.

Few millennials had the wisdom to understand that as we hit the job market. Instead, we believed that if opportunities didn't arise, it was a personal problem. We acknowledged how competitive the market was, how much lower we'd set our standards, but we were also certain that if we just worked hard enough, we'd triumph—or at least find stability, or happiness, or arrive at some other nebulous goal, even if it was increasingly unclear why we were searching for it.

We fought that losing battle for years. For many, including myself, it's hard not to feel embarrassed about it: I settled for so little because I was certain that with enough hard work, things would be different. But you can only work as an "independent contractor" at a job paying minimum wage with no benefits while shouldering a $400-a-month loan payment—even if it's in a field you're "passionate" about—for so many years before realizing that something's deeply wrong. It took burning out for many of us to arrive at this point. But the new millennial refrain of "Fuck passion, pay me" feels more persuasive and powerful every day.

5

How Work Got So Shitty

IN THE 1970S, THE TEMP AGENCY WAS ASCENDANT. Built on the labor, at least outwardly, of wives eager for quick pocket money, temping was sold as a quick and incredibly easy fix to a company's immediate labor needs. An ad for one of the leading firms, offering "Kelly Girls," promised that a temp worker

- never takes a vacation or holiday
- never asks for a raise
- never costs you a dime of slack time (when the work drops, you drop her)
- never has a cold, slipped disc, or loose tooth (not on your time, anyway!)
- never costs you for unemployment taxes and Social Security payments (none of the paperwork, either!)

- never costs you for fringe benefits (they add up to 30 percent of every payroll dollar)
- never fails to please (if your Kelly Girl employee doesn't work out, you don't pay)

In short, you didn't have to treat a Kelly Girl like an employee at all — or at least not like what unions and companies had agreed employment looked like. Temps, like overseas labor, provided a way for companies to circumvent the demands of unions without looking like union-busters. They also enabled companies to decrease their costs, while excusing themselves from any contract of responsibility between employer and employee — and in so doing, shifted the risks of everyday life back onto the individual employee. And as will become clear, it also provided the template for the contemporary work model, in which adjuncts, independent contractors, freelancers, gig employees, or any other sort of "contingent" laborer make up a new, ever-expanding societal classification: the precariat.

The precariat is not the vision of the working class held by many Americans. As the theorist Guy Standing points out, the working class, at least how it's remembered, had "long-term, stable, fixed-hour jobs with established routes of advancement, subject to unionization and collective agreements, with job titles their fathers and mothers would have understood, facing local employers whose names and features they were familiar with."[1] The precariat has almost none of those things. Uber drivers are part of the precariat. So are retail workers, Amazon warehouse employees, adjunct professors, freelance writers, Instacart grocery shoppers, corporate cleaners, MTV digital producers, in-home nursing assistants, Wal-Mart stockers, fast food servers, and people who cobble together several of these jobs to make ends meet.

A precariat worker knows few of their coworkers, and those that they do know turn over quickly. They often have a college degree, or have completed several semesters toward one. Some, like the adjuncts and freelance writers, find themselves in the precariat as they continue to pursue their "passion," no matter the cost. Others find themselves there through desperation. Their economic and class status is *precarious,* which renders them ever vigilant for even the smallest piece of bad luck that could sink them into poverty.

Above all, precariat workers are exhausted—and, regardless of the specifics of their job, burnt out. "Those in the precariat have lives dominated by insecurity, uncertainty, debt and humiliation," Standing writes. "They are denizens rather than citizens, losing cultural, civil, social, political and economic rights built up over generations. Most importantly, the precariat is the first class in history expected to labour and work at a lower level than the schooling it typically requires. In an ever more unequal society, its relative deprivation is severe."[2] They are angry at and are anxious about the broken promises of the American Dream, but they keep grinding to try to position themselves closer to it.

Depending on whether or not you're a part of the precariat, this might all sound dire. It is—but one of the greatest cruelties of the American class system is that no one, not even those whose lives are now defined by precariousness, wants to admit as much. They are "told they should be grateful and happy that they are in jobs and should be 'positive,'" Standing explains.[3] After all, the economy is booming! Unemployment is low! But that's not how a growing number of Americans are experiencing it.

If you think you're insulated from the precariat—through your current job, or your education, or your parents' standing —you're wrong. You might currently be part of what Standing calls the "salariat"—the class of workers who are salaried, have agency within their jobs, and report feeling that their opinion counts within the company. But every day, the salariat continues its "drift," as Standing puts it, into the precariat: full-time workers are laid off and replaced by independent contractors; the new "innovative" tech companies refuse to even categorize the bulk of their workforce as employees.

Workers aren't getting lazier, or worse at multitasking. We don't lack grit or ambition. Instead, work is bad and getting worse, precarious and getting more so. But to understand how work got this shitty for so many requires a significant detour into the past — into the history of the temp, but also into the interlocking histories of consulting, private equity, and investment banking. We have to understand how the workplace "fissured" — that is, broke apart at its very foundation — and how the resultant instability has affected us all.

*   *   *

We've covered this before, but here it is once more: In the 1950s and '60s, big unions, big corporations, and robust government regulation helped produce an unprecedented era of growth and economic stability. The stagflation of the 1970s and the mini-recessions of the 1980s, sparked and exacerbated by the reality of global markets and competition, made people desperate for a change, any change, that could return the company to that postwar prosperity, that "great compression" that expanded the middle class. Across the country, people began to buy in to the logic of the "free market": the idea that an economy free of government intervention will sort itself out naturally, and the self it sorts out will be stronger than ever before.

It's easy to see the allure: The postwar period had bolstered the belief that hard work would always be rewarded, despite the fact that deliberate, sometimes surgical intervention in the economy, coupled with wide-scale union protections, were what made it flourish. But that's the thing about American governmental intervention: When it's effective, it's enveloped in a narrative of "American ingenuity and hard work"; when it's ineffective, it's proof of the fundamentally immoral nature of government assistance.

The promise that the free market would fix everything was a persuasive one, and, over the course of the '80s and '90s, politicians on all levels began to roll back union protections and dramatically reduce government regulation, especially in regards to the financial markets. The heads of public corporations, desperate for increased stock valuations in an increasingly volatile market (and beholden to investors who could potentially oust them at any point) began sloughing off any non-essential components of their business, from janitors to entire arms of a company, in order to make it as lean and "agile" as possible. You might know this strategy by the more common but vague name of *downsizing*.

The rhetoric of downsizing suggests that whatever is being cut was never really necessary: You downsize from a sprawling McMansion to a home that fits you *just fine;* you reduce greed and redundancy and extravagance. That understanding followed it into the workplace, too. Sure, more Americans had enjoyed economic prosperity and stability during the Great Compression. But the companies had become, at least from the profit-margin-obsessed perspective of Wall Street, bloated. That "bloat," however, was often related to the compensation packages and structures that made work better for more people. It might have made life good, but that didn't mean it wasn't disposable.

But why did companies want to be so "lean"? Because it'd raise their stock value. And who was putting them on a starvation diet? Consultants. Guns for hire, brought in to offer cold assessments of companies after a period of observation. In *Temp: How American Work, American Business, and the American Dream Became Temporary*, Louis Hyman traces the development of consulting, along with accounting, as means to apply order to the sprawling corporations that grew over the course of the postwar boom. And while accountants' major task was keeping the books straight, consultants' task was more theoretical: analyzing how a company ran, and then telling it how to make it run *better*.

"Better," however, is a subjective term: Does a company run better when its employees are happy and provide livable income for their families? When its profit margins are larger? Because consultants had no investment in the firms themselves, their advice was in line with the aims of unfettered capitalism: How can companies make the most money, with the biggest profit margins, over the least amount of time? "The corporation, under the consultants' helm, was no longer an enduring venture," Hyman writes. "It became a momentary assemblage whose value was not in tomorrow's progress but in today's stock price."[4]

To understand how consultants affect the companies that employ them, you have to understand the way they work. The vast majority are recruited out of college, then assigned "projects," that is, companies in need of consultation. These days, consultants live in or near an urban center — but leave at dawn on Monday morning to travel to the site of the company they are assessing, whether in Grand Rapids, Michigan, or Miami. During the week, they stay in a hotel, they eat out or order room service, and most of all, they work: interviewing every employee under their purview, in search of inefficiencies and redundancies. They fly back home Thursday evenings, generally spend Fridays in the office, and after an established period of reviewing the company — be it a month or two years — they make their recommendations: Here's where, and how, to cut the fat. George Clooney in

Up in the Air is a consultant. So are a solid percentage of the people sitting in first class on a given flight.

Consultants' distance from the companies they're consulting — both literal and figurative — is a huge part of their value. They don't know, or have attachments to, any of the workers, which allows them a certain clarity when it comes to cuts. Unlike direct supervisors or CEOs, they'll never see the workers that get downsized again. They don't know about their family lives, or what ramifications their recommendations will have on the life of this town or region that is not theirs. It's hard not see them as ice-cold killers. But it's equally important to remember that they are doing what the company itself, often desperate to appease stockholders, has requested. A consultant makes recommendations; a company approves and executes them.

Over the course of the 1980s and '90s, consultants' recommendations became more and more focused on identifying the "core competencies" of a company — that is, what it does best, in a way that wasn't already replicated elsewhere — and quietly getting rid of anything and anyone that didn't contribute to them. As David Weil points out in *The Fissured Workplace,* that meant spinning off parts of companies, eliminating entire departments, and outsourcing "non-essential" labor (e.g., temp workers), who could be relied on to provide the same service at significantly lower cost to the company.[5]

Some of these workers came from outside services, like cleaning companies, who provided janitorial services to multiple companies. And some of them came from temp agencies. Before the 1970s, most temps worked for just one company, and filled in for different positions as needed, effectively making vacation and sick days possible (and guilt-free) for full-time workers. They did not *replace* workers; they temporarily filled in for them, as the name suggests. But by the 1970s, with the massive rise in the number and demand for temp workers, their role changed. More and more people were temping as a full-time job, and that meant shifting from company to company, working with multiple temp agencies, with little idea when or if the next job would come, or what it would require.

For companies attempting to downsize and shed labor costs, temps were cherished as "flexible," but what they really were was disposable. They could be hired for a short period of time, then let go without fanfare. They couldn't join the company union, if one existed, and as the Kelly Girl advertisement suggests, they didn't have any of the other rights afforded to actual employees.

And because of the overarching narrative about who temped and why, it was seen as easy, and acceptable, to treat them as such. As Hyman shows, the early narrative of the postwar temp was that she was a "luxury-seeking hausfrau," out to make a little extra money to buy the things she wanted in the home. The temp's family didn't *need* the money; the temp just wanted a little money-making fun. And because the income was considered superfluous, it wasn't as if firing them, or creating unstable job conditions, was actually harming anyone. After all, they always had the option to just not temp. But that narrative never bore much relation to fact — even more so in the 1970s, when the economy bottomed out and laborers, many laid off by the same sort of companies now relying on temp labor, just needed a job, any job.

Still, the narrative of temp work as actually temporary, or at least voluntary, stuck. Ultimately, temp work was so thoroughly feminized, and effectively trivialized, that little thought was paid to whether or not it was exploitative. As we'll see, similar narratives have accumulated around gig and freelance work in the wake of the Great Recession: When driving for Uber is framed as a voluntary side gig instead of a desperate attempt to supplement a dwindling teacher's salary, then it's all the easier to ignore the reality of the economic situation and the companies that take advantage of the workers they've failed.

*   *   *

The logic behind downsizing, reorganizations, and sloughing full-time employees was ultimately straightforward: Trimming the company meant short-term profits; short term profits meant higher stock prices and satisfied stockholders; satisfied stockholders meant the CEO and board members got to keep their jobs, even as the remaining non-temp, non-outsourced workers at the company were given less and less in terms of benefits and pay increases.

All of this seems like common sense today: That's just how the market works. But that's because that's how the market has worked *during millennials' lifetimes.* Before the 1970s, a public company's stock market value was often steady, rooted in long-term projections of growth and stability. But then something peculiar happened: As companies shed employee benefits like pensions, more and more Americans began investing in mutual funds, via the 401ks that had been offered up to replace the pension. In 1980, mutual funds were considered a "backwater" investment—they held a relatively paltry $134 billion in assets. By 2011, that number had exploded to $11.6 trillion.[6]

And here's where it gets interesting: Every day, mutual funds like Vanguard and Fidelity are investing for millions of people's retirements. But they care little about the long-term security of a company they're investing in, instead focusing on short-term profits that can show up in 401k statement as gains. The money going through these accounts is, in the economist David Weil's words, "impatient, and moves frequently in search of better returns."[7] In 2011, for example, the average turnover in mutual fund portfolios was 52 percent. These mutual funds, like the few large pension funds that remain, helped reify the market's mindset about layoffs, outsourcing, and massive CEO compensation: They're all great, so long as they continue to inspire the sort of profits these funds crave.

That logic is bolstered by private equity and venture capital firms, which buy "troubled" companies, reorganize them, and then resell them, oftentimes after leaning them to the point of bare bones. Private equity firms have little long-term investment in the companies they buy or what they may do for a community. They buy and sell all sorts of companies — often bundling many together and killing off the brand, no matter how old or beloved, in the process. One of the most vivid examples of the effects of private equity acquisition might be local newspapers. In the early 2000s, newspapers all over began to falter, as their business model collapsed under the challenge of the internet and Craigslist. Many family-owned papers were sold at fire sale prices: to a chain that controlled other papers, or eventually to a private equity firm that acquired the chain.

For papers under private equity, the last decade has been a disaster, with all but the most essential employees laid off. The *Denver Post,* for example, is owned, along with more than ninety other newspapers, by Alden Global Capital; between 2013 and 2018, the company slashed the number of journalists from 142 to fewer than 75.[8] The end result is a parable for the fissured marketplace: The newspapers maintain (very slight) profitability, but their overall value as institutions has plummeted. At the same time, the journalists, copyeditors, and photographers left there have watched their benefits dwindle and their pay remain stubbornly low. They spend every day frantically trying to do the work that five journalists used to do — all while wondering if

they might be the next cut necessary in order for the private equity company to eventually sell the newspaper at a profit.

And then there's the example of Toys "R" Us, a foundational
brand to so many millennial childhoods. In 2005, Toys "R" Us was
bought by a collection of private equity firms, which loaded the
company with debt; by 2007, 97 percent of its profits were directed toward paying down the interest.[9] In practice, that meant
no time for innovation, or remodeling stores, or devising new
strategies to compete with competitors. The private equity owners cut the fat, and then they cut down to the bone, and then, in
2017, the company went bankrupt. The stores were liquidated.
Every employee was let go. "A lot of people assume Amazon or
Walmart killed Toys "R" Us, but it was selling massive numbers of
toys until the very end," the anti-monopoly activist Matt Stoller
writes. "What destroyed the company were financiers, and public policies that allowed the divorcing of ownership from responsibility."[10]

It's easy to see how private equity has developed a reputation
as vultures, vampires, looters, pirates, and pillagers, destroying
whatever good or potential remains out of the already shelled-
out space of American capitalism. In 2019, a study compiled by
six progressive nonprofits found that private equity firms had
been responsible for over 1.3 million job losses over the last decade. At least one million jobs were later added back to the economy in some capacity, but that doesn't negate the effect of layoffs,
loss of benefits and promised pensions, and overall disruption,
which, according to the study, disproportionally affected women
and people of color.[11]

It's not that profits in and of themselves are morally bad. But
the logic of the current market is that a refusal to *increase* profits,
year after year, is a failure. A steady profit, or even a break-even
proposition that yields nonfinancial dividends to a community,

has no value to stockholders. This isn't a knock against capitalism so much as this particular *type* of capitalism: one whose goal is creating short-term profits for people with no connection to the product or the laborers behind it; to award people who have seemingly no awareness of, let alone guilt about, what their investment dollars may have done to the livelihood and working conditions of another.

This is the paradigm shift that's so hard to confront: that in the current iteration of capitalism, fueled by Wall Street and private equity, the vast majority of employees do not benefit, in any way, from the profits that the company creates for its shareholders. In fact, those profits are often contingent upon workers suffering.

* * *

This shift in financial goals — from long-term, gradual, stable profits to short-term spikes in stock price — helped create the increasingly shitty and alienated workplace we now know. It might seem like a long way from what's happening on Wall Street to the exhaustion of your daily life, but that's part of the point: the stock market thrives on decisions that generally make work and life worse for the average laborer. Indeed, a company's stock price often *rises,* at least in the short term, with the announcement of "restructuring" and the layoffs that accompany it.[12] Workers are no longer conceived of as assets. We're expensive, begrudged necessities. Get rid of as many of us as possible and watch company value soar.

Your workplace has probably already been "leaned" and you don't even know it. Think about the person who cleans your work space. Or the people who work at the lunch counter, or handle payroll, or tend to the tasteful lawn outside, or provide customer service. Maybe you are one of those people. Chances are high that the people doing these jobs aren't actually employed by the company that they outwardly seem to represent.

It didn't used to be this way. Companies used to employ the people who made work possible at all levels. The ramifications of this arrangement were huge: If you worked as a janitor at, say, 3M, you were entitled to the same benefits as my Granddad, who worked there as an accountant. Not the same salary—but the same pension structure, the same healthcare, the same *stability*. This was a massive equalizing force: You might not have the same earning potential, but you had the same protection from risk—and, at least in some cases, an opportunity for advancement, which could include moving up and out of janitorial work altogether.

But that mode of employment was also expensive—and because it didn't contribute "directly" to a company's profits, easily shed. Secretarial work and data input could go to temps, who don't need to be treated like employees at all. Accounting and payroll could go to companies specifically created to serve that purpose. Same for janitorial and food and security and customer service.

This model could theoretically work well for everyone involved: Cleaning companies know best how to be cleaning companies—why trouble another company with training and supervising one or two employees in an area totally outside its expertise? The pay and quality of work conditions could even, potentially, be the same. But within what David Weil calls the "fissured workplace," companies have become so devoted to their "core competencies" and brand maintenance that they've largely shed the responsibilities that accompany being a direct employer.

You can find examples of the fissured workplace in every

corner of your life. The federal government is filled with contractors—in part to circumvent the incredibly slow gears of federal hiring practices, but also as a cost-cutting measure. In nonprofits, grant writers are often contractors. IT is perhaps the most commonly outsourced department, but in many cases so is HR, payroll, admin, and maintenance. I talked to an animator who works for a university but is actually employed by a totally different company, and a lawyer whose company is subcontracted by other firms during "discovery"—an increasingly common practice. When you buy a garbage disposal from Lowe's and pay for its installation, the person who comes to your home often doesn't work for Lowe's. Many substitute teachers aren't employed by the school district, but by a subcontractor.

Walk downtown in Seattle, especially within a ten-block radius of the sprawling Amazon campus that's taken over South Lake Union, and you'll see thousands of people wearing performance vests and Amazon lanyards. But a large percentage of the people who show up every day at the Amazon campus and contribute to and otherwise maintain Amazon's services are in fact "contract" workers—employed by a secondary entity with a name no one can remember that shields Amazon from direct responsibility for those employees. And Amazon's far from an outlier: Subcontractors make up between 40 to 50 percent of the workforce in tech. They are software developers, software testers, people working in UX or UI design, entire teams and subsections of development.

At Google, subcontracted employees and temps (121,000 worldwide as of 2019) outnumber actual employees (102,000).[13] They work alongside each other—and are, at least ostensibly, equal. But temps and contractors make less money, have worse benefits, and in the United States earn no paid vacation time. And because of nondisclosure agreements signed upon hiring, no one's supposed to talk about it—publicly or privately. As Pradeep Chauhan, who runs a service that places contract workers, told the *New York Times,* "It's creating a caste system inside companies."[14]

Subcontracting also means that companies can deny wrongdoing when workers' rights are violated. If there's a sexual harassment complaint, the contracting company handles it (or, in most cases, doesn't—especially if the alleged harasser is employed by the actual company and not the subcontractor). Same for an issue with healthcare benefits, or pay equity. In some cases, a subcontractor—in charge of, say, providing food options in the cafeteria in the workplace—might hire *another* subcontractor to do the job. Which is why, Weil argues, it's so difficult to affix blame to, well, anyone: for pay, for working conditions, for lack of training. Subcontracting also makes advancement incredibly difficult: "In my company, we used to have people on the manufacturing lines make the jump to engineering teams, receptionists becoming administration assistants, etc. etc.," one worker told me. "The outsourcing trend killed those foot-in-door career paths."

The net result of this fissuring isn't higher pay, or even equal pay, to what the employee would've received if they hadn't been subcontracted out. Take the example of a cleaning company. They're competing with dozens of other cleaning companies to provide services for Cool Startup. Cool Startup will likely choose the cleaning company with the lowest bid—and the lowest bid comes from the company that pays its workers the least. Now, the owners of Cool Startup might never have deigned to pay its own employee so little—that would be bad PR!—but when services are subcontracted out, it can feign ignorance of the entire pay structure.

Outsourcing to subcontractors is also a handy way to get rid of unions, which are generally viewed, through the consultant mindset, as impediments to profit. (If workers in general are impediments to profit, then workers with power *definitely* are.) The solution to the union problem is simple: lay off everyone employed by the company and, in time, through a subcontractor, hire back people to do the very same jobs, without benefits. If the company had fired everyone and then just directly hired back all new, non-union members, they would be breaking the law. But the company didn't kill the union, per se—they just got rid of all the unionized employees. Labor law has not been updated to protect the new, highly fissured workplace in which there's no recourse for the "sloughed" unionized employee.

One crafty way to outsource risk is to become a franchise, a move that effectively cuts off corporate headquarters from direct responsibility for the thousands of iterations of the brand, owned by independent individuals, that dot the world. McDonald's, for example, has developed rigorous standards for how a food item must be prepared, how uniforms must be cleaned, and at what temperatures a meal must be served. But as Weil points out, a corporate entity itself "would recoil from being held responsible for franchises' failure to provide overtime pay for workers, or curbing sexual harassment of workers by supervisors, or for reducing exposure to dangerous cleaning materials."[15] The company wants the profits, and insists on brand maintenance —but shoulders none of the responsibility for what happens to franchise employees.

That much became apparent in 2019 when a group of McDonald's employees sued the company for its failure to address serious allegations of sexual harassment. One worker in Missouri accused her area manager of repeated sexual harassment—and then was accused of setting him up. After a Florida employee reported sexual harassment on the part of a male coworker, her manager cut her weekly hours from an average of twenty-four to as little as seven. And while McDonald's claims it's "committed to ensuring a harassment and bias-free workplace," the 2019 complaints were the third set of allegations to be filed in just three years.

Enduring sexual harassment — with no straightforward form of recourse, or with fear that if you do report it, you'll be fired — is just one of many symptoms of the fissured workplace. A 2016 study found that 40 percent of women in the fast food industry report experiencing sexual harassment on the job — and 42 percent of those women feel forced to simply accept it, lest they lose their jobs. And 21 percent reported that after raising the issue, they experienced retaliation of some sort: decreased hours, undesirable schedules, raise denials.[16]

And what happens in fast food is not unique: 80 percent of staffers at hotel franchises (Quality Inn, Motel 6, Doubletree, etc.) are employed by separate management companies.[17] In 2016, Unite Here, a union representing hospitality workers, surveyed its housekeeper members in Seattle: 53 percent reported facing some sort of harassment on the job[18]; in Chicago, the number topped 60 percent.[19] Two years before, 77 percent of Seattle voters had approved an initiative that required hotels to supply panic buttons for workers and the creation of a "ban list" for guests accused of sexual harassment. Hotels with over 100 rooms that didn't offer health insurance would be forced to provide a monthly stipend to help employees purchase their own. But the American Hotel and Lodging Association sued the state to overturn the initiative — and won.[20] It's one thing for companies to declare that sexual harassment is not tolerated at their hotels, or that they value their employees. It's quite another to actually dedicate the resources to substantiate the claim.

Companies looking to cut labor costs can rely on temps, outsource to subcontractors, kill a union — but they can also outsource by sending labor overseas, especially to countries where labor is cheap, because regulation and other forms of labor laws are slight, nonexistent, or unenforced. That's what Apple does—and why it directly employees only 63,000 of the 750,000 workers who manufacture, assemble, and sell Apple products across the world.[21]

Apple announced that trajectory back in 1993, with the publication of an essay entitled "The Changed Nature of Workers and Work" in the company magazine. "More and more companies are laying off permanent staff and relying on contract workers and outsourcing to carry out their business," Apple told its employees. "The emerging workplace has a head and no body. It centralizes free-floating talent resources as necessary to meet current needs, and changes size from moment to moment as the marketplace dictates."[22]

"A head and no body" is why Apple can claim that its hands are tied when it comes to evidence of extreme overwork in Chinese factories. In fact, it has no "hands" at all: Those companies aren't technically Apple factories; they just happen to produce the technology that becomes an Apple product. And the success of this philosophy is also a major reason why Apple is one of the most valuable companies on the stock exchange. Apple does all the good, brilliant stuff. All the messy, exploitative stuff that makes those good, brilliant things possible? Not their responsibility.

Outsourcing doesn't keep employee wages steady. It doesn't make employees' work-life better. What it does do is increase the overall value of a company on the stock market, which benefits stockholders and those lucky enough to have a 401k—while depressing wages for those who've been outsourced. And because so many people are willing or desperate to find a job, *any* job, the companies that employ these outsourced workers have little incitement to provide stability, regular scheduling, or benefits. These work situations don't just exacerbate burnout, but feel designed to create it. And at the heart of that design is a select few making a lot of money off of a lot of other people's lack of options.

*　　*　　*

Left to its own devices, capitalism is not benevolent. That's hard for many Americans to hear or think about, having been raised to adulate capitalism, but the fact remains: If the goal is always growth at any cost, then employees, like machine parts, are exploitable, as long as the productivity continues to go up and the profit margins continue to rise. But for a brief period of time, after the Great Depression and before the recessions of the 1970s, capitalism was — at least in America — somewhat more humane. Still imperfect, still exclusionary, still subject to market whims. But proof that the way we do things today doesn't have to be the way we do things in the future.

That period of (slightly) more worker-friendly capitalism wasn't the result of some sort of crisis of corporate conscience. Unions and government regulation forced companies to treat the humans who worked for them as, well, humans: humans who got sick, humans who had kids, humans who got injured on the job, humans who only had the energy to work one job, so should be paid enough to live on from that job, humans who had lives outside of their work.

Deregulation and anti-union legislation, along with new ways of getting around existing regulation, have returned us to capitalism's most ruthless form. The economy is "thriving," but the gap between the rich and poor keeps expanding, and the middle class — created through that period of relative corporate benevolence

—continues to shrink. "What is clearly unique in the recent history of capitalism," the Wall Street anthropologist Karen Ho explains, "is the complete divorce of what is perceived as the best interests of the corporation from the interests of most employees."[23]

With the stock market at all-time highs, the country is "prospering." Before the great risk shift, that prosperity trickled down to a huge percentage of the country through employee paychecks and benefits. Now the only way to share in that prosperity is to own stock. And as of 2017, only 54 percent of people in America own some form of stock—that includes 401ks and pensions.[24] When inflation is factored in, wages are largely stagnant. And no matter how low the unemployment figures are, they take on new meaning when compared to the number of people still living in poverty.

To be "employed" today does not mean you have a good job, or a stable job, or a job that pays well enough to bring a family over the poverty line. There's a startling disconnect between the ostensible health of the economy and the mental and physical health of those who power it. Which is why every time I hear unemployment numbers, I feel gaslit: like someone is telling us, over and over again, that what we know to be true is actually fiction. Same for every time I hear that the economy has never been stronger, and especially when I hear statements like that of the CEO who provides accounting services for Uber drivers: that the gig economy is a "lifestyle choice for millennials."[25]

Statements like that convince workers—and millennials in particular, who've had no other experience of the workplace—that if things feels shitty, then they've only got themselves to blame. Maybe you *are* lazy. Maybe you should just work harder. Maybe work is constant drudgery for everyone. Maybe everyone makes do. Sure, your best friend is struggling, and your sister is struggling, and your coworkers are struggling, but that's only anecdotal evidence against the larger narrative that *everything is great.*

This is how precarity becomes the status quo: We convince workers that poor conditions are normal; that rebelling against them is a symptom of generational entitlement; that free-market capitalism is what makes America great and this is free-market capitalism in action. It turns legitimate grievance, backed by a union or not, into "ungratefulness." And it standardizes overwork and surveillance and stress and instability—the very building blocks of burnout.

Bad jobs and the burnout that accompanies them are not the only option. Unions and regulation that address the realities of the changed economy will help. But there *are* also companies—big, profitable, companies—that prove that it doesn't have to be this way.

According to Zeynep Ton, whose 2014 book on "the good jobs strategy" became a mini-phenomenon, such companies provide "jobs with decent pay, decent benefits, and stable work schedules," "design jobs so that their employees can perform well and find meaning and dignity in their work," and, despite spending much more money on labor, nonetheless produce "excellent profits and growth."[26] The companies Ton profiles aren't little-known, experimental startups. They're Costco, QuikTrip, and Trader Joe's.

You can find QuikTrips—a pretty standard, if beloved, convenience store—in many areas of the US. It might seem like one of the least likely places to find a "good" job. But unlike most companies that hire workers without college degrees, QuikTrip offers affordable healthcare, a stable schedule, and significant training, and promotes managers exclusively from within—with corresponding pay increases. And the results are staggering: its lines are fast, its customers incredibly loyal. Its sales per square foot are 50 percent higher than the industry average. And employee turnover is just 13 percent, compared to 59 percent amongst the top quarter of the convenience store industry.

When Ton interviewed a QuikTrip worker named Patty in 2010, she'd been with the company since age nineteen, and was making more than $70,000 after more than seven years with the company. Asked what makes her excited to go to work every day, Patty responded: "It's knowing that you're going to be able to attend your kids' activities at school. You're going to be able to take care of your kids, and knowing that the company that you work for is growing each day. And you don't have to worry about, *Am I going to get laid off tomorrow?* Or, *Where's the next meal coming from?* There is no other company that will pay you your regular wage, a customer service bonus, a profit bonus, and even an attendance bonus. You go to work, you do your job, you're excited, and you know everything's pretty much taken care of. QuikTrip has never let me down."[27]

What Patty is describing is job security and satisfaction — a work scenario that doesn't cause burnout but helps protect against it. QuikTrip understands that when workers are happy, and safe, and respected, they just work *better.* That logic is straightforward, but, at least in our current moment, it feels radical. "QuikTrip's employees don't get treated well because its profits happen to be up," Ton argues. "QuickTrip's profits are up because it puts its employees at the center of its business. They are the creators of that success — not its lucky or occasional beneficiaries — and they are treated accordingly. That's what the company says, that's what its policies and procedures convey, and that's how its employees feel."[28] It's an anti-burnout strategy and a profit-producing strategy, but it's also just a *human* strategy.

The subjects of Ton's book are exceptional companies, and

what they've done is not easily replicable: It requires constant vigilance, and tinkering, and above all else, maintaining the understanding that workers who are treated as humans instead of disposable robots do indeed hold value. But these companies' success speaks truth to the lie that lousy jobs are "just the new normal." Bad jobs are not a necessity to achieve significant profits. They are a *strategy*, a choice. For millennials who've never experienced a different market logic, it requires some knowledge of that history—understanding it, refusing to shut up about it—to spread the good news. We know work doesn't have to be this way. Our very recent past is proof.

6

How Work Stays So Shitty

"In 2007, I broke my lease, packed my stuff into a van, and couch surfed in a brain fog. But then I faked my way into a startup as a designer in 2009, and life got better for me real fast. I was still in a codependent, abusive relationship, but suddenly I had the money to solve problems that had wrecked my life a few years before. All I had to do was work 60 hour weeks, so I did. It took two and a half years to figure out I was in a toxic work environment, underpaid for the work I was doing and literally the only person at the company who hadn't been offered stock. I've been working on unlearning the idea that putting in more work and being first in, last out is the only thing that makes me useful in the workplace. I dare myself to work 35 hours a week, but it just doesn't take."

— NINA, SOFTWARE DESIGNER, SAN FRANCISCO

"Sometimes I only know my schedule a few weeks in advance. Theaters can suddenly drop me from my contract a few days before it stops, and I am constantly sending emails to try and get work. I'm still covered by my parents' health insurance, but what happens when I turn twenty-six is a very real concern. In my previous job, my work was tracked by garments repaired per hours. For 'major' repairs (eight minutes or less), you were supposed to complete forty garments in six hours. For 'minor' repairs (two minutes or less), we had to do fifty garments in two hours. It was intensely stressful and intensely competitive. Going to the bathroom was both monitored and timed, and deducted from your repair speed. It did not foster any kind of good workplace."

— KAY, FREELANCE COSTUME TECHNICIAN, SEATTLE

"I was finally getting momentum as a writer and I wanted to chase it since I knew it was what I really wanted to be doing. But loneliness is a big one for me. There are days on end when I don't leave the house. I tend to get depressed. I don't see my friends as often I'd like. I am always chasing checks, which is spirit breaking. And I have no health insurance."

— CATE, FREELANCE FILM CRITIC, LOS ANGELES

YOU CAN TALK ABOUT THE FISSURED WORKPLACE IN AN abstract way, moving workers from one company to a subcompany like figurines in a tabletop game. But fissuring affects workers on a practical level, with effects that can be loosely divided into the rise and glorification of overwork, the spread and normalization of workplace surveillance, and the fetishization of freelance flexibility. Each of these trends contributes to burnout in its own noxious way. But the end result is the same: They make the everyday experience of work, across the income spectrum, undeniably and unceasingly shitty.

The Rise of Overwork

The American overwork ethic has become so standardized that there's no feeling of before or after: It's just how it is, how it always will be. But like every ideology, it has a source—it shouldn't be surprising that many of the same people responsible for the fissured workplace were *also* responsible for the fetishization of overwork. Chief amongst them: the consultant.

Elite consulting firms prided themselves on hiring the best and brightest from Ivy League universities—or, if they had to, from the most prestigious schools in a particular region. But their strategy was, and remains, perverse: They take the best students, work them into the ground, and then fire anyone who couldn't deal with spending their workweek away from friends and family or creating business plans that often required gutting long-term devoted employees.

The consultants who made the cut had to do more than establish themselves as workhorses. As Louis Hyman explains in *Temp,* drawing directly from McKinsey's own internal publications, the consultant was judged on whether "he ha[d] real promise for long-term success with the Firm based on his performance and his character."[1] Put differently: Did he dedicate his whole self, and his whole life, to his work? The initial culling usually took place a few years post-college. Oftentimes it was self-imposed: workers stuck around long enough to get their MBAs paid for, then willingly left the firm.

In the 1960s, researchers found that consultants had "more

emotional instability," and "less motivation to exercise power over others" than their peers who worked in stable corporations.[2] They'd downsized so many people that they were frightened of being downsized themselves, afflicted by the same omnipresent anxiety that their work had imposed on others.

But the people who quit or got fired from McKinsey didn't then start local boutiques, or go back and get their teaching degrees, or launch nonprofits. The consultancy cycle was so commonplace that leaving a firm wasn't a mark against you. Instead, former consultants quickly found new jobs, often with the very companies they once advised. After all, it's much cheaper to hire someone with McKinsey knowledge than to actually hire McKinsey. As more and more ex-consultants spread throughout corporate America, the employee-sloughing, core-competency-preserving, short-term-profits-at-all-costs ideology became commonplace. "The instability and high pay of the consulting world fed on itself, as the people who believed in this model of management cut the staffs of corporations, and when that was done, joined the staffs," Hyman explains. "It worked for them. Why would it not work for the rest of America?"[3] The same mindset extended to consultants' standards of overwork: It was an effective sorting mechanism for their business. Why shouldn't it be applied to *every* business?

Consultants, scattered to the corners of the American corporate world, helped create a new paradigm of work: what a "good" worker did, and how much of their lives they devoted to the company, and the level of stability they could expect in return (read: very little). But for all of their ubiquity, even consultants couldn't singlehandedly shift the culture of work in America. And in the rarified air of the investment bank, a similar attitude had already become accepted gospel.

Over the last twenty years, the office with the good snacks

and free lunch has become a cultural punchline: a way to high-light the absurdity of startup culture, or just the ridiculous perks millennials demand. But free food isn't just a benefit. It's a strat-egy to incentivize overwork, and the practice, along with so many other tenets of overwork, came directly from the culture of Wall Street.

That culture is what the anthropologist Karen Ho set out to study in the years leading up to and in the immediate aftermath of the Great Recession. In 1996, she took a sabbatical from her PhD in order to work at an investment bank, which she was able to pull off, despite a lack of finance training, because she was a grad student at Princeton—one of the handful of schools that investment banks conceive of as elite enough to produce invest-ment banker material.

For her research, Ho interviewed dozens of current and for-mer bankers, gaining a textured understanding of the day-to-day life on Wall Street as well as their overarching economic logic. Amongst her findings was that "organizational perks," standard across investment banks, acted to incentivize and perpetuate extremely long hours. Specifically, the free dinner and the free ride home. If an investment banker worked past seven p.m., they could order takeout on the company; because so many workers worked so late, they didn't ever have time to get groceries, let alone have the energy to make dinner. The cycle perpetuated it-self. If a banker stayed until seven p.m., they might as well stay until nine p.m.—when they can take a black car home, again on the company. For the bank, footing the bill for such perks was a small price to pay for the additional work hours.

Ho found that investment banks, especially the top tier, also clung to the notion that constant work is a signifier of eliteness, their version of "smartness." This logic was built on the fact that the banks hire their entry-level analysts almost exclusively out of the Ivy Leagues, and the Ivy Leagues only accept "the best of the best," which suggests the people at investment banks are also "the best of the best." It follows, then, that whatever work schedule they cultivate is superior — even if that work meant eighteen-hour days, nearly seven days a week, up to and past one's breaking point. "If you're single, and your family lives far away, like California, the better analyst you will be," a vice president at a major finance bank told Ho. Analysts often start work with a significant other but, as that same vice president explained, "all of a sudden, after a few months, everyone starts finding out that they are single."[4] "The point is to create a post-college atmosphere where within days of beginning work, analysts and associates begin to 'live' there," Ho argues, "comparing notes about who is staying the latest and 'getting slammed' the most, not to mention participating in the makeshift Nerf football game at 1 a.m."[5]

Some first-year analysts experienced a brief period of shock once initiated into this lifestyle. But Ho found that they quickly internalized the ethic of overwork the same way they had back in high school, and then in college: as a badge of honor, and proof of their own excellence. As one Harvard editorial put it, writing about investment banks' interest in the school's graduates: "They know that four years ago, we wanted the absolute best. We did not settle for number three or four on the college rankings. They prey on our desire to find the 'Harvard' of everything: activities, summer jobs, relationships, and now careers."[6] In other words, those high school students who refused to "settle" for anything other than Harvard lifted the bar on what constituted "hard work" for everyone else.

And for most, that overwork actually was worth it. As Ho points out, elite Wall Street bankers are among the very few in the American economy who "still experience a link between hard work and monetary rewards and upward mobility." Overwork, in their case, meant massive bonuses. Historically, most middle-class Americans experienced some version of this scenario: If their company was extremely productive and profitable, those profits trickled down to workers in the form of salary, benefits, and even bonuses (although never as big as on Wall Street). Now, after the great risk shift, those profits go to shareholders and CEOs — and to the bankers who recommend and enact the trades of those profitable companies.

Because investment bankers still benefit from the link between overwork and compensation, many also internalize the idea that if someone's not making much money, it's because the rest of the world, off Wall Street, lacks work ethic. An associate at Goldman Sachs gave Ho an extensive rundown of the way he's come to see the world, which is worth reading in full:

> If you go to the outside world and you start working with people, people just are not motivated in the same way. It is just a pain in the ass to get anything done in the real world. People leave work at five, six p.m. People take one-hour lunch breaks, and people do this and that and whatever. Believe me, it makes a big deal, because if you are working with people who all work real hard to do whatever it takes to get things done, it just makes things so much easier. And doing things is what makes people feel good about their life and makes them feel important. This is the whole self-worth thing — to complete and do things. In a big corporation or in the academy, it is hard to get things done. [On Wall Street], you work with so many people where anyone you talk to is so responsive and pretty bright and really motivated, it just makes for a pretty good environment. I think in the old days, back in the fifties or sixties, people kind of just had a set pattern of life. They went to work, climbed up the ladder slowly, and did whatever they were told. I think now that people are so seduced by the

capabilities that you can jump ahead and how much of a difference you can make, how important you can feel or whatever it is that gets you off. . . . It feels like now, you can get a lot done, be really productive, and it is seductive. And that is why people who have more than enough money . . . more than enough respect, still are involved in this at the expense of their families because they need to feel needed. And there is nothing better than to complete things on a regular basis.

I've read this account more than a dozen times, and the line that sticks out the most is the one that gets to the motivating engine of burnout culture: "There is nothing better than getting to complete things on a regular basis." Anything that gets in the way of "completing things" (and by "things," here, the associate means "work") is understood as a lack of devotion, or work ethic, or, it's strongly inferred, a lack of intelligence. And the effects of this mindset go far beyond mere elitism. It affirms the righteousness of downsizing, layoffs, and outsourcing: Those people in the "real world" were lazy anyway. In fact, if anything, Wall Street is doing them a favor: "We've made everyone smarter," an associate at Salomon Smith Barney told Ho. "Before, in the 1970s, corporations were so sloppy; now they are advanced. We're the grease that makes things turn more efficiently." Which is to say, they're the grease that's made everyone else's work lives as miserable as their own, and with far less compensation.

It doesn't help that beginning in the 1990s, corporations began hiring MBAs and ex-investment bankers directly from Wall Street instead of hiring leadership from within—as had been customary for decades.[7] Once in a leadership role, ex–finance bankers could explicitly and implicitly reproduce the understanding of "hard work" they internalized during their time on Wall Street. (It's worth noting that Jeff Bezos, who has fashioned a "bruising" workplace culture at Amazon, worked at the same firm as Ho.)[8] The phenomenon is similar to the spread of consulting "alums" across the corporate sector: Barring a significant, psychology-altering intervention, once someone equates "good" work with overwork, that conception will stay with them—and anyone under their power—for the rest of their lives.

We tell ourselves all sorts of stories to justify our overwork. Some, like Wall Street bankers, have decided that it's the best way of working, regardless of the fact that many readily admit that they spend a lot of their time inefficiently: bullshitting, spellchecking, or just waiting for edits on a presentation. Wall Street work isn't necessarily better or more productive work. In truth, it's just *more* work. But that doesn't mean it hasn't accumulated outsize power and influence on the way that *other* Americans work.

When I'm stressed by work, I find myself resenting the amount of sleep I need. Even though I know that sleep actually increases productivity, what I understand is that it decreases available working hours. All I want is to wake up and start, as that Goldman Sachs analyst put it so bluntly, "completing things on a regular basis." Sometimes I read about physically and psychologically anomalous "short sleepers," like the dozens of CEOs who survive and thrive on just a few hours of sleep a day—and feel deep pangs of jealousy. All of those people are talented, but their talent is ameliorated by their ability to let their work feed on even more parts of their lives.

You know who doesn't need sleep? Robots. We might say we hate the idea of turning into them, but for many millennials, we robotize ourselves willingly in hopes of gaining that elusive stability we so desperately crave. That means increasingly ignoring our own needs, including biological ones. As theorist Jonathan Crary points out, even our "sleep" is increasingly a version of machines in "sleep mode" that's not rest so much as "a deferred or diminished condition of operation and access."[9] In sleep mode, you're never actually off; you're just waiting to be turned back on again.

This sounds dystopic, but so are accounts of people stringing together two or three all-nighters to distinguish themselves, either in school or at work; or the lived reality of those in the precariat who work an eight-hour shift as a nurse's aide, grab a few hours of sleep, and go out to spend the night driving Uber before dropping their kids at school and heading back to their day job. We've conditioned ourselves to ignore every signal from the body saying *This is too much,* and we call that conditioning "grit" or "hustle."

This mindset was crystallized in a 2017 ad for Fiverr — an app through which "lean entrepreneurs" can pitch their services, starting at five dollars — that for a brief period of time was inescapable on the New York subway system. In the ad, a close-up of a harried, gaunt, yet miraculously still attractive woman is overlaid with the text YOU EAT A COFFEE FOR LUNCH. YOU FOLLOW THROUGH ON YOUR FOLLOW THROUGH. SLEEP DEPRIVATION IS YOUR DRUG OF CHOICE. YOU MIGHT BE A DOER.

"Doers" — the only type of person fit to survive the gig economy — have effectively silenced their body's warning system. After all, it's far easier to take some 5-Hour Energy than to look straight in the brutal face of our current economic system and call it what it is. As Jia Tolentino pointed out in *The New Yorker,* "At the root of this is the American obsession with self-reliance, which makes it more acceptable to applaud an individual for working himself to death than to argue that an individual working himself to death is evidence of a flawed economic system."[10]

The ideology of overwork has become so pernicious, so pervasive, that we attribute its conditions to our own failures, our own ignorance of the right life hack that will suddenly make everything easier. That's why books like *Grit* and *Unf*ck Yourself* and other titles with asterisks to blunt the profanity and the frustration have become such massive bestsellers: They suggest that the fix is right there, within our grasp. Because the problem, these books suggest, isn't the current economic system, or the companies that exploit and profit from it. It's us.

Surveillance Culture

I hope it's clear at this point just how misguided that assertion is: No amount of hustle or sleeplessness can permanently bend a broken system to your benefit. Your value as a worker is always unstable. What's deeply messed up, then, is that whatever value we *do* have is subject to continued optimization. And that optimization is achieved through ever-more noxious forms of employee surveillance.

Take the "open office," which doubles as both a cost-cutting method and a way for everyone in the office to know what everyone else in the office is doing at a particular moment. Unlike the private offices that were once *de rigeur,* for most, open offices make actually completing work incredibly difficult, subject to constant interruptions or, if you put on headphones, suggestions that you're a cold bitch — *not much of a team player.*

Stevie, who works as a copyeditor in an open office, told me she'd been told to make sure to look like she's "doing serious work ALL THE TIME in case the big boss walks by." Similarly, in the open office at BuzzFeed, the editor-in-chief periodically walks around, starting small talk, seeing what everyone's up to. There's very little you could be doing or watching on your computer at BuzzFeed to get you into trouble (save porn, which could still theoretically be rationalized). But even when my editor was nowhere to be seen, the visibility of my computer made me feel like I should always be typing or looking at something important. In a more traditional workplace, where, say, spending three hours on Reddit threads about furries would be frowned upon, the open office makes it stressful to do anything, even respond to an email from your kid's school, that could be construed as "off-task."

The goal of surveillance might be productivity, or quality control—but the psychological effects on workers is substantial. I spoke to a woman named Bri who worked for two years as a photo editor at an international photography agency, editing sets of images for various clients from movie premieres, award shows, breaking news events, etc. The company used a proprietary software to edit images that allowed managers to track every click and action. The actions weren't reviewed until a month later, but then they were scrutinized closely. "It was very difficult and degrading to have a conversation with a manager over a set of images I barely had any memory of," she explained.

"There was always this cloud of distrust that hung around our office. No one at my level felt like they were doing good work, or could do anything right," Bri continued. "Morale plummeted, and I began having imposter syndrome, even though I've worked in my field for over seven years—my every move was being monitored, and the only feedback I ever received from management was negative."

At Microsoft, managers can access data on employees' chats, emails, and calendar appointments to measure "employee productivity, management efficacy, and work-life balance." A growing number of companies are enlisting "tonal analysis" services that monitor meetings, calls, and Slack.[11] Sabrina, who identifies as white Hispanic, lives in an urban area, has a bachelor's degree, and makes around $30,000 a year. She was thrilled to be hired in a "research position" at a small startup before she discovered that it was in fact hours of rote data entry. Every day, she was asked to document, down to the minute, how long it took to complete each task on a Google Sheet, which was then shared with her boss, who would tell her if she was going too slow. She had to track not only how many minutes she spent inputting each segment of data, but also how many minutes she spent sending emails, or looking up how to do things, no matter if it took just a single minute.

"Having to track every single second of my productivity made me nervous to even use the bathroom," Sabrina explained. "Do I literally write 'bathroom' on my time sheet? So I started to use the bathroom while I sent emails so as to not mess with my data totals and earn myself a reprimand. But then I was scared that if I entered six minutes for sending email into my time sheet, that would seem like too long of a time to be sending emails. This circulation thinking, and the looming, unknown consequences, made me miserable."

Like so many heavily surveilled employees, Sabrina dreaded going to work every day. The tasks were mind-numbing. Her forearms and hands ached from typing so fast for so long without breaks. But she stayed with it because her boss, who was a mini-celebrity in her field, promised that "hard work" could bring a chance to "prove" yourself: "To get what, exactly, I'm not sure," she said. "The prestige of associating with him? But in the moment, those promises made it difficult to protest anything, and made me eager to please and accept his surveillance."

This sort of monitoring is often soft-sold in the name of efficiency or happens so incrementally that employees have few avenues for resistance. "Your employer controls your livelihood," Ben Waber, an MIT scientist who's studied workplace surveillance, explains. "And if they say 'give me this data,' it's very hard to say no."[12] When there are so few options for stable employment, you don't get to decide whether or not you want to be surveilled. You just figure out how to manage the suffering it creates.

There's significant evidence that the more surveilled—and less trusted—you feel, the less productive you are. In *The Job: Work and Its Future in a Time of Radical Change*, the organizational psychologist Amy Wrzesniewski tells Ellen Ruppel Shell that close monitoring by supervisors "makes it difficult for us to think independently and act proactively" and "nearly impossible for us to make meaning of our work."[13]

Ruppel Shell points to the example of a nanny: Until recently, most nannies had total control over what they did during the day with their charges. They fed them and put them down for naps at certain times, but that autonomy helped make their experiences bearable, even enjoyable.

When I was nannying, that autonomy—paired with a living wage—did indeed make the job fun. My two-year-old charge and I rode the bus all over the city. We explored a new park every day of the week. We went to museums and street fairs and sometimes, when the rain wouldn't stop for the fifth day in a row, we watched a movie in the theater together. And while I had a cell phone for emergencies, we did all of this totally untracked, in and outside the home. The year before, I had been nannying for an infant on the swanky Eastside of Seattle, when, unexpectedly, his grandmother came to stay in the house for several months. Every move I made, every word I used, every cry the child made, I felt watched and reported. I hated the commute, which is the reason I gave when I quit the job. But I hated the surveillance more.

Today, surveillance of childcare workers is increasingly normalized—whether in the form of hidden nanny cams, crib cam-

eras (viewable from the parent's phone) that show the exact moment when the child goes to sleep and wakes up, or constant text
updates. When I was nannying, I'd write a brief note detailing
what the toddler ate and what we did at the end of each day. Now
I'd be entering it into an app, which would allow my employers to
approve every decision in real time.

And then there's the trackers. In order to decrease health insurance premiums, more and more companies are instituting
programs that offer free Fitbits and calorie counters to workers.
The deal is straightforward: Get in your 10,000 steps a day, or
lose weight, and we all win! In practice, though, it's one more in-
cursion of the workplace into the personal, and a normalization
of a deeply dystopian idea: that a good worker is a worker who
permits their company to monitor their movements.

In September 2017, Amazon won two patents for wristband
technology that tracks warehouse workers' movements and provides "haptic feedback" (i.e., light buzzes) when you're close to
the right (or picking up the wrong) item for delivery. The disclo-
sure of the patents raised concern that Amazon would be treating
its workers like robots — but in truth, they are already are: "After
a year working on the floor, I felt like I had become a version of
the robots I was working with," one former Amazon warehouse
worker told the *New York Times.*[14] "They want to turn people into
machines. The robotic technology isn't up to scratch yet, so until
it is, they will use human robots."

Or consider the Spire Stone: a small, beautifully designed
tracker meant to be worn near the skin. When, through a series
of different sensors, the Spire thinks that the worker is stressed,
it guides them through a brief meditation. Theoretically, Spire
is a tool to *alleviate* stress at work — and thereby optimize the
worker for, well, more work. A surefire way to increase your level

of stress is to be stressed out all the time over whether or not the weird pulsing rock on your skin is telling your manager that you're stressed.

Some of these tactics feel limited to a certain echelon of worker, working for a certain sort of "paradigm-shifting" company. But technological surveillance, intended to "optimize" the worker and increase profits, has become standard within the fast food and retail industries. In *Vox*, Emily Guendelsberger describes how the particular stresses of the fast food workplace create a scenario similar to what one neuroscientist, in his attempts to create conditions that trigger depression in rats, called "the pit of despair."

Employees are constantly supervised, and not just by annoying managers. "Everything is timed and monitored digitally, second by second," Guendelsberger explains. "If you're not keeping up, the system will notify a manager, and you will hear about it."[15] The pit of despair isn't just what it feels like, on the job, working the cash register or the grill. It's the whole suite of anxieties that accumulate around the minimum-wage worker.

To start, there's the digital time clock, which penalizes workers for checking in even a minute after a shift begins, and the general stress of the worker's schedule, which uses an algorithm and past data to determine exactly when the store needs more or fewer employees. In practice, this means ever-changing, totally unstable schedules, generally distributed to employees just two days ahead of time. (Except in selected cities like New York, San Francisco, and Seattle, where labor laws mandate that a schedule must be distributed two weeks in advance.) One longtime hotel front desk manager told me that before 2015, all the hotels she worked for posted schedules at least two weeks in advance. After 2015, that became impossible: The algorithms produced last-minute variations that made it so that the schedules were often available just a day ahead of time. At the same time, staffing budgets were tightened—forcing her and her coworkers to work sixty- to seventy-hour weeks. She usually had just one day off a week, which she dedicated to sleeping.

At one big-name fashion retailer, a worker told me that the algorithm was based on sales from the year before—with no accounting for holidays, weather, etc. Some companies now schedule "clopen" shifts, in which an employee comes in for a few hours to close, goes home for a few hours of sleep, and then returns to the store for an early open. Brooke, who works as a server at a high-end fast casual restaurant, is regularly assigned such shifts: "It makes getting consistent sleep very difficult," she says. The same goes for "understaffing," in which *just the right amount* of workers are scheduled for a particular moment in the day.

When there's a sudden rush, unanticipated by the algorithm, everyone starts yelling for backup, creating, in Guendelsberger's words, "maximized misery for workers *and* customers." Sure, it's inhumane. But it's profitable.

The work schedule for Holly, who recently started a job as a front desk agent at a hotel, is based on the projected number of arrivals and departures on any given day. More senior staff gets more consistent scheduling with regular days off; those who are newer to the company, like her, are scheduled "all over the place." In addition to "clopen" shifts, there's no guarantee of time-off requests, "which means a lot of canceling plans on the fly, and coping with disappointment/irate family and friends because you're unable to commit to anything except for the job." There's no guarantee that she'll get forty hours a week, but her schedule's not consistent enough to find another job. "Trying to draw up a budget," she says, "is a big scribble nightmare."

When you're barely making enough money to survive, or supporting a child, as a quarter of fast food workers do, the options for stress "relief" or amelioration dwindle. You might have an hour for the gym, but not enough money to pay for it. You have less money and less wherewithal to try to buy or make healthier food. Your body begins to bear the physical signs of your labor: in burns, as reported by 79 percent of fast food workers in 2015, or flat-out exhaustion.[16] You're paid so little, and certainly not enough to save, and are so exhausted by the work you do that it's often hard to see a way out.

Holly told me that her job has resurfaced her "long-seemingly-neutralized, painstakingly managed" panic disorder. She's tried telling her managers that erratic scheduling makes it incredibly difficult to manage her anxiety; they respond, "That's just the way it is." The only option to manage her health is to quit the job — but she can't do that until she has something lined up, and in the midst of an anxious episode, job hunting feels impossible. "Thankfully I have some solid friends to keep me from slipping into the dark place," she says. "But for the people without strong social/familial scaffolding, it could be devastating."

Stress is not just something you experience while trying to fulfill an order, or make it into work fifteen minutes early because you can't trust public transportation to get you there on time. Stress disintegrates the body, and can make it unsuitable for any other type of work. A stressful job isn't just a route to burnout. It also traps you, creating a situation in which you can see no option other than to keep doing it.

The same goes for all sorts of contingent labor: An undocumented worker, whether in the fields or as a nanny, has no legal standing, no means of reporting exploitation, no recourse when wages are withheld. "Off the books" laborers, as domestic workers often are, don't have to be paid overtime. That's what happens when you don't have options: You have no negotiating power, or power of any sort, at least when it comes to the workplace.

Which is why freelance work, with the "options" that accompany it, has become so alluring: The structure of formal work, whether in a fast food restaurant or a law firm, has become so stressful that going freelance, either within one's field or working in the gig economy, seems like a perfect solution.

The Fetishization of Freelance Labor

Over the course of the Great Recession, over 8.8 million jobs were eliminated in the United States alone. Americans lost jobs in construction, at colleges, at nonprofits, at law firms, and at big-box stores going out of business. They lost jobs in recreation, at newspapers, at public radio stations, at car factories and start-ups, in finance, in advertising, and in publishing. In the past, recessions have busted the job market, but then recovery has rebuilt it: The jobs disappeared as companies tightened their belts, then reappeared as they felt confident expanding.

That's not what happened this time — which is one of the main reasons why millennials, many of whom were struggling to find their first job, any job, during this era, have had such a negative experience of work. To be clear, it's not that jobs weren't created. In fact, strong job creation numbers were flouted every day — first by Obama, then by Trump. It's just that they weren't the same sort of jobs as before. A "job" can be a temp position given to a freelancer, a seasonal gig, even a part-time job. According to one study, nearly *all* of the jobs "added" to the economy between 2005 and 2015 were "contingent" or "alternative" in some way.[17]

But for those desperate for work, especially millennials graduating into the post-recession market, these jobs nonetheless provided a much-needed paycheck, however meager — and the freelance and gig economy exploded. The willingness of workers to settle for these job conditions helped foster an even deeper fissuring of the workplace: first, by normalizing the low standards of the freelance economy; second, by "redefining" what it meant to be "employed."

The general logic behind freelancing goes something like this: You have a marketable skill, maybe in graphic design, photography, writing, digital editing, or web design. Various companies are in need of that skill. In the past, medium- and large-size companies would've hired full-time employees with that skill. But in the fissured workplace, those same companies are reticent to hire any more full-time employees than absolutely necessary. So they hire multiple freelancers to do the work of a full-time staffer, which gives the company high-quality work, without the added responsibility to shoulder freelancers' health benefits or ensure fair working conditions.

From the outside, freelancing seems like a dream: You work when you want to work; you're ostensibly in control of your own destiny. But if you're a freelancer, you're familiar with the dark side of these "benefits." The "freedom to set your own hours" also means the "freedom to pay for your own healthcare." The passage of the Affordable Care Act has made it easier to purchase an individual plan off the marketplace. But before that — and given the concerted attempt to undercut the ACA — obtaining affordable healthcare as a freelancer has become increasingly untenable.

In California, one person told me that the *cheapest* insurance they could find — for one person, with very little coverage and a high deductible — goes for $330 a month. I talked to a dog walker in Seattle who pays $675 — without dental coverage. Another person reported that their bargain basement plan in Minnesota costs $250 a month. In Dallas, $378 a month for a catastrophic plan with a $10,000 deductible. And that's if there's just one of you: A freelance writer told me she'd had breast cancer, and her husband, a freelance photographer and photo editor, is an insulin-dependent Type 2 diabetic. They live in suburban New York, and currently pay $1,484 a month for coverage. Many freelancers told me their deductibles were so high that they avoided going to the doctor if at all possible, which frequently ended with even *higher* bills when they were finally forced to seek care—and, because they were freelancers, there was no such thing as paid time off to recover.

Freelancing also means no employer-facilitated 401k, no employee match, and no subsidized or concerted means, other than the portion of your freelance checks that go to Social Security every month, to save for retirement. It often means hiring an accountant to deal with labyrinthian tax structures, and getting paid a flat fee for the end product or service, regardless of how many hours you put into it. It means complete independence, which in the current capitalist marketplace is another way of saying it means complete insecurity.

"I get no general or consistent feedback on my skills," Alex, who works as a freelance designer and illustrator, told me. "I accept pay less than my worth just to get a job. There's consistent price undercutting. And there's the anxiety over the lack of control over my own life." "Clients," after all, owe you nothing. When the supply of freelancers with a given skill or service is greater than the demand, wages cannot be negotiated. You adjust your rate to whatever a client is willing to pay.

Take the example of journalism: Every writer used to dream about the freedom of the freelance lifestyle. Pitch only the stories *you* want to write; write only for the publications *you* want to write for. And back when magazine publishing was healthy, you could make bank: two dollars a word (on the moderate side of things) for a 5,000-word feature meant $10,000 for a few months' work.

But when the journalism market bottomed out with the Great Recession, everything reset. Laid-off journalists flooded the market, desperate for freelance gigs. The amount of competition drove down rates, which was about what most outlets could afford to pay. And then there were people like me: non-journalists who'd honed their voice online, on *LiveJournal* and *WordPress,* for free. In 2010, I started reading the *Hairpin,* a website that had sprung from the ashes of the recession.

The business model, like a lot of business models at that time, was contingent on publishing anything good by anyone who was willing to write for free. I began writing pieces, rooted in my academic research, on the history of celebrity gossip and classic Hollywood scandal. Like a typical millennial, I was chuffed that they'd even publish them. I wanted an audience for my passion far more than I wanted to be paid. This model made it possible for hundreds of people to break into writing. You can trace the careers of many prominent contemporary writers back to the *Hairpin,* its sister site, the *Awl,* its cousin site, the *Toast.* Same for dozens of sports writers, blogging for free on sites like the *Bleacher Report.* We "made it" because writing wasn't our main gig, which allowed us to write for nothing or, as the sites gained traction and the recession faded, we wrote for what my grandmother would've called "pin money": extra, surplus, gravy.

But because we were all writing as a side gig—which is why we could afford to do it for free—we also helped to drive rates way, way down. Why pay a freelance writer their established rate, the rate that would help keep them paying rent, when you could pay a graduate student in art history zero dollars for their insight?

That's the sort of desperation that actual companies—far more than esoteric little websites—took advantage of. And no one took more advantage of it than the newly ascendant gig employers: Uber, Handy, DoorDash, and dozens of others. When we look back on the period following the Great Recession, it will be remembered not as a time of great innovation, but of great exploitation, when tech companies reached "unicorn" status (valued over $1 billion) on the backs of employees they refused to even deign to label, let alone respect, as such.

*   *   *

The dynamics and overarching philosophy of Silicon Valley create the perfect conditions for fissured workplaces. Silicon Valley thinks the "old" way of work is broken. It *loves* overwork. Its ideology of "disruption" — to "move fast and break things," as Mark Zuckerberg famously put it — is contingent on a willingness to destroy any semblance of a stable workplace. In the startup world, the ultimate goal is "going public": creating a high enough stock valuation, and, afterward, unmitigated growth, no matter the human cost. That's how these companies pay back the venture capital firms that invested in them — and that's how they make their founders, boards, and early employees very rich.

Talking about how Silicon Valley and shifting concepts of work means talking about Uber. You might be as sick of talking about Uber as I am, but its impact is widespread and undeniable. "Under our noses, the company has ushered in a wave of changes touching most aspects of society, be it family life or childcare arrangements, worker conditions or management practices, commuting patterns or urban planning, or racial equality campaigns and labor rights initiatives," Alex Rosenblat argues in *Uberland.* It "confuses categories such as innovation and lawlessness, work and consumption, algorithms and managers, neutrality and control, sharing and employment."[18] The number of Americans who've actually driven for Uber is proportionally small. But the changes it set in motion are slowly infiltrating the rest of the economy and our everyday lives—especially those who, in any capacity, rely on the gig economy.

Like so many other startup companies of the post-recession era, Uber was founded on the premise of disruption: taking an old industry, oftentimes one that was a bit clunky, and analog, but that paid its workers a living wage, and using digital technologies to change it into something sleeker, easier, and cheaper that would funnel money to the disrupting company. Uber, along with Lyft, Juno, and a handful of other ride-hailing companies, disrupted what has traditionally been known as the "livery" business: picking people up and taking them places. Their popularity launched an entire cottage industry of services reconceptualizing quotidian tasks: Rover disrupted pet care. Airbnb disrupted lodging. Handy disrupted handymen. Postmates and Seamless and DoorDash disrupted takeout. And while these apps have made vacationing and ordering in and getting from one place to another easier for consumers, they also created a massive swath of bad jobs—bad jobs that workers, still desperate from the fallout of the recession, were (at least temporarily) thrilled to take.

For a short period of time, companies like Uber were viewed as economic saviors. They sold themselves as a means of using and distributing resources—cars, drivers, cleaners, bedrooms—with far more efficiency than the old systems, all while creating the jobs that the clawing middle class were desperate to land. The secret of these jobs, though, were that they weren't even technically jobs, and certainly not the sort of jobs that could mend the broken class ladder. Instead, these jobs have created what the tech columnist Farhad Manjoo calls "a permanent digital underclass," both in the United States and around the world, "who will toil permanently without decent protections."[19]

That's because, at least at Uber, the tens of thousands of people who drove for the company weren't even considered employees. In external messaging, Uber's posture toward these men and women remained steady: The drivers were, in fact, a sort of *customer*. The app merely connected one set of customers, in need of rides, with another set of customers, willing to provide it. As Sarah Kessler, author of *Gigged*, points out, "Uber merely took a trend among corporations—employing as few people as possible—and adapted it for the smartphone era."[20]

After all, actually hiring employees, even if you're just paying minimum wage, is "expensive"—and requires the company to take on all sorts of responsibilities. When you're a startup burning through millions in venture capital, the goal is growth, always growth, and responsibility is an impediment to growth. Uber solved the problem by calling their employees "customers" and by officially designating them as "independent contractors."

"Independence" meant those who drove for Uber could make their own schedule, had no real boss, and worked for themselves. But it also meant these pseudo-employees had no right to unionize, and Uber had no responsibility to train them or provide benefits. Gig economies lured workers with a promise of that independence—with work that could actually bend to fit our lives, our children's schedules, our other responsibilities. This work was framed as particularly suitable for supposedly self-centered, picky, self-righteous millennials; as the gig economy grew in visibility, *Forbes* declared, "The 9 to 5 job may soon be a relic of the past, if millennials have their way."[21]

But that's not how it worked out. Not for Handy cleaners, or TaskRabbits, or laborers on Amazon's Mechanical Turk, who bid to complete menial online tasks (clicking on every photo with a picture of a bird, for example, in order to assist with AI recognition) for pennies. Not for Door Dashers, who until a massive online backlash was using tips to cover their independent contractors' base pay—meaning that if a Dasher was guaranteed $6.85 per delivery and received a $3 tip, they still received just $6.85; users were essentially tipping DoorDash itself. And despite Uber's past (and thoroughly debunked) claims that an Uber driver could make $90,000 a year, the majority of people driving or cleaning or renting their spare bedroom or clicking relentlessly on a mouse in the gig economy are doing it as a second or third job—a shitty job to supplement a different shitty job.[22] The gig economy isn't replacing the traditional economy. It's propping it up in a way that convinces people it's not broken.

Freelance and gigging don't make drudgery or anxiety disappear. Instead, they exacerbate them. Any time that you do take off is tinged with regret or anxiousness that you could be working. That hour at a birthday party could be thirty dollars from Uber. That hour on a run could be spent pitching to new clients. That hour reading a book could be used to seek out another writing assignment. In today's economy, going freelance means internalizing the fact that you could and should always be working more. Nick, who does freelance stats analysis through Upwork, described the internalized pressure to be "working eternally and at all times"; Jane, a freelance writer, explains that "there is such a sense in freelancing that you are never doing enough—that you should be doing more, making more, hustling more—and that every failure you have (real or perceived) is entirely your fault. In an office job, you're still getting paid for those five minutes it takes to make a cup of tea; when you're freelancing, every minute you're not working, you're losing money."

In practice, freelancing often means developing the mindset that "everything bad is good, everything good is bad"—a mantra I threw around with my friends during grad school to describe the perverse alchemy of overwork, in which drudgery feels "great," and actually pleasurable activities become indelibly lined with guilt. As Kessler reports in *Gigged,* Uber directly exploits this mindset: When a driver attempts to close the app and refuse future calls, it responds with a variation on "Are you sure you want to go offline? Demand is very high in your area. Make more money. Don't stop now!"[23]

Your ability to work is never as "free" as the word *freelance* suggests. If your car has to be repaired, you're sick for a long period of time, or you simply don't want to drive, Uber makes it difficult to start working again. You're repeatedly subjected to the whimsy of drunk passengers who give a single star for fun. And as Guy Standing points out, "The person who works for himself works for a tyrant — you are only as good as your last job and your performance. You are constantly being evaluated and graded. Having to worry so much about where the next bit of bread is coming from means people losing control over their lives."[24] Or, as one Uber driver told Rosenblat, "you don't have a boss over your head — you have a phone over your head."[25]

Freelancing is exhausting and anxiety-building enough. But that's compounded by the widespread refusal to see what you do as *work*. Just as the work of teachers or mothers is devalued (or unvalued), jobs within the sharing economy aren't figured as jobs at all — they're attempts to monetize your hobby, to have fun conversations while driving around the city, to invite people into your home. Even calling these jobs "gigs," with all the inherent connotation of brevity and enjoyability, elides their status as labor. It's not the gig economy after all; it's the always-frantically-seeking-the-*next-gig* economy.

*   *   *

"We've idealized the idea of portable work, promoting the notion of people roaming about with a portfolio of skills they can sell at a price they set themselves," Standing argues. "Some are able to do that, of course. But to think that we can build a society on this platform, with no protections, is fanciful."[26]

Many of Uber's employees continue to fight for the right to bargain with their employer. Freelancers in media from all over the United States have created their own iteration of union, in which they collectively set rates and, when media employees are laid off from an organization or strike, refuse to "scab" into their former roles. More and more freelancers, gig economy laborers, and temps are realizing that flexibility is meaningless without stability to accompany it.

But the only way to call for these types of action is to have leverage: to have options, but also to be acknowledged as an employee. This means an overhauling of our current system, an action that may need governmental intervention. If lawmakers force companies like Uber to stop misclassifying its employees as independent contractors, it would reinforce the social contract between companies and laborers—the idea that companies are responsible for the livelihoods of those who labor for them, and that the profits gleaned through this labor should trickle down, in some form, to them. That might seem incredibly radical, but if you look back just sixty years, it was also an incredibly American way of conceiving of profits.

It's a solution that's especially difficult to implement when the head of the company is saying there's no problem in the first place: "I think a lot of the question about whether this is employee versus independent contractor misses a little bit of the point," Tony Xu, CEO of DoorDash, told *ReCode Decode*. "I mean, if you think about what is the root problem, the root problem is, how do we maximize all this flexibility, which Dashers love, and provide a security blanket for those who need it?"[27]

One very obvious way: Hire them as employees. Masking exploitation in the rhetoric of freelancing and independent contractors' "flexibility" avoids talking about why that flexibility is coveted: because the supposedly "thriving economy" is built on millions of people being treated as robots. "What worries me most is that this is just the beginning," Manjoo wrote in the aftermath of the DoorDash tipping backlash. "The software-driven policies of exploitation and servility will metastasize across the economic value chain. Taking DoorDash workers' tips today will pave the way for taking advantage of everyone else tomorrow."

Manjoo's right. But the people it's most poised to take advantage of in the immediate future are those who have no other options — and those, like millennials and Gen Z, who don't realize there's any other way. Which underlines the current conundrum: Shitty work conditions produce burnout, but burnout — and the resultant inability, either through lack of energy or lack of resources, to resist exploitation — helps keep work shitty. Significant legislation to updates labor laws to respond to current workplace realitics can and will help. But so will solidarity: an old-fashioned word that simply means consensus, amongst a wide variety of people of like mind, that resistance is possible.

7

Technology Makes
Everything Work

THE FIRST THING I HEAR IN THE MORNING IS MY SLEEP-
Cycle app, which is supposedly monitoring my movements in order to "gently" wake me as I emerge from sleep. I swipe it off and
see the first alerts from the various news apps on my phone: bad
things, getting worse. As I lie in bed, my thumb goes to Instagram for truly unknown reasons, but I'm less interested in seeing what others have posted than how many people have liked
whatever photo I posted the night before. I check my personal
email. I check my work email. I deleted the Twitter app off my
phone, but don't worry: You can always just open Chrome and go
to Twitter.com.

I get out of bed and yell at Alexa a few times to turn on NPR. I
turn on the shower. As it warms up, I check Slack to see if there's
anything I need to attend to as the East Coast wakes up. When

I get out of the shower, the radio's playing something interesting, so while I'm standing there in my towel, I look it up online and tweet it. I look at Slack again, this time to "check in" with my team on what I'm doing for the day. I get dressed and get my coffee and sit down to the computer, where I spent a solid half hour reading things, tweeting things and waiting for them to get fav'ed. I post one of the stories I read to the Facebook page of 43,000 followers that I've been running for a decade. I check back in five minutes to see if anyone's commented on it. I tell myself I should try to get to work while forgetting this is kind of my work.

I think, *I should really start writing.* I go to the Google Doc draft open in my browser. Oops, I mean I go to the clothing website to see if the thing I put in my cart last week is on sale. Oops, I actually mean I go back to Slack to drop in a link to make sure everyone knows I'm online and working. I write two hundred words in my draft before deciding I should sign that contract for a speaking engagement that's been sitting in my Inbox of Shame. I don't have a printer or scanner, and I can't remember the password for the online document signer. I try to reset the password but it says, quite nicely, that I can't use any of my last three passwords. Someone is calling with a Seattle area code; they don't leave a message because my voicemail is full and has been for six months.

I'm in my email and the "Promotions" tab has somehow grown from two to forty-two over the course of three hours. The unsubscribe widget I installed a few months ago stopped working when the tech people at work made everyone change their passwords, and now I spend a lot of time deleting emails from West Elm. But wait there's a Facebook notification: A new post in the group page for the dog rescue where I adopted my puppy! Someone I haven't spoken to directly since high school has posted something new!

Over on LinkedIn, my book agent is celebrating her fifth work anniversary; so is a former student whose face I vaguely remember. I have lunch and hate-skim a blog I've been hate-skimming for years. Trump does a bad tweet. Someone else wrote a bad take. I eke out some more writing between very important-seeming Slack conversations about Joe Jonas's musculature.

I go to the gym. On the spin bike, I read things I saw on Twitter and stored in my Pocket app. I get interrupted once, twice, fifteen times by one of my group texts. I read something I like and slow down on the bike to take a drink of water and tweet it. I end my workout and go to the bathroom, where I have just enough time to look at my phone again. I drive to the grocery store and get stuck at a long stoplight. I pick up my phone, which says, "It looks like you are driving." I lie to my phone.

I'm checking out at the grocery store and I'm checking Slack. I'm getting into the car to drive home and I'm texting my friend an inside joke. I'm five minutes from home and I'm checking in with my boyfriend. I'm walking my dog on the beautiful trails and I keep taking out my phone to take pictures. I'm back at home with a beer and sitting in the backyard and "relaxing" by reading the internet and tweeting and finalizing edits on a piece. I'm texting my mom instead of calling her. I'm posting a dog walk photo to Instagram and wondering if I've posted too many dog photos lately. I'm making dinner while asking Alexa to play a podcast where people talk about the news I didn't really internalize.

I get into bed with the best intention of reading the book on my nightstand but wow, that's a really funny TikTok. I check my Instagram likes on the dog photo I did indeed post. I check my email and my other email and Facebook. There's nothing else to check, so somehow I decide it's a good time to open my Delta app and check on my frequent flyer mile count. Oops, I ran out of book time; better set SleepCycle.

I'm equally ashamed and exhausted writing that description of a pretty standard day in my digital life — and it doesn't even include all of the additional times I looked at my phone, or checked social media, or went back and forth between a draft and the internet, as I did *twice just while writing this sentence.* In the United States, one 2013 study found that millennials check their phone 150 times day; a different 2016 study claimed we log an average of six hours and nineteen minutes of scrolling and texting and stressing out over emails per week.[1] No one I know likes their phone. Most people I know even realize that whatever benefits the phone allows — Google Maps, Emergency Calling — are far outweighed by the distraction that accompanies it.

We know this. We know our phones suck. We even know the apps on them were engineered to be addictive. We know that the utopian promises of technology — to make work more efficient, to make connections stronger, to make photos better and more shareable, to make the news more accessible, to make communication easier — have in fact created *more* work, more responsibility, more opportunities to fail like a failure.

Part of the problem is that these digital technologies, from cell phones to Apple Watches, from Instagram to Slack, encourage our worst habits. They stymie our best-laid plans for self-preservation. They ransack our free time. They make it increasingly impossible to do the things that actually ground us. They turn a run in the woods into an opportunity for self-optimization. They are the neediest and most selfish entity in every interaction I have with others. They compel us to frame experiences, *as we are experiencing them,* with future captions, and to conceive of travel as worthwhile only when documented for public consumption. They steal joy and solitude and leave only exhaustion and regret. I hate them and resent them and find it increasingly difficult to live without them.

Digital detoxes don't fix the problem. The only long-term fix is making the background into foreground: calling out the exact ways digital technologies have colonized our lives, aggravating and expanding our burnout in the name of efficiency.

What these technologies do best is remind us of what we're not doing: who's hanging out without us, who's working more than us, what news we're not reading. It refuses to allow our consciousness off the hook, in order to do the essential, protective, regenerative work of sublimating and repressing. Instead, it provides the opposite: a nonstop barrage of notifications and reminders and interactions. It brings every detail of our lives and others' to the forefront in a way that makes it impossible to ignore. Of *course* we do more.

*   *   *

Like so many aspects of burnout, digital exhaustion isn't unique to millennials. But our generation has a relationship with digital technologies that, at least in this moment, is uniquely aggravating. Our young adult lives were profoundly shaped by them, but we also have distinct memories of what life was like *before* their existence. Those memories are age and class dependent, but the commonality remains: Our childhoods weren't textured by smartphones, yet our college years and young adulthoods were contoured by digital cameras and early Facebook and constant accessibility, even if it was via a flip phone.

These technologies changed how many millennials made plans, how we flirted, how we behaved and were then held accountable for that behavior in public spaces. They changed how we took photos, how we acquired music and listened to it, what we did when we were on our computers, and how long we spent on those computers. Everything seemed to be changing, becoming easier or cheaper or simpler, but it still felt *gradual*. My original "smart" phone had a shit camera and took ten minutes to load a single email. I still listened to CDs in my apartment and in the car. I watched Netflix DVDs on my laptop. I blogged on *WordPress*. I knew people were out there with Blackberries, but that wasn't yet my world.

Slowly, and then seemingly all at once, all of that changed. The iPhone became available outside of AT&T. Netflix started streaming. So did Hulu and Amazon and HBO. Twitter took off and largely demolished the blogging world. Young millennials stopped using Facebook as their parents signed on. Instagram took off, and with it the mandate to aestheticize and package experiences for public consumption.

Our phones became extensions of ourselves—and the primary means of organizing our lives. I check email on my phone. I deposit checks using my phone. I schedule Airbnbs on my phone. I order groceries, and takeout food, and clothes on my phone. I split the bill for drinks using my phone, and figure out my subway route on my phone, and use my phone to make funny faces at my friends' newborn children. I stopped bringing magazines to the gym and started just bringing . . . my phone. I exchanged cable for an AppleTV. I stopped using my iPod, and my digital camera, and my address book, and my tape recorder, and the DVD drive on my computer. When I got a new computer, it didn't even *have* a DVD drive.

It took a decade, but the lives of most millennials I know have followed a similar technological consolidation. My brother resisted a smartphone until 2017 before capitulating; others have successfully quit or altogether ignored social media. But those cases increasingly feel like the outliers. For most of us, our lives now flow through our phones and the apps on them: They are the primary mediators of our errands, our travel, our work, our exercise, our organization, our memories, our connections, our finances, and our friendships.

Which is why it's so difficult to moderate our relationship with our phones, let alone disengage with them entirely. For so many of us, disengaging from our phone means disengaging from life. There's a fair amount of shame affixed to this new reality: that those more connected to their phones are lesser people, or at least people with lesser wills. But the phone (or, more specifically, the apps on the phone) was engineered to first create a need, then fill that need in a way that would be impossible to re-create—all under the *guise* of productivity and efficiency. To succumb to its promises doesn't mean you're weak; it simply means you're a human, frantically trying to complete everything required of you.

But before we get into the specific ways that phones encourage our worst habits and aggravate our burnout, we should be on the same page about why an object with services that we hate is engineered to keep making us feel like crap. In short: It makes money. That money comes from manipulating, sustaining, and beguiling our attention, which is sold to advertisers, which in turn makes the app money—and makes our phones indispensable.

When people talk about "the attention economy," they're talking about the buying and selling of our time: time we used to spend with our minds "turned off," meandering on a walk, staring into space at a traffic light, those seventeen minutes before you fall asleep. It's an economy based on taking up residency in the interstitial moments of our lives but also through subtle, repeated disruption of the main events—so much so that Netflix's CEO famously joked that the company's main competitor is sleep.[2]

Dozens of studies and articles confirm what we already intuitively understand: Checking social media, at least when you find something positive or interesting, releases a small amount of dopamine, the pleasure-seeking chemical in our brain. Our brain loves dopamine, so it keeps seeking it out, addicted to the possibility of incremental changes: new photos, new likes, new comments—what the man who engineered the Like button calls "bright dings of pseudo-pleasure."[3] The same principle applies to our phones, generally: It doesn't matter if there's always something new on the home screen each time we pick it up. What matters is that *sometimes* there's something new and worth our time.

But social media wasn't always this way. Think back on your first memories of Facebook: pre-Newsfeed, pre–Like button. You'd go to the website (on your computer!) and then maybe a day would go by, and you'd check it again. But the addition of the Like button—and changing the "alerts" from blue to red, so that people couldn't ignore them—incentivized repeated, obsessive returns to the site. For years, if you wanted to read more on Facebook or Twitter or Instagram, you'd have to refresh the site; in 2010, Loren Brichter introduced the "pull to refresh" function on the Tweetie app, which has now become standard on social media apps and beyond. These days, "pull to refresh" isn't really necessary—there's technology that could automatically refresh your app—but it functions as a sort of slot machine lever, keeping the user engaged far beyond when they'd normally have clicked out of the app.

Again, it wasn't always this way. Snapchat didn't always alert you when someone was simply *typing.* News sites didn't always send push alerts. Neither did apps for meditation, or Starbucks, or dating, or the New England Patriots, or learning Spanish, or the number matching game 2048. Sephora didn't alert you when you were close to a store, and Google didn't ask you to rate your subway trip after you finished it. But without your attention— your repeated, compulsive attention—these apps would become worthless. Or, at the very least, far less valuable. So they softly urge, manipulate, and command it: through notifications, but also through gamification, which use game-like elements to draw you into otherwise very un-fun activities, like following my Delta Frequent Flyer progress.

These days, the phone is where most millennials do our bank account checking, Amazon ordering, ride hailing, route finding, music playing, TikTok watching, photo taking, secondhand clothes selling, recipe finding, sleeping baby monitoring, and ticket (plane, movie, bus, concert) storing. Some of those tasks can still be done off the phone, but they're increasingly designed to be performed through an app. That's how phones root themselves in our lives: not through one app or five, but via a whole maelstrom of assault on our attention. The user is the ostensible benefactor of all this technological advancement, but our reliance on our phones is a net loss: a loss of privacy, of attention, of autonomy. The winners are the companies that have so effectively exploited our drive for convenience, over and over again, for profit.

When I first got an iPhone, it felt so bizarre to be able to look anything up at any time. Now separation from my phone is like phantom limb syndrome. In those early iPhone years, I could still leave it at home all day and not even notice its absence. Last year, I forgot it at home on a weekend trip and felt totally unmoored. I know exactly how alerts and push notifications manipulate me and am still delighted when I step out of the Lyft and feel a buzz in my pocket: Who could it be? Oh, right, it's just the app asking me to rate my driver, just like it's done the last five hundred times. I am the rat pushing the lever to feed myself poison that tastes, ever so briefly, like candy.

Granted, I have a job that keeps me more online than most, more wed to Twitter than nearly all. But there are other tethers, shared and unique: Pinterest, Instagram stories, Poshmark, sports, crosswords, Slack, school apps, fertility apps, meal-planning apps, fitness apps, and text chains that ironically feel like the only thing tethering us to our non-phone lives. And it doesn't matter if you follow the tips for reducing your phone dependence: Getting rid of the pushes and email alerts might stop the notifications, but the behaviors themselves have already been internalized. You can delete an app, like I deleted Twitter, and still figure out other ways to access it. You can put your phone on airplane mode after eight p.m., which I do, and still find your tendencies unchecked at eight a.m.

Why is the allure so strong? The dopamine explanation is part of it, for sure. But for me, I think the larger draw is a shared delusion: that with my phone, I can multitask like a motherfucker, and be all things to everyone, including myself. It's not the shiny black rectangle that's beguiling; it's the idea that your life could be so ruthlessly, beautifully efficient, seamless, *under control,* that makes it appealing.

That's a lie, of course. It doesn't matter how many times we read studies about how multitasking actually inhibits your ability to complete tasks: We convince ourselves that the internet makes us *better,* more efficient, right about to really start killing it. We'll concentrate at work; we'll master that errand paralysis through *apps;* we'll keep our household in order through *other apps;* we'll figure out a social media strategy that at once develops and refines our personal brand while also demanding very little of our attention; we'll make everyone in our lives feel recognized and special because of *texting!*

When all that fails to occur, we stress out, which makes us want to multitask even more to try to get a handle on the situation, which makes us even more inefficient. It's an attention death spiral for all of us. I think it's valuable, though, to parse the forms of the internet that are particularly propellent for burnout: 1) millennial-oriented social media; 2) the news; 3) technologies that spread work into what remains of our nonwork lives.

*   *   *

For millennials, Facebook shaped (and messed up) many of our social lives when we were in our teens and twenties. But these days, most millennials I know have largely abandoned it. Facebook is toxic, Facebook is political — and the knowledge of the ways the company has exploited our personal information is too difficult to ignore. Most of my millennial friends have started using it almost exclusively for the groups: private, public, and secret, oriented around podcasts and hobbies and discussion interests.

A portion of young millennials still use Snapchat; Twitter remains the compulsion of choice for many writers and academics and wonks; Pinterest has its own psychological attractions. The communities of Reddit have an addictive pull. LinkedIn is Twitter for people with MBAs. But the social media platform most overtly responsible for burnout is Instagram. This might seem counterintuitive: Instagram's appeal has long been that it's Facebook without drama, a distillation of what made Facebook truly interesting in the first place, that is, *cute pics.* But generating those cute, curated pics is exhausting. So, in its own way, is looking at them: a never-ending scroll of lives that don't just seem cooler than yours, but also more balanced, more put together. The Instagram feed becomes a constant, low-key lecture on the ways in which you haven't figured your shit out.

I look at my feed right now and I see a picture of a well-behaved puppy in beautiful morning light, a husband posting a picture of his wife's perfect Natasha Lyonne shaggy haircut, a friend from college holding her baby in an Oregon pot field, a Montana reporter on a rocky traverse outside Glacier National Park, another reporter's glam wedding look in Bulgaria, an ad for a swimsuit I was looking at yesterday, a blurry photo of a quasi friend's epic karaoke weekday night, a writer I haven't spoken to in two years finishing a draft of his book, a really well-lit photo of a friend's baby I've met once, a local friend out on the river after fishing, my best friend from college at a pool party with no one else I know.

I broke down the anxieties each one of these sparks:

Cute Well-Behaved Puppy →
    I should take cuter pictures of my puppy.

Wife's Perfect Natasha Lyonne Shaggy Haircut →
    God, my hair is uncool.

College friend in pot field →
    That seems like a lot of work.

Montana Reporter in Glacier →
    I am not hardcore.

Glam Bulgarian Wedding Look →
    I have gone feral out here in Montana.

Swimsuit →
    Is it time to go for the late-thirties one-piece look?

Epic Karaoke →
 Am I an old lady with no friends?

Book Finish →
 Remember how I haven't finished my book?

Well-Lit Photo of Baby →
 What if I regret not having a baby?

Local Friend on River →
 I spend too much time on my computer.

Best Friend at Pool Party →
 She has new friends that aren't me and I hate it.

Are these rational takeaways? Sort of. They're regular anxieties, the type of worries that could pop up from looking at a magazine or a friend's postcard. But on Instagram, they're all jammed into one continuous line, piquing every corner of our potential anxiety. They form a personalized mosaic of the lives we're not living, choices we're not making, and they force a type of pernicious comparison cycle. Each photo is just one in a tall stack of evidence, posted over months and years, pointing to how others are living the millennial dream: working at a cool job but not working too much; hanging out with a fun and supportive partner; if desired, raising cute and not cloying kids; taking unique vacations and making time for interesting hobbies.

We all know that Instagram, like any other social media platform, isn't "real." It's a curated version of life. But that doesn't mean that we don't judge ourselves against it. I find that millennials are far less jealous of objects or belongings than the holistic experiences represented there, the sort of thing that prompts people to comment, *I want your life*. The millennial dream depicted on Instagram isn't just desirable — it's balanced, satisfied, and unaffiliated with burnout.

The photos and videos that induce the most jealousy are those that suggest a perfect equilibrium (work hard, play hard!) has been reached. Work is rarely pictured in the millennial Instagram life, but it's always there. Periodically, it's photographed as a space that's fun or zany or has a good view — and it's always framed as rewarding or satisfying. But most of the time, it's the thing you're getting away from: You worked hard enough to enjoy *life*.

But few of us have even come close to reaching that equilibrium. Posting on social media is a means of narrativizing our own lives: We're telling ourselves what our lives are like. And when we can't find the satisfaction we've been told we should receive from a good, "fulfilling" job and a balanced personal life, the best way to convince ourselves is to illustrate it for others.

If you look at my Instagram, it'd be easy to extrapolate that I spend all my time hiking, communing with nature and my dogs, running or walking or cross-country skiing — all while managing to travel somewhere equally beautiful every other week. I do spend a lot of time outdoors with my dogs, and I do spend a lot of time traveling for my job. But I post the outdoor pictures to try to prove to myself and others that the bulk of my Montana life isn't spent behind a computer, and the other shots are to convince myself and others that constant travel isn't an alienating slog, but a thrill. The truth of my real, lived life lies somewhere in between what's pictured and what's intended. But there's a reason I sometimes find myself scrolling through my own account as I fight that before-sleep anxiety: When I don't feel connected to myself or my life, Instagram reminds me of who I've decided I am.

For knowledge workers, a well-curated Instagram, like a popular Twitter presence, can be a gateway to a job, or #sponcon. The purest example of this concept is the social media influencer, whose entire income source is performing and mediating the self online. Most people's lives aren't so explicitly monetizable, but that doesn't mean they're not cultivating a brand to project to the larger world. To wit: I have a friend whose brand is "Parenting is hard but always worth it." Others include "My kids are so bizarre!"; "I'm a Cool Dad"; "Wilderness overposter"; "Books are life"; "Wheels up"; "Culinary adventuress"; "Cosmopolitan nomad"; "I ride multiple bikes"; "I am yoga"; "I have friends and we drink alcohol" and "Creative being creative."

A powerful brand requires constant maintenance and optimization. We might not curate our "squares" as ruthlessly as Gen Z—who often keep just a handful of photos posted at a time—but most of us think about how often to post, when something's "story" content versus when it's a post, how much photo editing is acceptable and how much is too obvious. And then there's the never-ending search for content: At its most pronounced, it's people risking their lives in extreme locations "for the 'gram"; in most people's lives, it's just oscillating between actually experiencing a thing and thinking about how to best present that thing on Instagram in an on-brand way. We post, therefore we are.

That's how Instagram further blurs whatever boundaries remain between work and play. There is no "off the clock" when every hour is an opportunity for content generation, facilitated by smartphones that make every moment capturable and brandable. Even when you're somewhere without phone service—traveling internationally, in the woods, on the water—you can still take the picture and save it for later. Instagram's photo compression system means that even the crappiest of internet signals can get the job done. And then you wait to see measurable approval of your life roll in.

Whether or not you explicitly conceive of Instagram in this way—as a window unto others' balanced lives; as an opportunity to portray your own—even casual users find themselves resentful of the place it comes to occupy in their minds. Open the app and discover a dose of newness—and, if you posted yourself, an opportunity to see each and every person who's liked the latest slice of your life, who's watched your story, who's messaged you a torrent of 100s in affirmation. It's quietly thrilling, at least until you think about just how little has changed since the last time you opened the app.

Which explains the twinned pleasure and pain of social media, the sharp contrast between our draw to it and the continually unsatisfying experience of actually being on it. Instagram provides such low-effort distraction, and is so effective in posturing as actual leisure, that we find ourselves there when we'd rather be elsewhere—deep in a book, talking with a friend, taking a walk, staring into space.

When I have fifteen minutes before bed and I'm exhausted, I know the best thing to ease myself into rest is reading a book. But just making that choice to put down the phone demands discipline. Opening the Instagram app is easy—even if it makes me feel like shit, and even more in need of the sort of actual escape the book could've provided. Same for the moment the plane lands: What if I keep reading whatever I'm reading? Or rest my eyes, or do a quick meditation, or just observe the packed humanity around me? Instead, I get anxious for the LTE to kick in so that I can check all the incremental changes and affirmations on my social media.

That's how social media robs of us of the moments that could counterbalance our burnout. It distances us from actual experiences as we obsess over documenting them. It turns us into needless multitaskers. As you'll see in the next chapter, it erodes what used to be known as leisure time. And perhaps most damagingly, it destroys opportunities for solitude: what Cal Newport, drawing on the definition of Raymond Kethledge and Michael Erwin, describes as the "subjective state in which your mind is free from input from other minds."⁴ In other words, hanging out with your own mind and all the emotions and ideas that experience promises and threatens to unearth.

Ask yourself: When was the last time you were really bored? Not bored with social media, or bored with a book, but truly, expansively, bored, a boredom that seemed to have no beginning or end, the sort of boredom that characterized so many of our childhoods? Until recently, it'd been years for me—at least as long as I've had a smartphone, with its limitless aptitude for distraction.

But then I spent three weeks in remote parts of Southeast Asia, where traveling required long hours on winding roads. There was no internet, and it was too bumpy to even attempt to read. So I listened to music, and stared out the window, and allowed my mind to wander places it hadn't been in years: memories, thought experiments, new ideas. My memory of childhood boredom is that it was always painful—something I was desperate to escape from. But now I find myself desperate to escape to it, and repeatedly foiled by the easy proximity of the phone.

I want to never think of Instagram again, yet feel a deep mournfulness for what I'd lose if I were to abandon it. It's an unrewarding part-time job that's also my only connection to friends I've become too busy to spend actual time with. And it's become so intertwined with my performance of self that I fear there's no self without it. That's an exaggeration, maybe. But the prospect of relearning who I am—and who others are—remains daunting. I'm already exhausted, I tell myself. Where would I find the energy to do something that hard?

* * *

Up until the 2016 election, keeping up with the news cycle felt generally achievable. Read a few websites, listen to the news, maybe a political podcast, and you've got it. But Trump sent the news cycle into hyperdrive. Through the election and early days of his presidency, I began to feel increasingly out of control, a sense that seemed to extend to the state of the government, society, the presidency, democracy, the global world order. Every time I tried to get a handle on what was happening around me, and tried to really root myself in the facts and the context, the ground began to shift. Trump tweeted; someone else lied; Trump tweeted; someone else published a big investigative piece; Trump tweeted something racist; #MeToo happened; Trump tweeted something else racist; someone from the cabinet resigned.

Katherine Miller, a longtime politics editor and writer at BuzzFeed, best described the feeling just months into Trump's presidency: "Everything might seem so normal," she wrote, "then you unlock your phone and—*bam*—everything gets LOUD again. You have almost certainly had this experience: You wake up in the morning or from a nap, or walk out of a movie, then check Facebook, Twitter, your texts to find people mid-thought, context-free, frozen in emotion, angry at Trump or the Trump people or the anti-Trump people or the media, angry and mocking at hypocrisy whose details aren't yet clear to you, angry at how ineffectual someone is, or maybe they're doing something even more indecipherable—it's not anger, it's just a meme or a quotation or a screenshot with 'lol' or '2017' or just an emoji. The mystery begins: What happened? What has Trump done now?"[5]

Miller's experience of the news cycle, like my own, is elevated: our notifications are filled with people who are relentlessly, indefatigably online, and many of them are yelling at us or, since we're members of "the media," in our general direction. But journalists aren't the only ones assaulted by the news. Boomers text their millennial kids to check whether they've seen what Trump's done; all sorts of seemingly well-meaning people post sincere reactions and pleas to PAY ATTENTION, REFUSE TO BECOME COMPLACENT on Instagram and Facebook.

I appreciate Miller's use of the word "mystery," though, to describe the frantic attempt at catch-up: It captures both the compulsive, serialized aspect of the contemporary news cycle, but also the constant frustration at never actually wrapping up the story. Like social media, reading the news—with all its *new*ness —activates the dopamine machine in our brains. In *Riveted,* the cognitive scientist Jim Davies explains that dopamine makes "everything look significant": a switch in Oval Office personnel, a gossip item about Ivanka's ability to land dinner reservations, a major policy reversal, a new meme retweeted by the president, it all feels equally, desperately important to understand.

And while some of those reports are indeed significant, experiencing them online, either through push notifications or Twitter or other people's texts, flattens them into one long plane of dubious import. A major policy reversal is far more crucial to understand than Ivanka's dinner reservations, but when both are reported with equal urgency and fervor, who's to know? It's increasingly difficult to parse where to allocate your most rapt attention. Which helps explain why, at least fifty times over the last three years, I've watched a "revelation" break across my Twitter timeline and had no idea how to react. "Is this actually a big deal?" I'd ask a politics reporter. Usually, the answer was "potentially—but most likely no."

Part of the problem, of course, is that events that *would* have been a big deal during previous presidencies simply aren't under Trump. There are multiple reasons for the muting of would-be scandals: the refusal of the much of the political right to be publicly scandalized, morally, financially, behaviorally, or otherwise, by his behavior, but also Trump's own ability to redirect the news cycle via new false and/or outlandish and/or racist statements. If you're a Trump supporter, the dynamics are inverted: Trump does something that should be celebrated and isn't; when that celebration fails to arrive, he rightly redirects toward another deserved point of celebration.

In practice, the Trump-directed news cycle has all the notes of a horribly plotted film: narrative threads continually dead end; punchlines fail to land or arrive at all; characters don't develop and their actions have no consequences. It's impossible to tell which plot points need to be remembered and which ones are meaningless. And, worst of all, there's never any closure or catharsis. There are cliffhangers from week to week like a bad soap opera, but you never figure out what's really going on, what's really going to happen, who'll be held responsible.

Likening the news to a movie isn't meant to trivialize it. Trump's actions, like any political figure's, have had very real consequences in the world; multiple reputable studies have underlined the ways in which anti-Semitic violence, bullying, xenophobia, and white supremacy increased under his administration. People argue about whether or not it's okay to characterize one of his tweets as racist, but there are millions of people who actually experience harm from the racist attitudes Trump has espoused, propagated, and normalized. There's also the generalized anxiety of living under this administration as a trans person, or an immigrant, or an undocumented person, or a queer non–birth parent, or a Jewish person, or a Native person, or even just as a woman. Some of it stems from living in low- or high-grade fear that people you love will be taken from you. Or an overwhelming sense that hard-fought-for rights are being eroded. Or the slow-burning revelation that you are now living in a country in decline. Even if you think that others shouldn't feel this way doesn't change the fact that they do.

Everyone has different ways of coping with anxiety and fear and sadness. But one of the most prevalent, now and for centuries, has been to turn it into stories that feel morally legible. That's what melodrama did for societal tensions in the eighteenth and nineteenth centuries; that's what film melodrama and protest music did in the twentieth century. The news has long served this societal function, but it's never provided omnipresent dramatization in quite the way it does now.

Sometimes we find these narratives on deeply partisan sites, or by following deeply partisan figures. Sometimes we find them in the dry play-by-play of the *New York Times,* the richly investigative pieces of *ProPublica,* or the palace intrigue of *Vanity Fair.* Political profiles are the new celebrity profiles; celebrity gossip has expanded to include the love lives and peccadilloes and best tweets of everyone from Kellyanne Conway to Alexandria Ocasio-Cortez. We're not reading this information because we're curious; we're reading it because we're desperately, continuously confused—and each click promises something approximating meaning. And while Trump is the inciting factor, there's little hope that our broken media cycle will mend itself after he leaves office.

The same principle applies outside the realm of explicitly presidential politics, in the chasm between the tragedies that surround us and the apparent inability to do anything about them. Gun violence, broken healthcare, refugee crises, global climate change, police brutality, children in government custody at the border, mental health crises, the opioid crises, violence against trans women and Native women—to cope, you can choose darkness, or apathy, or obsessive self-edification.

Consuming news makes it feel like you're doing *something,* even if it's just bearing witness.

Of course, bearing witness takes a toll—especially when the news is structured to emotionally aggravate more than educate. Plus, as Brad Stulberg argues in a piece about breaking digital addiction, it can provide a false illusion of participation: "Instead of worrying about illness you can exercise," he points out. "Instead of despairing about the political situation and making comments on Facebook you can contact your elected officials. Instead of feeling awful for people in unfortunate circumstances you can volunteer."[6]

All of this is true. But those are options for people who aren't already so exhausted by the rest of their lives, people with the wherewithal for proactiveness instead of the reactive, frantic Band-Aid-applying approach so many of us have settled into. When you're burnt out, sometimes the best you feel like you can do, as a responsible citizen with an open heart, is try to keep up with the news. But then the heavy, inescapable load of that same news burns you out even more: The world becomes *work.*

For many, there is a struggle to acknowledge that more information, like more friends, or more photos, or more work ethic, is actually worse—that you can fuck yourself over with your own good intentions. In a piece on "the new FOMO," *Wired* journalist Nick Stockton acknowledges what we all know: Checking Facebook, reading the news, being online all the time, makes us feel worse. There are studies that clearly show as much. Smart people, lots of them, say that we should all engage in social media breaks.

But as Stockton writes, "I don't want to take a break. The internet is doing exactly what it's supposed to: give me all the information, all the time. And I want to hold that fire hose of information right up to my face and gulp down as much as I can. I just don't want to feel bad about it."[7] Recovering from burnout doesn't mean extracting yourself from the world. It just means thinking a lot more actively, and carefully, about the way you've convinced yourself is the best way to interact with it.

*   *   *

A year into my job at BuzzFeed, Slack arrived. We'd had a group chat system, but Slack was different: It promised a revolution. Its goal was to "kill email" by switching workplace communication to direct messages and group discussion channels. It promised easier collaboration (true) and less clogged inboxes (maybe). And most importantly, it had a sophisticated mobile app. Like email, Slack allowed work to spread into the crevices of life where until that point it couldn't fit. In a more efficient, instantaneous manner than email, it brings the *entire office* into your phone, which is to say, into your bed, when you land on the plane, when you walk down the street, as you stand in line at the grocery store, or as you wait, half naked, on the exam table for your doctor.

Granted, work has long been able to follow people home. Doctors would review their "dictation," or notes on a patient visit, after hours, and you could always whip out some memos on the Apple IIe at home. But none of those processes were "live": Whatever work you accomplished on your own wouldn't be known to others, or force others to respond in kind, until the next workday. Workaholism could be a personal problem.

But the spread of email—on the desktop, then on the Wi-Fi enabled laptop, then the Blackberry, and now all manner of smartphones, smart watches, and "smart appliances," including your exercise bike—changed all that. It didn't just accelerate communication; it standardized a new, far more addictive form of communication, with a casualness that cloaked its destructiveness. When you "shoot off a few emails" on a Sunday afternoon, for example, you might convince yourself you're just getting on top of things for the week ahead—which might *feel* true. But what you're really doing is giving work access to be everywhere you are. And once allowed in, it spreads without your permission: to the dinner table, the couch, the kid's soccer game, the grocery store, the car, the family vacation.

Sites of digital *leisure* increasingly double as sites of digital labor: If you help run your company's social media, every time you log into Facebook or Twitter or Instagram you face bombardment from your work accounts. If someone emails you and you don't immediately respond, they'll move straight to your social media accounts—even when you have an auto-responder indicating that you're not available. Fewer and fewer employers supply work phones (either on the actual desk or in the form of work cell phones); calls and texts to your "work phone" (from sources, from clients, from employers) are just calls and texts to *your phone*. "Back in the day, AIM was the thing," one Silicon Valley CEO explained. "You had an away message. You were literally away from your device. Now you can't. You're 100 percent on at all times."[8]

It's the emails, but it's more: It's the Google Docs, and the conference calls you listen to on mute while making your kids' breakfast, and the databases you can log in to from home, and your manager texting on Sunday night with "the plan for tomorrow." Some of these developments are heralded as time-saving schedule optimizers: fewer meetings, more conference calls! Less rigid workplace hours, more flexibility! You can start your workday at home, spend an extra day at the cabin, even take off early to pick up your kid from school and wrap up loose ends later. But all that digitally enabled flexibility really means digitally enabling *more work*—with fewer boundaries. And Slack, like work email, makes workplace communication feel casual, even as participants internalize it as compulsory.

Granted, only a fraction of the workforce currently uses Slack —as of April 2019, around 95,000 companies paid for its services.[9] But many other workplaces use similar programs, or will soon; given the unabated rise of remote work, its influence feels inescapable. There were remote workers before Slack, but unlike email, or phone calls, or Gchat, Slack is able to digitally re-create the workplace, complete with standards of decorum, and participation, and "presentism," however unspoken. It was intended to make work *easier,* or at least more streamlined, but like so many work optimization tactics, it just makes those who use it work *more,* and with more anxiety.

Slack thus becomes a way to LARP—Live Action Role Play —your job. "LARPing your job" was coined by the technology writer John Herrman, who, all the way back in 2015, predicted the ways in which Slack would screw with our conception of work: "Slack is where people make jokes and register their presence; it is where stories and editing and administrating are discussed as much for self-justification as for the completion of *actual goals.* Working in an active Slack . . . is a productivity nightmare, especially if you don't hate your coworkers. Anyone who suggests otherwise is either rationalizing or delusional."[10]

As more work becomes remote, it's something so many of us think about: How do we demonstrate that we're "in the office" when we're in our sweatpants on the couch? I do it by dropping links to articles (to show that I'm reading), by commenting on other people's links (to show that I'm reading Slack), and by participating in conversations (to show that I'm engaged). I work very hard to produce *evidence* that I'm constantly doing work instead of, well, actually doing work.

My editors would say that there's no need to compulsively perform on Slack. But what would they say if I just didn't use Slack at all? People who do "knowledge work" — those whose products are often intangible, like ideas on a page — often struggle with the feeling that there's little to show for the hours we spend sitting in front of our computers. And the compulsion is heightened for those of us who worked, job searched, or were laid off during the post-2008 recession: We're desperate to show we're worthy of a salaried job, and eager to demonstrate how much labor and engagement we're willing to give in exchange for full-time employment and health insurance. That was certainly the case for me, especially in a field like culture writing, where full-time gigs remain rare.

This mindset may be delusional: Yes, of course, managers do think about how much work we're producing, but only the worst of them are clocking how many hours the green "active" dot is showing up next to your name on Slack. And most of our co-workers are too worried about LARPing their own jobs to worry about how much you're LARPing yours.

We're performing, in other words, largely for ourselves. Justifying to *ourselves* that we deserve our job. Justifying to *ourselves* that writing for the internet is a vocation that deserves steady payment. At heart, this is a manifestation of a general undervaluing of our own work: Many of us still navigate the workplace as if getting paid to produce knowledge means we're getting away with something, and have to do everything possible to make sure no one realizes they've made a massive mistake.

Of course, there are myriad cultural and societal forces that have led us to this point of disbelief. Every time someone makes fun of a millennial's undergrad or grad degree, or denigrates a job that somehow manages to funnel the passion that we were told by the adults in our lives to follow; every time someone is befuddled by a job description (social media manager!) that doesn't match their personal understanding of hard work and chooses to ridicule it instead—all of those messages come together to tell us that our work is either easy or pointless. No wonder we spend so much time trying to communicate how hard we work.

*   *   *

Midway through writing this book, I went to the woods. Beforehand, I bought a solar panel setup to power my laptop. And then I spent a week at a campsite on a lake in the Swan Valley, with no internet, and no phone signal—save a very small corner of camp, and even then, just enough to send out a very slow text message. Otherwise it was just me, my draft, my books, and what felt like luscious, expansive pools of time.

Every day was a variation of the same: Wake up, walk for an hour with the dogs, work for a few hours, take a run, read a novel over lunch, take another walk with the dogs, work for a few hours, have a beer while editing what I just wrote, take the dogs for a swim, get in the tent, read my novel, and go to bed. I did that for six days. I wrote over 20,000 words.

The number of actual writing hours wasn't that huge—probably around six to seven a day. The difference was that I spent those hours *actually* writing. When my mind wandered, I'd pet a dog. Or I'd pick up my phone and look at a photo I took of my dog, but do nothing with it because there was nothing to do. Or I'd just stare into space. Then I'd return to what I was writing, my concentration and direction miraculously intact.

I should've been thrilled with my progress, but I was racked with ambivalence: If I could just work this way in the non-woods world, I could be producing so much more—and, at least theoretically, working so much *less*.

Of course, I was able to write with that intensity because I was essentially without obligations. I didn't have to care for children. I didn't have to make small talk. I didn't have to pack anyone a lunch. I didn't have to commute, or do laundry, or clean, save the daily excavation of pine needles from my tent. I didn't have to shower or worry about my appearance. My work email was on an out-of-office auto-responder. I was getting nine hours of sleep a night, and had time to exercise, and money to purchase food that made me feel full and good. The only thing I really had to worry about was whether or not my solar panel was in the sun. My life — and productivity — was not unlike that of an independently wealthy white man writing in the nineteenth century.

Ultimately, that productivity had less to do with the lack of internet and more to do with the centrality of my work: It wasn't constantly vying with distractions, but it also wasn't vying with every other thing I had to do. Digital technologies allow work to spread into the rest of our lives, but they also allow the rest of our lives to spread into work. As I attempted to write these past three paragraphs, I was paying my credit card bill, reading a breaking news story, and figuring out how to transfer my new puppy's microchip registration to my name. Everything — especially writing this section — was taking far longer than it should have. And none of it felt good, or fulfilling, or cathartic.

But that's the reality of millennial, internet-ridden life: I need to be an insanely productive writer *and* be funny on Slack *and* post good links on Twitter *and* keep the house clean *and* cook a fun new recipe from Pinterest *and* track my exercise on Map-MyRun *and* text my friends to ask questions about their growing children *and* check in with my mom *and* grow tomatoes in the backyard *and* enjoy Montana *and* Instagram myself enjoying Montana *and* shower *and* put on cute clothes for that thirty-minute video call with my coworkers *and and and and.*

The internet isn't the root cause of our burnout. But its promise to "make our lives easier" is a profoundly broken one, responsible for the illusion that "doing it all" isn't just possible, but mandatory. When we fail to do so, we don't blame the broken tools. We blame ourselves. Deep down, millennials know the primary exacerbator of burnout isn't really email, or Instagram, or a constant stream of news alerts. It's the continuous failure to reach the impossible expectations we've set for ourselves.

8

What Is a Weekend?

THERE ARE SIX DAYS BETWEEN CHRISTMAS AND NEW Year's. And I have come to hate every one of them.

It didn't used to be this way. As a child, I luxuriated in what felt like a much-deserved and much-needed break from school, filled with the afterglow of Christmas, sledding and cross-country skiing, and devoting hours to reading in bed. Even in college, I'd come home for break, exhausted and usually on the brink of some illness, but reveling in the catharsis of a semester over and done. There was no reading to catch up on, no papers to start organizing. Sometimes I'd babysit for extra cash, or my mom would put me to work on chores around the house. It was long enough "off" that I eventually got bored with it, and craved the return to school and the schedule that accompanied it.

In grad school and as a professor, I came to understand that time — like all time formally labeled a "break" — was actually just meant for working. But when I started writing for BuzzFeed, the days became a weird, liminal space: About half the office was on vacation, but the half who remained didn't seem to be doing much? Confronted with generalized low work expectations, I don't know what to do with myself. I feel itchy, unsettled — unable to give myself permission to work *less,* or even not work at all.

But it's not just Dead Week that makes me anxious. For millennials who've internalized the burnout mentality — that more work is always better, and that all time can and should be used to optimize oneself or one's performance — "leisure" time is often fraught and rarely restful. And that's if we have it in the first place: Leisure numbers are notoriously difficult to track, as they depend on self-reporting and some (male) sociologists historically considered "childcare" to be a form of leisure. But in 2018, adults aged twenty-five through thirty-four reported an average of 4.2 hours of leisure a day. Two of those hours were spent watching television. A bleak 20.4 minutes were dedicated to "thinking/relaxing."[1]

If, when you think about your own life, those numbers still sound a little high, you're not alone. Those reports are based on the American Time Use Diaries, which ask participants to faithfully categorize the events of each day. But the quantity of leisure ultimately matters far less than its quality. Is texting your mom "leisure"? Is going to the gym to put in thirty-five minutes on the elliptical trainer? Is mindless scrolling on Instagram, or trying to read the latest political news in bed, or supervising your kids at the park?

Part of our problem is that we work more. But the other problem is that the hours when we're not technically working never feel free from optimization — either of the body, the mind, or one's social status. The word *leisure* comes from the Latin *licere,* variously translated as "to be permitted or "or to be free." Leisure, then, is time you are *allowed* to do what you'd like, *free* from the compunction to generate value. But when all hours can be theoretically converted to *more work,* the hours when you're not working feel like a lost opportunity, or just an abject failure.

"I'm the most unleisured person I know," Caroline, a white writer and podcaster in her thirties, told me. The combination of her first work experiences (in the post-recession economy) and her place in the freelance market (where you can *always* be doing more) have made her that way. "I've never had a hobby that I didn't monetize, whether I meant to or not," she told me. She travels, ostensibly on "vacation," and finds herself returning, again and again, to her work.

For Caroline, every task has to feel like it's clearly moving her life forward. Doing errands is okay, because it's part of the "work" of organizing her home and life; so is tweeting and Instagramming, because it contributes to her overall brand, which keeps her employed. "I don't even think I'm financially motivated so much as motivated by the fear that I don't have the tools or talent to carry me through the rest of my life," she explained. "Doctors can always be doctors, lawyers can always be lawyers, but I've made a living as part of this creative class, and I don't know what that looks like in fifteen, thirty, fifty years."

Every chance, every book deal, every podcast, could be her last. "The thing is, I've found a lot of success in this hustle," she said. "And knowing that this mentality has paid off in big dividends further reinforces the behavior." She reads about cultivating rest, and doing nothing, and thinks that's fine for other people. But if she tries to relax, hang out, read a book at the pool, it has serious ramifications on her mental health. At this point, Caroline fears she's been working this way for so long that her attitude is too broken to ever be fixed.

*   *   *

That's a word I heard over and over again as millennials told me about their relationship to leisure: It's broken. Historically, leisure was the time to "do what you will," the eight hours of the day not spent on working or resting. People cultivated hobbies, anything from walking aimlessly to constructing model airplanes. What mattered is that it wasn't done to make yourself a more desirable match, to declare your societal status, or make some extra money on the side. It was done for *pleasure*. Which is again why it's so ironic that millennials, stereotyped as the most self-obsessed generation, have lost sight of what doing something simply for personal pleasure looks like.

Our leisure rarely feels restorative, or self-guided, or even *fun*. Hanging out with friends? Exhausting to coordinate. Dating? An online slog. A dinner party? Way too much work. I'm unclear whether I spend my Saturday mornings on long runs because I like it, or because it's a "productive" way to discipline my body. Do I read fiction because I love to read fiction, or to say that I have read fiction? These aren't entirely new phenomena, but they help explain the prevalence of millennial burnout: It's hard to recover from days spent laboring when your "time off" feels like work.

Two hundred years ago, formal leisure was the provenance of the aristocracy. You went to university not because you needed a good degree on your CV, but because you wanted to join the clergy, or liked books, and what else would you do with your days? Maybe go on a walk, call on a friend, or learn an instrument, or play cards, or embroider. But none of those things was done to make money—you had well enough of it, and everyone knew as much, because you spent your days wholly engaged in leisure.

Most non-aristocrats had only the briefest swatches of leisure: for religious services and holidays and harvest celebrations. The rhythms of work — on the farm, in the kitchen — were the rhythms of life. It wasn't until the first industrial revolution, and the mass movement of workers into the city and into the factory, that the first labor reformers called for the creation of a five-day week. Leisure was, in many important ways, "democratized," especially for those in the cities, who flocked to the bevy of so-called cheap amusements (amusement parks, movie theaters, dance halls) that popped up to serve them.

In 1926, increased mechanization and automation (and resultant productivity) meant that Henry Ford could announce a five-day workweek. In 1930, the British economist John Maynard Keynes predicted that his grandchildren would work only fifteen hours a week. With abundant time for leisure across the classes, society would flourish. Democratic participation would go up, reformers argued, as would societal cohesion, familial bonds, philanthropic and volunteer work. People would have the time and space to engage with ideas and seek out new ones, to delight in friends and family, to experiment with new skills simply because they please us. These things had been the provenance of the rich, or at the very least the rich man, for some time. But soon, theoretically, they would be available for all.

Today, that vision sounds utopian — or, at the very least, fantastical. In *Free Time: The Forgotten American Dream,* Benjamin Hunnicutt points out that as productivity continued to increase, and unions began to successfully advocate for decreased work hours, public and private society embarked on a massive expansion of the infrastructure of leisure. They built camps and vacation resorts; they started community sports leagues and launched "a vigorous parks and recreation movement," including the development of thousands of public parks spaces we enjoy today. These spaces weren't built so we could sit in them while hunched over a sandwich from Pret-a-Manger and respond to emails on our phone, but in anticipation of mass leisure.

But something curious happened on the path to the fifteen-hour workweek. At first, as productivity went up, the number of expected hours at work did indeed decrease. But starting in the 1970s, they began to rise again. Part of the reason was classic American capitalism. If you can make a hundred widgets in less time, that doesn't mean everyone should work less—instead, they should work the *same* number of hours and make *more* widgets. But part of it, too, had to do with the rise of a different sort of work, "knowledge work," with a different sort of widget.

Knowledge workers have "outcomes" and "products," but unlike a factory product, they were difficult to measure. As a result, these workers are salaried, as in, paid for the entire year instead of by the hour. During the Great Compression era, most salaried workers still worked a forty-hour week, but without the rigidity of clocking in or out—and, depending on your contract, a legal demand to pay overtime. You might assume that most salaried workers would never exceed forty hours, or maybe even straight-up waste some of those forty hours. And, at least for part of the twentieth century, that was the case: Think of the storied boozy lunch, the *Mad Men*–style in-office liquor carts, the couch naps. After all, most of these salaried men, and they were almost always men, had secretaries to do everything save the most essential components of their jobs.

Up until the 1970s, the middle-class male, whether in factory or in the office, still had hours of delineated leisure time to enjoy outside of work. But as the economy began to falter, the number of hours spent at work continued to increase. With massive downsizing and layoffs across the business sector, every worker had to prove their worth, both to their supervisors, but also to consultants sent in to identify redundancies and inefficiencies.

And the easiest way to signal that you were working harder and were more essential to the company than the person sitting next to you was to work *longer.* At the same time, payment in hourly jobs ceased to keep pace with inflation, and many hourly workers clamored for overtime pay (or a second job) to cover household expenses in the same manner as before.

One of the easiest ways for a company to reduce its bottom line was to drastically cut benefits. But benefit cuts hurt company morale. So instead, they hired fewer people — and thus paid out fewer benefits — and simply expected them to do more work.[2] Even as actual productivity continued to rise, year after year, companies continued to reduce paid time off. In an attitude that should sound familiar today, in a tight job market, workers had little choice but to agree to the increased hours and demands.

In her landmark book *The Overworked American,* Juliet B. Schor found what at the time of the book's publication in 1990, felt almost scandalous. Since 1970, there'd been a steady, year-after-year increase in the amount of work Americans performed, and a dramatic decrease in average leisure time: down to just 16.5 hours a week.[3] Schor wasn't the first to ring the alarm: In 1988, the *New York Times* attempted to explain "Why All Those People Feel They Never Have Any Time." *Time* published a cover story declaring "American Has Run Out of Time" the next year. It's no coincidence workaholism became a broad cultural anxiety around this period: What had been perceived as hard work for more than a decade was suddenly recognized for the strangeness that it was.

But that was the strangeness that reared us, that millennials observed in our parents, even if it wasn't called workaholism, and that we would internalize as we went through school toward college. Sure, no one *liked* working all the time. But that didn't make it seem any less *necessary*. Today, the workaholism first diagnosed amongst boomers has become so commonplace as to no longer even be considered a pathology. Whether you're putting in sixty hours a week at your salaried job or cobbling together thirty-seven at Walmart plus thirteen driving Uber, it's just the way it is.

There are countless other ways that work seeps into our best attempts at leisure time. Today's work crises always seem to de-mand immediate attention—even when nothing about them, or their ramifications, would change if you just waited to han-dle them in the morning. The continued globalization of work means that you might be needed on a conference call at three p.m. in Berlin—or, six a.m. in Portland. A manager who is too frazzled during the day to keep up with her email attends to it in bed at ten pm. Her responses compel people to respond by ten fifteen p.m.

Some office cultures demand self-sacrificing presentism: Last one out of the office "wins." But for most millennials I know, the only person "forcing" them to work long hours is themselves. Not because we're masochists, but because we've internalized the idea that the only way to keep excelling at our jobs is to work all the time. The problem with this attitude is that working all the time doesn't mean producing all the time, but it nonetheless creates a self-satisfying fiction of "productivity."

That ceaseless drive for productivity isn't a natural human force—and, at least in its current form, is a relatively recent phe-nomenon. In *Counterproductive: Time Management in the Knowl-edge Economy*, the Intel engineer Melissa Gregg examines the his-tory of the "productivity" craze, which she dates to the 1970s, with subsequent spikes in the 1990s and the present. Gregg con-nects each wave of productivity management guides, self-help books, and, today, apps to periods of anxiety over downsizing and the perceived need to prove oneself as more productive—and, as such, more theoretically valuable — than one's peers. Amidst our current climate of economic precarity, the only way to create and maintain a semblance of order is to adhere to the gospel of productivity, whether blasting through your email to get to Inbox Zero or ignoring it altogether.

A variety of lucrative businesses have emerged to facilitate peak productivity, catering to a mix of those desperate to pack *even more* work into their day, and others whose workload makes them feel if they're drowning in the most basic of adult responsibilities. As Anna Wiener makes clear in *Uncanny Valley*, so many of the innovations of Silicon Valley of the last decade were designed to speak to the "affluent and the overextended," selling everything from toothbrushes to vitamins directly through our Instagram accounts. "On any given night in America, exhausted parents and New Year's–resolution cooks were unpacking identical cardboard boxes shipped by meal-prep startups, disposing of identical piles of plastic packaging, and sitting down to identical dishes," she writes. "Homogeneity was a small price to pay for the erasure of decision fatigue. It liberated our minds to pursue other endeavors, like work."[4]

One result of this drive for productivity is a new hierarchy of labor: On the top end, there are salaried, hyperproductive knowledge workers. Below, there are the people who perform the "mundane" tasks that make that productivity possible: nannies, TaskRabbits, Uber Eats drivers, house cleaners, personal organizers, Trunk Club stylists, Blue Apron packagers, Amazon warehouse workers and drivers, FreshDirect shoppers. Rich people have always had servants. The difference, then, is that those servants made it so that they *didn't* have to work — not so that they could work *more*. The people who facilitate these productivity-facilitating tasks, however, are almost always independent contractors, underpaid, with little job security or recourse for mistreatment. Many are driven by their own set of unrealistic productivity standards, but instead of getting paid hundreds of thousands of dollars to grind themselves into the ground to meet them, they're barely making minimum wage.

In the modern workplace, it seems that everyone in the salaried work space — from managers to workers themselves — is so anxious about proving their value that we neglect a veritable cornucopia of evidence that better work is almost always achieved through *less* work. The head of a very staid New Zealand trust company read about a study that found that office workers, working a standard forty-hour week, were only productive for between 1.5 and 2.5 hours every day.[5] So he decided to try something revolutionary: institute a four-day workweek wherein every employee would be paid the same, so long as they continued to reach their previous productivity goals, just in 80 percent of the time. At the end of a two-month-long trial, they found that productivity had risen 20 percent — while "work-life balance" satisfaction scores rose from 54 percent to 78 percent. In 2019, a similar trial at Microsoft Japan resulted in a 40 percent rise in productivity.[6] Rest doesn't just make workers happier, but makes them more efficient when they're actually on the job.[7]

To admit as much, though, means confronting ossified American ideologies around work: that more work is good, and less work is bad, no matter how much evidence suggests otherwise. Which is why opting out of work, at least in our current situation, doesn't feel possible. Earlier this year, a friend took a day off for a much-needed weekend away from her job as a lawyer at a startup. She told them that she could be reached, *in case of emergency,* on her cell. Hours later, the phone lit up: It wasn't an emergency, but her boss could sure use her input. The same scenario applies across the workforce: Flight attendants, service workers, janitorial staff, all can be called, even if it's their day off, and compelled to come back in to work. Each of us has become, in our individual ways, essential.

That's why my friend received that call: She was the only person who could answer her boss's question. But that's also why people feel guilty for taking time off: Someone has to do their work, so it'll either be them drowning in a firehose of accumulated work when they return, or their coworkers simmering in resentment when they have to pull a double shift. In our current setup, any attempt to draw clear lines around work and leisure, or to deal with one's own burnout, means creating burnout in others. What feels like the only solution is also the least useful one: We just keep working more.

*   *   *

Instead of shaping business around our own bodily rhythms, we bend, blunt, and otherwise ignore our body's demands in order to work at all times. The theorist Jonathan Crary situates this work seepage as part of a mentality of "24/7," in which "one's personal and social identity has been reorganized to conform to the uninterrupted operation of markets, information networks, and other systems." Some of us work these body- and mind-breaking hours because we must. Others simply work them because we *can*.

Granted, before the industrial revolution, many people's jobs — as farmers, or doctors, or wetnurses — would periodically require working into the night, and even on holy days. It wasn't until the second industrial revolution, however, and the demand to operate factories at full capacity, around the clock, that every hour became a workable hour. But even as the day, swing, and night shifts became regular features of factory life across America, "blue laws" banning the operation of most types of business on Sundays helped preserve at least one day of rest.

Many of the laws specifically applied to the sale of alcohol—an extension of moralizing Christian forces who wanted to preserve the Sabbath from some debauched fate. Which is part of why such laws have been challenged: Why should those who are nonreligious adhere to a religious day? But the courts have repeatedly evoked the "secular benefits" of a workless Sunday. "Upon no subject is there such a concurrence of opinion, among philosophers, moralists and statesman of all nations, as on the necessity of periodical cessation from labor," Chief Justice Stephen Johnson Field of the California Supreme Court wrote in 1858. "One day in seven is the rule, founded in experience, and sustained by science."[8]

Philosophers, moralists, and statesman still agree that rest would be *nice*. But it's repeatedly rejected as *necessary*. The blue laws that persist today are mostly regarded as an annoyance. Most mid-to-large-size businesses, save those owned by the most pious, remain open on Sunday. In *The Sabbath World*, Judith Shulevitz suggests that the process began with the gradual commercialization of leisure in the twentieth century.[9] Before, Sundays were largely spent in and around the home and church. People ate at home or with family members, using food items purchased earlier in the week. For the pious, time was spent in meditation or devotion. For the less so, spare hours could be used for reading, or playing, or other forms of diversion.

But then people began seeking out structured activities that cost money on the weekend—which, in turn, required others to work, whether in the form of the person checking tickets at the movie theater or the person selling concessions. And when enough of those people start working, even *more* people are enlisted to tap the market, from convenience store employees to grocery stockers. The need for public services increases as well: You need an employee to unlock the bathrooms at the park, and many more to drive buses and subways.

The desire for services becomes the normalization of services. Today, 31 percent of full-time employees — and 56 percent of people with multiple jobs — work on the weekends. Only a handful of government holidays (Fourth of July, Thanksgiving, Christmas, New Year's) feel "observed" in a meaningful way, and even then, many retail service employees *still* work. During the Christmas season, even mail carriers have begun to work Sundays. Not because we need our Christmas presents any faster, but because the United States Postal Service sees it as a possible way to compete with its private competitors.

And while the class-secure (or union-protected) can still refuse to work on certain days, or at certain times, those without leverage — particularly the undocumented, the undereducated, or those working multiple jobs — mangle the rhythms of their lives to correspond with the demands of capital. The ever-broadening class divide isn't just between the haves and the have-nots, or the productive and those facilitating their productiveness, but those who can protect a modicum of hours devoted to sleep and those who cannot.

Work hasn't colonized our weekends and holidays because we simply can't get enough of it. Before, the logic of capitalism had been legally cordoned off from Sundays. Now it's been let loose on all of our "leisure time" — and our attitudes about what that time's "potential" is have changed accordingly. Leisure scholars point to economist Staffan B. Linder's *The Harried Leisure Class,* published in 1970, as the first text to identify the consequences of a market seeking ever more growth, ever larger markets, and ever more consumption to fuel them. Within that model, every hour of every day becomes increasingly valuable: to a company, but also to oneself.

In this way, any time spent not working—that, is, leisure time—is money that's effectively lost. In order to reconcile ourselves to that idea, we cram in as many activities and as much consumption as possible into our leisure time, so as to make it valuable in some way. To evoke this style of manic consumption, Linder describes the man who, after dinner, fills his leisure by "drinking Brazilian coffee, sipping a French cognac, reading the *New York Times,* listening to a Brandenburg Concerto and his Swedish wife—all at the same time, with varying degrees of success." Today's version might be the woman who drinks her seven-dollar cold brew, with a four-dollar coconut water in her purse, on her way to yoga, while listening to *The Daily* on her headphones, while sending appropriate reaction GIFs to her group text about their upcoming girls' weekend.

The strategy of "maximizing" what leisure we do have—for ourselves, for our families, with our peers—has everything to do with, big surprise, class anxiety. In *The Sum of Small Things: A Theory of the Aspirational Class,* Elizabeth Currid-Halkett argues that a subsection of Americans have become increasingly concerned with expressing their class position through "cultural signifiers that convey their acquisition of knowledge and value system."[10] In other words, talking about, Instagramming, and otherwise broadcasting engagement with the sort of leisure activities, media products, and purchases that underline "elite" status. You are what you eat, read, watch, and wear, but it doesn't end there. You're also the gym you belong to, the filters you use to post vacation photos, where you go on that vacation.

It's not enough to listen to NPR, read the latest nonfiction National Book Award winner, or run a half marathon. You have to make sure *others* know that you are the type of person who

makes that particular sort of productive, self-edifying, optimized use of your leisure time. And while many of the products
and experiences associated with the "aspirational class" are fairly
old-school middlebrow (reading best-selling literary fiction,
watching Oscar-bait movies), the current mark of the cultured
bourgeois is a taste for the highbrow and lowbrow, the ballet and
the best dancers on TikTok, the best of prestige television and
the plot turns of the entire *Real Housewives* franchise. To be cultured is to be culturally omnivorous, no matter how much time
it takes.

When people complain about "too much television," this is
part of what they're complaining about: not that there's an abundance of options, for all manner of tastes, available in the marketplace, but that the amount of consumption necessary to keep
up in conversation just keeps growing. Episodes, podcasts, even
sporting events come to feel like checklists. It doesn't matter if
you actually like any of these things, or even actually consume
them in entirety, so much as signal, on social media and in person,
that you are the type of person who consumes them. And when
you only have so much time to dedicate to leisure, there's a constant demand to make the very best use your time, consuming
the products and engaging in leisure that most effectively dem-
onstrates your status as a cultural omnivore. You open (and then
aspirationally save for later) dozens of articles recommended by
others. You buy some yarn and a how-to-knit book, and never
cast a stitch. You start a book, then wonder if you should be
reading that other, cooler book. You dabble, and then you look
over your shoulder—or scroll your Instagram—for something
better.

As Currid-Halkett points out, this practice transcends actual
income levels—adjunct professors with PhDs barely making
ends meet often consume and broadcast the same aspirational

class materials as Ivy-League-educated lawyers. It obscures the sort of economic stability a degree can actually provide, but provides a different sort of class salve: It's okay if you're hundreds of thousands of dollars in debt, will never buy a home, and are terrified of what a medical catastrophe could bring, so long as you can still blend in with higher incomes in a social setting. In a profile of Michael Barbaro, the host of *The Daily*—the massively popular *New York Times* podcast, and a perfect example of aspirational consumption—producer Jenna Weiss-Berman pinpoints the show's appeal: "You listen to *The Daily* and you're better equipped to speak at a dinner party," she explained. "And that's all you really want."

We love to think that our cultural and leisure tastes are, to some extent, "natural"—I sign up for this triathlon, I watch this show, I download this podcast *because I like it!*—but every choice is muddled by our understanding of what it says about us, and the conversations from which we'll be excluded if we opt out. It's okay to skip one TV show, or franchise, or trend, but opt out entirely and you'll be out of the loop the next time you hang out with your similarly class-aspirational friends. It's not enough just to hang out, after all: There has to be a purpose. The popularity of the book club isn't just about people reading more. It's also about needing a productive affixation to the simple desire to be with other people.

A similar dynamic happens with travel and exercise: If you don't have enough money to plan a trip to Japan, you can still talk about the best new Japanese restaurant in town; if you can't afford SoulCycle or a road bike, you can still talk about training for your weekly Saturday-long run; if you can't donate to a political campaign, you can still authoritatively talk about a candidate's strategy after listening to *Pod Save America*. Which is one of the reasons that newsletters like the *Skimm,* which currently boasts more than 7 million subscribers and was last valued at upwards of $55 million, have become so popular: They're a cheat sheet for aspirational consumption, offering bite-size briefings on every topic that could come up at drinks after work. They make it easier, as the *Skimm* tagline declares, "to live smarter," or at least to appear as if you are.[11]

Is watching movies, going to yoga, and listening to podcasts work? Of course not, not technically. A whole lot of people would love to feel pressure to watch more television instead of being forced to spend those hours on the job. But when this type of cultural consumption becomes the only way to buy a ticket into your aspirational class, it feels less like a choice, and more of an obligation: a form of unpaid labor. Which explains why "relaxing" by engaging in these activities can feel so exhausting, so unfulfilling, so frustratingly unrestorative.

*   *   *

Cramming your leisure with "aspirational" class value might quell some anxieties about class security. But an even more effective way to feel secure in one's class is to *make more money* — specifically, by monetizing your hobby.

A hobby is technically an activity performed during leisure time for the sheer purpose of pleasure. If you try an activity once, you're a dabbler; somewhere in the process of doing it again, and again, and again, it becomes a hobby. Many of today's hobbies involve cultivating skills that machines have made obsolete, or at least technically unnecessary: knitting, baking, tinkering. Others provide the pleasure of collecting and categorizing, or incredible concentration and attention to detail, or harmony, literal and figurative, with others. Singing in a choir, that's a hobby. So is a bowling league, a quilting circle, a running club. A video game can definitely be a hobby—especially community-building, strategy-refining games like Minecraft or The Sims.

Some hobbies, especially ones involving exercise, double as a means to build aspirational capital. In most places in the country, being a person who downhill skis is to underline that you have the means to outfit yourself and pay for a hundred-dollar lift ticket. But many hobbies, especially ones related to craft, feel like throwbacks, cool only insomuch as they're proudly *uncool*. Sometimes we pick up them up as adults, but many hobbies start when we're kids, passed down from family and community. I hike and camp because my dad hikes and camps. I garden because my mom gardens; she gardens because her mom gardened.

Hobbies are evacuated of ambition; any "purpose" is secondary. They're pleasure for pleasure's sake. But when your entire life has been geared toward building value for college, hobbies feel like foreign, almost obscene dreams: Every activity must be a means to an end. Growing up, my partner only read books for class, only sang when in choirs that would look good on his resume, only participated in rowing because the best colleges wanted a sport. It wasn't until he hit his thirties and we moved to Montana that he finally found the space to try to figure out what he actually liked doing instead of what he *should* do to add value to himself. Today, he describes the process as "fraught with guilt and self-doubt."

For many millennials, there's a drive to make anything you dedicate yourself to as perfect as possible. "I can't be a mediocre cyclist or dancer or hiker," Aly, a white woman on the trajectory toward upper-middle class, told me. "I have to be balls-to-the-walls amazing at it." Lara, who identifies as Jewish and middle class, remembers a time in her twenties when she had hobbies: "I sang in bands, I learned guitar, and started to learn drums," she recalls. "But then I got into graduate school and figured I wouldn't have the time or resources to keep it up. I felt guilty devoting time to something that wasn't furthering my writing career." Recently, she got her drum set from back at home, but still struggles to find the time she'd like to devote to it. "I don't like to do anything half assed," she said. "But of course that would require a lot more leisure time than I have."

Some of the people who have most time for leisure — and feel the least pressure to monetize their hobbies — are those with what some might call the most boring jobs. Ethan, who's white and currently lives in Nashville, works as a claims processor for a major insurance company. He works exactly forty hours a week, and considers himself lower-middle class. There's a clear delineation between when he's working and when he's not, and that allows him to protect his leisure hours, which he largely devotes to playing and writing about Dungeons and Dragons.

When people do find the time and mental space to cultivate a hobby, especially if you're "good" at it, then pressure to monetize it begins to accumulate. If someone loves to bake and starts bringing her creations to parties, the only way we know how to really compliment them is to suggest, *You could do this for money!* Janique, who's thirty-one, Black, and middle class, prides herself on maintaining time for singing and songwriting — but since she's joined a band, the pressure from others to get paid for it in some way has ramped up considerably.

Gina, who identifies as Asian American and middle class, knows that the idea that you should make money from the things that give you pleasure is societal. "I've learned a lot about the exploitation that that kind of mindset allows," she told me, "and I don't want the 'pure' love I have for my hobbies to be polluted by the false promise that I might be able to make some bucks from my efforts. I have seen friends try to monetize, and I have seen friends *succeed* at monetizing, I have seen friends grow to hate or feel shackled by what once brought them joy. No thank you!"

In today's economy, though, it's often a privilege to "protect" one's hobbies from monetization. Jimmie, who lives in southern Wisconsin and describes his class position as "not homeless anymore and owns a home," works eighty to one hundred hours a week patching together gigs in broadcasting, social media, digital content creation, and design. "I've monetized almost every aspect of my life that isn't being a parent, and I'm a couple medical bills away from starting a dad blog," he explained. "I even broadcast my video game tournaments." He'd love to keep things to himself, but he has two kids to support. "We need money and I don't have time to waste being unproductive," he told me. "It's not as fun, but we have a roof over our heads."

Jimmie estimates that he has around five to seven hours of leisure time a week: his commute, and then the half hour he spends passed out on the couch when he comes home from work. He doesn't consider broadcasting a video game tournament leisure, or even a hobby. When he monetized it, he changed the very nature of the activity. A monetized hobby might be periodically enjoyable, but when the activity becomes a means to an end— whether profit or perfection or entrance into school—it loses its essential, and essentially restorative, quality.

I've found that the people who do have hobbies—and find solace in them—are the ones who've given themselves the broadest permission for failure and imperfection. They revel in the process of making a table rather than feel pressure to sell it once its finished, or they just enjoy the experience of a hike rather than the Instagram of their view at the top, and the fetishization of being the sort of person who hikes. They understand that reading a book matters not because others know about it, but because you took pleasure in it. That attitude might sound simple, or maybe just obvious. But for so many millennials, it's often feels impossible.

*   *   *

Millennials have stopped going to religious services in massive numbers. We stream Netflix at home instead of going to the movies. The country club, the Elks Club, the volunteer fire department, the unpaid governmental committees that make local government run — all are struggling.[12] We go on Tinder dates instead of simply showing up at the bar. We group text instead of hanging out with our friend group, because finding a time when everyone's schedules align means planning four months in advance.

Back in 2000, the book *Bowling Alone*, written by the political scientist Robert Putnam, argued that American participation in groups, clubs, and organizations — religious, cultural, or otherwise — had precipitously dropped, as had the "social cohesion" that sprang from regular participation in them. Putnam's findings were controversial and contested, and many argued that community had simply shifted locations: maybe no one was going to bowling league, but they were hanging out online (in AOL chatrooms, on message boards) instead. Twenty years later, and our burnout levels, like our political and cultural polarization, speak to the prescience of Putnam's findings.

Following publication of *Bowling Alone*, several of Putnam's critics embarked on their own research, looking to either counter or confirm Putnam's claims. In 2011, they found significant decreases in both familial and nonfamilial networks — but nonfamilial most of all. "Americans' social networks are collapsing inward," Putnam wrote in his 2015 follow-up, *Our Kids*, "and now consist of fewer, denser, more homogenous, more familiar (and less nonkin) ties."[13]

But why aren't we hanging out with other people? Part of the problem is that the ability to easily coordinate schedules disintegrated alongside standardized working hours. If your schedule shifts from week to week—either due to algorithmic recalculations or your own inclination to stretch work hours—it can feel impossible to make plans or weekly commitments. Add in the increased pressure to arrange and supervise children's activities, and your available hours become even more difficult to overlap with others'. No one wants to admit just how difficult it will be to actually make plans happen, so people declare their best intentions to meet up—for a drink, for a playdate, for dinner—and then cycle into an endless cycle of "that doesn't work for me, could we do next week?" and last-minute cancellations.

In *Palaces for the People,* Erik Klinenberg suggests that part of the decline in social ties is rooted in our preference for efficiency: He points to a study that found that a daycare that made pickup as seamless and quick as possible meant that the parents hardly got to know each other. But when you forced the parents to come inside, wait around, and pick up their kids at the same time, boom, social connections began to form.[14] But part of the problem, too, is a decline in social infrastructure: the spaces, public and private, from libraries to supper clubs and synagogues, that made it easy to cultivate informal, nonmonetary ties.

These places still exist, of course, but they have become less central, and less vital, and, most importantly, less accessible. Because of liability issues, more and more churches are limiting the ability of members to use the space off-hours, even if they pay for it. Many public beaches and parks charge exclusionary fees—for parking and entrance—in areas without public transportation. Public playing fields and tracks are now locked or monop-

olized by teams that have paid to practice. A woman in upstate
New York decided to convene a book club of people with similar
interests she'd met on the internet. She didn't want to just host
it in her home — and spent weeks trying to find a space that was
accessible and affordable to everyone.

"We used to enjoy seeing AAA baseball downtown," one parent told me. "Then they turned the 'family zone' (open grassy
berms where the kids liked to play) into pay 'group/party areas.'
Then they moved into a new stadium on the rich side of town.
Then we stopped going." A woman in the D.C. area told me that
the Wegmans grocery store in an upper-middle-class, predominantly Black neighborhood had a small area in the front room
to drink coffee and eat. "People often used that areas for church
meetings, board games, and study groups," she said. "There are
now signs discouraging that."

Teresa, a postdoctoral researcher in Boston, consciously chose
to join a gaming group because there was a set meeting time every week, always at the same place. "Otherwise my friends and
I only play like once a month," she said, "because it just takes so
much effort to find a time and place that works." That's what social infrastructure helps provide: a relief from endless planning
and replanning. The Lions, Eagles, Moose, or Elks Club meetings were like clockwork, and in a space — with parking! — that
was always available. Same with church and Bible study, PEO and
the Junior League, the NAACP and League of Women's Voters.
Their reliability was part of what made them easier to engage in.

But as work and parenting expectations continued to expand,
and priorities continued to shift inward, group commitments
were one of the easiest time-consuming activities to jettison. As
fewer and fewer people attended, the groups themselves began
to disappear, with little to replace them — at least little that's affordable, that has regular meetings, that isn't religiously specific,

or doesn't center on children. We can talk about the value of group sports all we want, but attending a child's soccer game — and spending most of your time on the sidelines attending to work email — is not the same as playing on a team yourself.

I'm not the first person to tell you any of this. Most of us have read all about the studies that show that volunteering makes you happier, that in-person conversation and laughter is more nourishing than digital communication, that time for contemplation, religious or otherwise, makes us feel more balanced and less anxious. We know that leisure, especially the sort that Putnam describes as foundational to social ties, makes us feel better.

But for many people, just the *idea* of any of those activities seems to require an insurmountable expenditure of energy. In short, we're too tired to actually rest and restore ourselves. Meghan, who's white and lives in Albany, works a full-time job as an administrative assistant and a part-time job as a bookseller. She finds an hour or so a day, plus one day on the weekend, for leisure time, but she increasingly finds personal interactions, and dating especially, to be "emotionally daunting and draining." Even hanging out with her best friend wipes her out.

Rosie, a literary agent in New York, cannot extract leisure activities from their costs: "Lying in bed scrolling Twitter is free," she points out, "and living in New York just requires more energy, both physical (walking everywhere) and mental (researching service changes to the subway and buses). Plus, she says, "if I don't get a good Instagram post of the leisure activity, I might as well not have done it." Laura, who lives in Chicago and works as a special ed teacher, never wants to see her friends, or date, or cook — she's so tired, she just wants to melt into the couch. "But then I can't focus on what I'm watching, and end up unfocused again, and not completely relaxing," she explained. "Here I am telling you I don't even relax right! I feel bad about feeling bad! But by the time I have leisure time, I just want to be alone!"

And the pressure seems to build even more with kids. Claire, age twenty-nine, lives with her husband and two children in eastern Pennsylvania. Her husband works two jobs (in an office, and as a freelance writer) while she works part-time (twelve to sixteen hours a week) and stays home to take care of her kids. She's also learning a new trade on the side (computer networking) since her current job has no room for advancement. She gets out of the house every few weeks with friends, but there have been periods where she didn't see friends for months at a time: It was simply too hard to coordinate. Once, maybe twice a month, she and her husband find a sitter to go out. "I have to really push myself and plan ahead if I want to attend a meetup or event, because the shock waves it sends through my routine are so hard to absorb," she admitted. "Way too often, I cancel at the last minute because I am worn out from the day."

It's important to pause with that scenario—one that I've heard over and over, and that I've articulated myself. Being with our friends, the people who love and cherish us, is too unsettling to our schedules. But our schedules *are* our lives. And what are our lives without others?

We watch television, we smoke more weed and drink to *force* our bodies to relax, we elevate and celebrate introvert behavior with T-shirts that read SORRY I'M LATE / I'D RATHER BE AT HOME. We try to feel okay with the way things are. But what haunts me is the truth that what you do with your leisure time now, when it's so rare and so overdetermined and so overladen with exhaustion, is not—at least not necessarily—what you would do if you had more of it. So many of our best intentions, our most curious and creative and compassionate selves, are right there, closer beneath the surface of our lives than we know. We simply need space, time, and rest to make them a reality.

* * *

Sometimes, I purposefully pick the longest line at the grocery store and watch myself react to my impatience — my inability to hang out, even for just a handful of extra minutes, with my own mind. I'm addicted to stimulation. I've forgotten not just how to wait, but even how to let my mind wander and play. In *How to Do Nothing: Resisting the Attention Economy,* Jenny Odell makes a deeply compelling case for ignoring all of the impulses toward productivity and perfection that have come to imbue our lives, leisure, and otherwise. That means doing, well, *nothing* — at least nothing that is conceived of as value-making under capitalism.

Odell describes the deep pleasures of learning the names of the flora and fauna in her local park. Learning their names means being able to actually notice them — see them, and spend time recognizing them, simply because they occupy the same space as us. They matter, and are valuable, simply because they *are* — not because they make us better workers, or more desirable partners, or more economically secure.

There are all sorts of ways to do "nothing", and they don't (necessarily) even involve sequestering ourselves from the internet, or purposefully choosing the longest line at the grocery store. Caring for others, worshiping, singing, and talking, and hanging out with your own mind — all of it can be blissfully, radically unproductive. It matters because it nourishes you and others. Full stop.

Odell argues that we've come to the point where we downplay all of the competing forces for our attention, using words like "annoying" or "distracting" to describe the engineered addiction of social media, the fear of missing an important email, the compulsion to render leisure in some way financially and personally "productive." But distractions, Odell writes, "keep us from doing the things we want to do"—which then "accumulate and keep us from living the lives we want to live." In this way, the "best, most alive parts" of ourselves are "paved over by a ruthless logic of use."

A reckoning with burnout is so often a reckoning with the fact that the things you fill your day with—*the things you fill your life with*—feel unrecognizable from the sort of life you want to live, and the sort of meaning you want to make of it. That's why the burnout condition is more than just addiction to work. It's an alienation from the self, and from desire. If you subtract your ability to work, who are you? Is there a self left to excavate? Do you know what you like and don't like when there's no one there to watch, and no exhaustion to force you to choose the path of least resistance? Do you know how to move without always moving forward?

A recommitment to and cherishing of oneself isn't self-care, or self-centered-ness, at least not in the contemporary connotations of those words. Instead, it's a declaration of value: not because you labor, not because you consume, not because you produce, but simply because you *are*. To emerge from burnout, and ultimately resist its return, is to remember as much.

9

The Exhausted Millennial Parent

IT'S EASY TO SEE HOW HAVING A KID CAN EXACERBATE all of the tendencies, anxieties, and exhaustion that characterize millennial burnout. But it's another thing, especially if you don't have kids, to try to understand how that exacerbation actually *feels*.

"You think you have it under control until something throws it all off and you have a breakdown," Lisa, a mother of two from suburban Pennsylvania, told me. "You suddenly realize your kid's shoes are two sizes too small, and you burst into tears: You're a horrible mom who has abused her kid because you were caught up in the day-to-day. Toddlers never tell you when shoes are too tight. You agree to split the weekend with your spouse, and he goes off golfing for seven hours and you are so filled with rage when he gets home that you don't even care that tomorrow is 'your day,' because you have nothing planned and don't know what you to do because there are no female hobbies that last seven hours."

"It's the kind of exhaustion where you can't really have other feelings," Lauren, who recently moved from the US to Britain, explained. "I'd wake up some mornings and just stare out my window, wanting to cry, but mostly I didn't have the luxury of *having* feelings. Either I'd get told, 'This is what being a mom is like!' or some kind of authority would come around for Concerned Looks and postpartum depression quizzes. I don't think I was ever a danger to my kids. I think I was just exhausted, given no help, and blamed for any feelings of resentment in my life."

"Parenting burnout makes me feel like I don't want to take care of anyone anymore, ever," Amy, who's white and lives in a major American city, said. "I don't want to have to remember the minutiae of anyone's day. I find myself being irritable and short-fused with my kids over the smallest things. I tend to lose perspective on the socks that have been left in the middle of the living room for too long, and I can easily fly off the handle if I'm asked for one more thing in the middle of the seven others I'm already doing. I hate that I resent my husband for getting to work outside the home, and having the privilege of forgetting that he was supposed to be home at a certain time because he got caught up with work. At times I feel too small for the momentous title of Mom."

"I'm not quite on board with the concept of 'burnout,'" Jenny, who parents in small town in a western state, explained. "It's like that quote from David Foster Wallace about goldfish and water: One fish asks another fish, 'How's the water?' The other fish replies, 'What the hell is water?'"

*   *   *

Historically, parents have been forced to make decisions about which child will have to drop out of school to work, or which child will get more food. Those choices are gruesome and have never been easy—but they have always been acknowledged as such. Contemporary parenting culture, meanwhile, is a particularly complicated and deceptive kind of difficult, made all the more so because its difficulty is so often denied or erased. It enforces ideals that are impossible to achieve within our current caregiving scenarios and squares the blame for societal failures on individual parents. It breeds resentment and despair—particularly for women who placed stock in the idea of an equal partnership. Similar to the paradigm of overwork, it equates exhaustion with skill, or aptitude, or devotion: The "best" parents are the ones who give until there's nothing left of themselves. And, worst of all, there's little evidence that it actually makes kids' lives better.

Instead of the "problem that has no name," famously described in Betty Friedan's landmark 1963 book, *The Feminine Mystique,* this problem has a name, and that name is parenting burnout. It's the result of shifting ideas about what constitutes "good parenting," stubborn ideas about whose labor gets "counted," and the overflow of work outside of the workplace. But first and foremost, it's an outgrowth of the fact that American society is still arranged as if every family has a caretaker who stays home, even as fewer and fewer families are arranged that way.

Parenting burnout does not uniquely affect mothers. But because mothers continue to perform the vast majority of the labor in homes with a mother and a father, it affects mothers *most.* The burden only increases when you consider growing rates of single parenthood: As of 2017, about one-fifth of the children in the United States lived with a solo mother.[1] Just because women have been liberated from many of the explicit forms of subjugation and sexism that accompanied domestic life, other forms continue to thrive, sublimated into the ideologies of ideal contemporary womanhood. Today's mothers are expected to gracefully manage and maintain a high-pressure job, her children, her relationship, her domestic space, and her body. She is "free" to be pressured to be everything to everyone at all times, save herself.

But how did it get this way? Squint at your parents' parenting practices, and you can see the outlines of what have become the expensive, anxious, and paranoid parenting practices of today. First, there was the fear of the ever-more-dangerous world — and the accompanying threats to children's well-being. Those threats could be subverted, but only through vigilance and knowledge, which gradually translated into total surveillance — of our children, but also of other people's parenting practices. Second, there was the fear of downward mobility: that a family's class position was unstable, and pouring literal or figurative resources into children was the only way to try to protect against that slippage.

Burnt-out boomer parents felt it; now their burnt-out millennial children feel it as well. Cue even more amped-up versions of the "concerted cultivation" that guided many middle-class childhoods, complete with packed schedules, bonus enrichment, and college planning that starts before birth, the necessity of which are reinforced through the Instagram accounts, Facebook parenting threads, blogs, newsletters, podcasts, and parenting books that fill bourgeois mothers' media diets.

But that doesn't entirely answer the question of how it got this bad for mothers in particular. The answer, of course, is patriarchy—but patriarchy cloaked in the deceptive language of equality and progress. As multiple historians have shown, women have long resented the mundane, stultifying tasks of domesticity, but rarely dared to contradict the public understanding of the joyful, self-abnegating mother. When women started entering the professional workplace in the 1960s and '70s, the freedom and choice which had long been allotted to men came into sharp relief. Not all women wanted lives outside the domestic sphere. But many women wanted the *choice*.

Of course, millions of poor women, especially Black and Brown women, had been working outside of the home for generations. They just did it, as so many poor people do now, in workplaces that were informal (someone else's home) or unstable (migrant farmwork). But when white middle-class women started doing it, and in the same spaces as white, middle-class men — well, that was cause for alarm.

Alarm, but also stability: For many families, a supplemental income was a godsend. But that stability was offset by the shame of the husband no longer being able to uniquely provide for his family, and all other manner of fragile masculinity manifestations. And how do you make men feel better about their masculinity? You assure them that nothing, really, will change: A woman might be working in the office eight hours a day, but she'll still be feminine and put together, and dinner will still be served at the same time, and the kids won't even notice a thing. In other words, she'll still be a full-time housewife — even if she's also a full-time worker outside the home. Hence the "second shift," a term popularized by Arlie Russell Hochschild's 1989 book of the same name, to describe the fact that these mothers were in fact pulling double shifts every day: one in the "formal" workplace, then another back at home.

Hochschild argues that women's entrance into the paid economy was "the basic social revolution" of our time.[2] But as she pointed out, the feminist component of that revolution was largely "stalled": Just because women were shouldering equal amounts of work outside the home didn't mean that the work inside the home was equally split as well. As a result, the "first" shift (a mother's job outside the home) was often compromised or devalued in order to keep maintaining the second one in the home. One-shift fathers, by contrast, could continue to cultivate their careers unimpeded.

Granted, these fathers did perform more domestic work than their own fathers: Between 1965 and 2003, men's portion of unpaid family work rose from under 20 percent to nearly 30 percent.[3] But since 2003, that figure has remained stubbornly in place. Time-use studies by the Bureau of Labor Statistics find that women who work for pay outside the home still shoulder 65 percent of childcare responsibilities.[4] Fathers, in other words, have never even approached performing an equal amount of household labor.

Societal programs have not addressed the shift toward the dual-parent work model, even as fewer and fewer families have a stay-at-home parent today. In America, there is still no mandatory paid parental leave; subsidized and affordable childcare is difficult if not impossible to find; school runs for just three quarters of the year and two thirds of the workday. In short, the societally compelled rhythms of a child's day and year are incompatible with the rhythms of most parents' working life.

In the past, even when millennials were children, this incompatibility was largely manageable: A kid could come home from school and hang out with a grandparent, or a slightly older sibling, or go to the neighbor's house. Some were "latchkey kids," named for keys worn around their necks, who'd spend hours at home after school before a parent returned from work. The cultural stereotypes around these kids soon became plagued with sweeping indictments on how this alone time could corrupt their character. Kids left alone started fires. They were lonely. They watched too much television. They ended up on a path toward juvenile delinquency. And with that image came an increasingly critical view of the parents who allowed their children to home unsupervised.

Today, we have even more working mothers and a dearth of childcare alternatives. But instead of returning to looser standards of supervision, or altering work hours, we've mandated *constant* supervision. Many elementary schools won't release a child after school—or even allow them off a school bus—without an approved adult present. To allow your late-elementary-school-age child to come home to an empty house is, as several people from across the country told me, to risk getting reported to CPS.

It doesn't matter if you, as a parent, think your child has the ability to safely be at home by herself. Other adults will report you. As Kim Brooks points out in *Small Animals: Parenthood in the Age of Fear,* when Barbara W. Sarnecka, a cognitive scientist at USC-Irvine, allowed her third-grader to play after school at an adjacent park—with many adults present but not herself—another parent emailed her husband, and the principal of the elementary school emailed her. Brooks also recalls the fallout after she made the decision to leave her four-year-old in her car for five minutes while she ran into the store to grab a pair of head-phones.[5] The police didn't "catch" her. Someone in the parking lot, someone she'd never met and never would, taped her on their cell phone—and then submitted the videotape to the police.

As with all things parenting, the standards are most exacting amongst middle class, urban and suburban parents. And while (white) middle-class parents often do the policing, they're also the ones most likely to avoid criminal consequences for their actions. As Brooks points out, when she was charged with "contributing to the delinquency of a minor" in the state of Virginia, she was able to afford the sort of nice clothes that signal to a prosecutor and judge, "I'm not a threat to my children or society." She was also able to afford a good lawyer, who made the process as seamless as possible—and earned her a sentence of community service and a parenting class. She endured the social censure and the sense of shame, but that was nothing compared to what could've happened to her or her children if she wasn't a white middle-class woman.

Which is why the new standard, enforced by teachers and principals and parents and their peers, is that if a parent can't alter their schedule in order to pick up and supervise their child after school, the understanding is that they'll pay someone else, or some service, to do it for them. The stats bear this out: Census data shows that between 1997 and 2013, the number of grade-school American children who spent time alone after school went down by nearly 40 percent—from one in five kids in 1997 to one in nine in 2013. Part of that shift can be linked to increased work flexibility (parents' jobs take up more hours, but some of those hours can be shifted around—which, in practice, usually just makes for more work, or distracted work, or distracted parenting). And part of it can be attributed to increased availability of afterschool programs, many funded by private/public partnerships like the Afterschool Alliance, which was founded in 2000.

To be clear: There's nothing wrong with afterschool programs. They're great! In many low-income areas, they're fully subsidized. But for millions of American families, paying for them is a burden. In one New Jersey school district, a parent told me they have no control over whether their kindergartener attends school in the morning or afternoon; if they need "full-day" school, it's an extra $600 a month, plus the cost of afterschool care. In the Ballard neighborhood of Seattle, the afterschool program had a waitlist of three years; a week's worth of care (three and a half hours a day) cost just under $500. At a YMCA in Kansas, a week's worth of care (around three hours a day) still costs $105.

It's very expensive, in other words, for both parents to work outside the home: The national average cost for childcare, according to one advocacy group, is nearly $8,700 a year. In some states, the average cost for a year of preschool care is roughly $13,000; overall, childcare costs for a family with a working mother went up 70 percent from 1985 to 2012. It's even more of a hardship for single parents: On average, 36 percent of a single parent's income is devoted to paying others to take care of their children[6]

Of course, families *do* make it work. They make it work by hodgepodging shifts, by relying on friends and family, by getting into gig work, by neglecting savings, or allowing their student loans to go into forbearance. But not everyone has reliable friends or available family — and gig work is not the same as full-time employment. Which is why some mothers who'd like to be in the workplace see no other option than to quit.

For years, the accepted wisdom was that a woman would stay home during a child's early years, then return to the workplace, if she wished, when the child reached later school age. But with childcare costs so much lower, that decision was rarely an economic imperative; it was just what many (middle-class) women did.

Many millennials who grew up in those homes — myself included — watched that scenario play out with their parents. In 2015, as part of a larger story, I heard from hundreds of millennial women about what they'd internalized about having children, co-parenting, and jobs from watching their boomer moms. They talked about hard work, and multitasking, but they also talked about their mothers' regret: "I know she put off a lot of the things she wanted to do in life (college) or compromised on them (career) because she had kids," one woman who grew up in Wyoming told me. "I always swore that would not be me."

Some of us watched our moms emerge from divorce with nonexistent career paths. Some just heard our moms talk, with thinly veiled or fully unveiled regret, about what became unavailable to them after leaving the workplace. Some of us saw how hard it was to make ends meet on one salary, especially when that salary went away for whatever reason. And some of us have decided to delay or not have kids. But most women I know simply decided that they'd avoid their mothers' regret by doing things differently. They'd keep their careers *and* have kids — even if that meant most of their salary, at least in those early years, was going to childcare. At least they'd have *options*.

*   *   *

As parents' time at work increased, the paradigm of what was "possible" or "acceptable" or even "affordable" parenting did not change with it. Wide-scale, sweeping legislation was not passed to address it; the vast majority of employers did not alter their policies to accommodate parents. Instead, the endless expectations of how to be a "good" parent — a parent whose child would be successful, and happy, and reproduce or reach above their current class status — expanded. More work outside of the home begat more work *at* home.

Let me say that again, because it's truly mind-boggling. Instead of being easier on ourselves as parents, given all of shifts in expectations at work, and our increasingly fraught class position, and the massive amounts of debt we've incurred in order to maintain that class position—we allowed expectations to go *up*. More parenting options hasn't been liberating; it's become nauseatingly claustrophobic.

This was true, in some fashion, for boomer parents—but it's more true, in more cases, for millennial parents. There's more information than ever on "good" parenting and thus more ways to fail at it. There's more speculation on ways you can mess up your kids and thus more fear that you're doing it. Kids are more expensive, and families have less money to devote to them after covering essentials. Parenting practices are more public and more scrutinized. Employers might offer ostensible flexibility but only while also requiring more work.

And contradictions—*options!*—abound. You should be involved but not *too* involved; you should direct kids toward college education at all costs even if you feel ambivalent about your own; you should cultivate your child's independence but never leave them unsupervised; you should praise women's empowerment even as women's work is devalued in the home; you should trumpet the benefits of diversity while obsessing over whether your child is in the "right" school; you should teach them healthy relationships with technology while maintaining an unhealthy relationship with your own technology. And that's if you have time, in the first place, to worry about any of these things: As Elizabeth Currid-Halkett points out, "To actually talk about the nuances and choices of motherhood (rather than simply being a mother and taking care of one's children) implies the luxury to do so."[7]

Modern parenting has always in some way been about doubting your own competence. But never before has that doubt arrived with such force from so many vectors. Like all expectations, ideals, and ideologies, the question of who's actually enforcing these parenting standards is a knotty one. No one likes them, and yet there they remain, providing a sort of informal parenting surveillance state, manifest in gossip and passive-aggressive Facebook comments and "well-intentioned" mom support group chatter.

At least that's the case amongst the bourgeois, the solidly upper-middle class, the largely white population that functions as the true originator and arbiter of these norms—the yardstick against which contemporary parenting is measured and found wanting. It doesn't matter if you don't have the extra income to buy organic food, or to set aside money to pay for a college fund, or to provide constant afterschool supervision. It doesn't matter if your refusal is principled or financially motivated—if you want different things for yourself or your kids. To refuse to *strive* is to declare yourself, in the eyes of society at large, as a willfully bad parent.

Take the much-debated subject of breastfeeding: a "best" mothering practice, vaunted, at least in part, because it is "free" —and, barring medical difficulties, theoretically available to all mothers. But access to a lactation consultant isn't free. Neither are the pumps, nursing pads, bottles, mini-fridges, and special bras and tops that make long-term nursing a reality for mothers who cannot be with their children throughout the day. Nursing takes massive amounts of time—a luxury many working mothers, especially poor ones, simply do not have. According to Cynthia Colen, a sociologist of public health, only 12 percent of female workers and 5 percent of female low-wage workers have access to any sort of paid leave; as a result, "most women are required to forgo income in order to breast feed."[8]

Or, after breastfeeding, there is an expectation to provide children with a healthy diet. The sociologist Caitlin Daniel found that poor parents knew exactly what types of foods were healthiest for their kids. But as any parent knows, introducing new foods and broadening a child's palate requires a significant amount of wasted food—which, when your food budget is governed by food stamps, is a huge risk. Daniel spotlights one poor mother from her research who attempted, the best she could, to provide healthy food on a budget, including seeking out bruised vegetables she could purchase at a discount, which she'd pair with rice, beans, or pasta. "These meals cost relatively little—if they're eaten," Daniel explains. "But when her children rejected them, an affordable dish became a financial burden. Grudgingly, this mother resorted to the frozen burritos and chicken nuggets that her family preferred."[9]

It's not that poor parents don't know what good parenting looks like. It's that various forces make it unavailable to them. For white middle-class people, a refusal to participate in such practices can entail social ostracization. But for a Black or Brown parent, such a refusal contributes to social stigma: the idea that your entire race is lazy or ignorant. And, in some cases, it can be used as evidence of criminal neglect. In 2014, a South Carolina woman allowed her nine-year-old daughter, out of school for the summer, to play at a popular park while she was at work.[10] Before, she'd allowed her daughter to play on a laptop in the space where she worked, but when the laptop was stolen, her daughter asked to go to the park instead. When an adult at the park asked where her mother was, she replied, "Work." The woman called the police, the mother was arrested for "unlawful conduct toward a child," and her daughter was placed in temporary foster care.

It's the same story, in many ways, as the UC-Irvine professor who allowed her son to go to the playground after school. But the consequences were markedly different: The professor just had to deal with a passive-aggressive email to her husband and a call from the principal. The South Carolina woman was charged with a crime and had her child taken from her. And those differences had everything to do with race and class: The South Carolina mother is Black, and her child was at the park while she worked at McDonald's. The professor is white, and, well, a professor.

Everyone ostensibly has the right to figure out how to parent, so long as it doesn't directly endanger the child. But in our current society, white middle-class people still set the standards around what sorts of parenting is *best*. Just because the rules make winning impossible doesn't mean these parents can't force everyone—themselves included—to play past the point of exhaustion.

*   *   *

Burnout occurs when the distance between the ideal and the possible lived reality becomes too much to bear. That's true of the workplace, and that's true of parenting. The common denominator amongst millennials, then, is that we've been inculcated with the idea of that failure—like our failure to find secure employment, or save enough money to buy a house, or stave off an avalanche of medical debt—can be chalked up to simply not trying hard enough. As the sociologist Veronica Tichenor puts it, "Work hasn't changed. Workplaces still act like everyone has a wife at home. Everyone should be the ideal worker and not have to leave to take care of a sick kid. If one family struggles to balance it all, it's a personal problem. All these families with the same problem? That's a social issue."[11]

And yet, we continue to treat this social issue as a personal issue. More specifically, a mother's issue. Women have long been freighted with the task of reconciling or soothing the anxieties that accompany societal change, and contemporary mothers are no different. When women began to move into the professional workplace, the resultant anxiety over "motherless" children and unkempt homes and feminized stay-at-home fathers had to be quelled in some way, lest a backlash erase whatever small progress had been made. The tacit agreement: Women could enter the workplace, but only if they fulfilled *every other* societal expectation. They could be ambitious, but still had to be nice; powerful, but still hot; hardworking, but still a good cook; multitasking, but still a conscientious housekeeper; a leader, but still feminine; a workaholic, but still a devoted parent. To be clear, many of these expectations were foisted on boomer moms as well—but there was less of an expectation to perform and package all of those qualities online for mass consumption.

Men participate in and reinforce these ideals, but the primary arbitrators of success or failure are other women. That's one of the most noxious elements of patriarchal control: It turns the very women it subjugates into the primary enforcers of its ideology. And it manifests most vividly in what many women described, in various forms of disgust, as competitive martyrdom: "White/WASPy women seem addicted to martyrdom as a parenting philosophy," Kaili, a white woman from Chicago, told me. "From BUYING ALL THE THINGS to the tyranny of breastfeeding to the baby gaining weight, there are endless ways to feel guilty. I think we are quick to make it as hard as possible for ourselves instead of just living."

Operating in this way—constantly re-inscribing the same standards that make life so un-neededly *hard*—is psychologically fucked. But it's also just flat-out *exhausting*. Even more so when all that unprocessed frustration has nowhere to go but toward competition with other moms: "Instead of offering a legitimate show of community or problem solving, moms almost universally will try to one-up your source of parenting frustration with their own similar but clearly much worse struggles," Lauren, who calls herself a "broke white college student" in the Pacific Northwest, explained. "We could easily offer each other an exchange of hosting playdates while one takes a few hours of alone time, but then we'd be admitting that we need help — and are clearly not up to the task of parenting. Better to cling to the torch of martyrdom with a white-knuckled death grip."

Katie, who lives in a New England suburb, sees the ethos of self-sacrifice intertwined with what she calls "Instagram parenting": "when you post all the beautiful stuff, great vacations, smiling kids, and never the craziness." Except for when you do post, or blog, about the craziness — "then it has to be emphasized." Instagram and Facebook have become the primary means through which friends and family keep track of a family. It's a place to document the (always well-lit, and very cute) everyday, but it's engineered to showcase the spectacular: the trips, the fancy birthday parties, the most adorable outfits, the most together family-ness. Sasha, a white upper-middle-class mom from Brooklyn, describes the Instagram Mom as the "cool, composed mom who keeps a super organized calendar with the family's appointments, wants to have exciting sex no matter what time the kids went to sleep, can compartmentalize work and home, and never lets her kids watch TV or eat cereal for dinner."

But Instagram parenting is just the contemporary manifestation of the cult of "busyness," which the communications scholar Ann Burnett has been tracking for years vis-à-vis family holiday letters: the long, descriptive summaries of a family's year sent around the holidays. As she amassed more and more, she noticed a trend in the way the authors of the letters — almost always mothers — were framing their family's lives: as an endless, packed, frenetic stream of *busyness*. She began to realize that they were, in fact, *competing:* "It's about showing status," Burnett told Brigid Schulte, author of *Overwhelmed.* "That if you're busy, you're important. You're leading a full and worthy life."[12] Busyness, in other words, as a very certain sort of *class.*

There's a common denominator here, between all the Insta-gram Mom–ing and the Mommy Martyrdom. It's work, all of it. First, you erase it by making motherhood look hectic but easy — "such an adventure!" — but always beautiful and effortless. Then, because it's not okay *not* to work, you emphasize it, to clarify to yourself and your partner and your family and your peers just how much you actually are working. It's contradictory, and man-aging that contradiction (on top of all of the perfect parenting and exasperating sacrifice) just creates *more* work.

The labor compounds in a way that makes you so exhausted you don't have energy to resist it, even when you know it's non-sense. Celia, who identifies as Latina and disabled, lives in an ur-ban Midwest city with her husband and their child. "So many of the demands seem like housewife busy-work to me," she said. "'Never let your child see a screen' just means you can never empty a dishwasher or wash your hair without an ordeal. Or the idea that if you sleep train your child, it'll damage your relation-ship with them forever, or that you should do 'baby-led weaning,' because if you feed your child purees, they will never have a de-veloped palate and will become fat from eating from pouches, even though you don't have time to make tiny diced food." Celia can articulate all of this clearly, and yet still admits to feeling ter-rified, every day, that she's messing up her child in some way.

Many women can list, in detail, the bevy of tasks, attitudes, and habits that accompany "good" motherhood — and then, in the same sentence, admit there are simply not enough hours in the day to even come close to doing them all. And yet women who can, try. It's the millennial way: If the system is rigged against you, just try harder. Which helps explain one of the most curi-ous stats of the last forty years: Women with jobs spend just as much time parenting as stay-at-home mothers did in the 1970s. The metaphor of the second shift isn't a metaphor at all: They are doing two full-time jobs.[13] And in order to make time for both of those jobs, they are sleeping less — and spending far, far less time on themselves, or their own leisure.

Indeed, they're spending more time on the "new domesticity," best manifest in what Rachel, who parents her five-year-old with her wife outside of Memphis, calls "GODDAMN MOTHERFUCKING PINTEREST."[14] "Out of the four semi-healthy items my kid eats, I'm supposed to make edible butterflies for her lunch each day," she says. "Then there are dress-up days at school, wholesome crafts that are supposed to improve fine-motor skills while avoiding screen time, and the need for everything to have a theme." If a traditional leisure activity like, say, knitting, is actually pleasurable, mothers feel pressure to monetize it: Erika, who lives in a Boston suburb and describes her family as "struggling financially," finds herself endlessly reading articles on Pinterest such as "21 Totally Legit Side Hustles for Stay-at-Home Moms." "I'm constantly wondering if I could start a knitting business," she says, "instead of just relaxing with a hobby I get pleasure out of."

"Time studies find that a mother, especially one who works outside the home for pay, is among the most time-poor humans on the planet," Schulte writes in *Overwhelmed,* "especially single mothers, weighed down not only by role overload but also what sociologists call 'task density' — the intense responsibility she bears and the multitude of jobs she performs in each of those roles."[15] Marielle Cloin, who studies family time use in the Netherlands, explains the problem to Schulte as "role overload": "the constant switching from one role to the next."[16] In five minutes, a mom can go from texting a friend who's been struggling to chopping fruit for a kid's snack to checking a recipe online to regulating a sibling argument in the next room to trying to listen to her partner tell her about their day at work.

Whatever leisure time remains is increasingly spent with, or constantly interrupted by, children. Women exercise — with their children. Women socialize — with their children. "I'm so desperate for alone time that I stay up far later than I should, just in an attempt to have moments to myself," Katie, who lives outside of Atlanta, explained. "I wind up making myself more exhausted by trying to take time for myself." Marie is white, identifies as middle class, and lives in Pomona, California, with her husband, who's Indian, and her mother-in-law. She finds herself constantly arguing about the length of her shower: "My husband will complain that I'm in the bathroom for thirty or forty-five minutes, and I realized that what I really mean when I say I want to take a shower is that I want some time for myself — to groom, to relax, to think."

If you work outside of the home, there's guilt that you're not using any leftover time to spend with your children. Amy, who works as a full-time librarian, was shocked at how difficult it was to return to her job, which often requires working on nights and weekends. "I put a lot of pressure on myself to make the most of the time we get to spend together, and I feel guilty taking any time for myself that I could be spending with my son," she says. Alternately, time away from parenting is spent *talking* about parenting. "I don't want to talk about my kids and their problems when I'm out with my neighbors or friends," Christine, who lives in Atlanta, says. "I have a life outside my kids and other interests. My mother definitely didn't spend time at block parties discussing my activities and I'm there doing that. Husbands get out of that BS."

Of course, contemporary fathers are expected to be present, to be involved — but the standards are far less exacting. "My husband doesn't have to strive/excel/constantly pursue improvement to be considered a great professor/husband/father/

community member," Brooke, who's white and middle class and lives in rural North Carolina, explains. "And maybe I don't have to either, but I constantly feel like I do. The most bullshit thing is the constant never-enoughness."

Dads, by contrast, can find "enoughness" by aspiring to a level of involvement best summarized as "more than what their own fathers did." That can run the spectrum from simply learning to change a diaper to taking on the role of full-time stay-at-home parent. On average, it still looks like 35 percent of the labor, even if the dads themselves don't want to admit it: 41 percent of fathers believe their childcare responsibilities were "shared equally."[17]

As Darcy Lockman puts it in *All the Rage: Mothers, Fathers, and the Myth of Equal Partnership,* "Reports of the modern, involved father have been greatly exaggerated."[18] The *culture* of fatherhood has changed, but that doesn't mean that fathers, even those committed to equality before the arrival of children, are enacting it in the home. A 2015 study by the Families and Work Institute found that only 35 percent of employed millennial men without children believed in "traditional" family roles: that "men should be breadwinners and women should be caregivers."[19] For those who already have kids, that number jumped to *53 percent.* As Alissa, who identifies as Hispanic, white, and Native American, put it, "I didn't know my progressive husband was not progressive until it came to the actual division of parenting tasks."

There are myriad explanations for this unequal distribution of labor: Men aren't as good at multitasking, men don't breastfeed and thus can't take the same sort of caregiving role in early infancy, women have unrealistic expectations for how men should complete tasks. Lockman methodically breaks down — and disabuses readers of — each notion. Men are not "naturally" bad at multitasking, for example. Men are *conditioned* not to have to be multitaskers; women are *conditioned* to be multitaskers. "Everything we call a sex difference, if you take a different perspective —what's the power angle on this—often explains things," the neuroscientist Lise Eliot tells Lockman. "It has served men very well to assume that male-female differences are hard-wired."[20]

Which isn't to entirely fault men: Like women, most have few models of truly equitable partnerships. Once patterns of caregiving (and "expertise" in that care) are established, it's extremely difficult to alter them. But even men who do attempt to do their share of the household labor— switching off on bedtimes, taking on the laundry— still seldom carry what can feel like the heaviest burden of all: "the mental load." The mental load, as the French cartoonist Emma describes, is carried by the person in the family (almost always a woman) who takes on a role akin to "household management project leader."

The manager doesn't just complete chores; they keep the entire household's schedule in their minds. They're ultimately responsible for the health of the family, the upkeep of the home and their own bodies, maintaining a sex life, cultivating an emotional bond with their children, overseeing aging parents' care, making sure bills are paid and neighbors are greeted and someone's home for a service call and holiday cards get in the mail and vacations are planned six months in advance and airline miles aren't expiring and the dog's getting exercise. The load is so heavy, made more so by the fact that no matter how many tasks you finish, it never seems to get any lighter.

Women have told me that reading Emma's cartoon, which has gone viral many times over, brought them to tears: They'd never seen the particular work that they do described, let alone acknowledged. It's largely invisible, but it's also so incredibly difficult to, well, un*load*, even to the most well-meaning of partners. "I call it the 'You should have asked' phenomenon," Debbie, an upper-class mom in Florida, says. "I love my husband and think he is really one of the good ones, but he only does things when asked. He only does dishes after dinner if I explicitly ask him to, and then he never actually gets the kitchen all the way clean. Even if I explicitly ask him to do something, I don't know if it is selective incompetence or regular incompetence, but he does it wrong."

As Michael Kimmel, author of *Manhood in America,* described to Lockman, men find all manner of ways to "opt out" of equal labor. "Men often tell me, 'My wife gets on me all the time because I don't vacuum, and I'm watching a baseball game, and she comes in and says, "At least you could vacuum." So I do, and then she comes back and tells me I didn't do it very thoroughly. So I just figure I won't do it anymore.' I say to them, 'Well, that's an interesting response! If I were your supervisor at work and I assigned you a report, and I wasn't happy with what you turned in, and I told you so, would your reply be, "Well, then, I'll never do *that* again!"'?"

When I've recounted that story, in person or online, some respond that the problem lies in viewing one partner (the mother) as the boss, and the other (the father) as an employee. It's true: This is not an ideal scenario. But it's what happens when one partner is reluctant, or actively refuses, to perform equal labor in the home.

"Men find ways of being so difficult that it's not worth it," the sociologist Lisa Wade explains.[21] So many women reconcile themselves to accept the inequality. "There is no fair in motherhood," a friend told me. "You'll drive yourself insane if you try. I just try to focus on what I need to be a whole person and let the imbalance go as much as I can." You feel grateful that "he's one of the better ones," even though this posture, as Lockman writes, "conceals a sort of female subordination that would otherwise be intolerable in many twenty-first-century-homes.... He's-happy-to-do-it-if-I-ask is yet another task; it's not a partnership."

Many women feel that because they have it better than others, they have no "right" to complain. Lockman borrows "relative-deprivation theory" from sociology to explain this reticence: "Only when one feels more deprived than other members of her reference group will she feel entitled to adamant protest." Your partner's not the worst; he's doing more than his father, or than your friend's husband, who's *really* the worst. As Sara, a middle-class mom from Washington, DC, put it to me, "Our division of labor is 70/30 and I consider myself lucky (which is bullshit)." Jill, who lives in a Midwest suburb, fought hard for a 55/45 split. "It took a lot of arguments and discussions to get this point, and even now it's not quite even," she said. "But I know I have a better parenting partnership than most everyone else I know, so I don't dare push my luck much farther."

That structural problems are *worse* for people with less money, or less help, or less flexibility, also makes some women feel ungrateful if they voice the ways in which the system still makes them feel like shit. "This is where I really hate myself," Sarah, an upper-middle class woman from a Midwestern suburb, explained. "We are very privileged. We have fairly secure jobs, we make over $200,000 a year, and we have minimal debt. I feel like I'm not allowed to complain about burnout because so many people have it worse than I do. I'm not scrimping or worrying about bills. I feel so guilty for complaining, so I keep a lot of my rage."

Just because inequality is not as dire does not mean that it is not felt. "I could talk for hours about burnout and how I feel *every fucking day* that I'm failing," Renee, who's middle class and lives in New Jersey, told me. "I get mad at everyone who has family help and support. And I have hated my husband like never before, because so much of the day-to-day and bigger scope is on me. We both work full-time, but it's on me. I'm just so, so angry." Rage seems to flare particularly wildly during periods of partner leisure: "The most telling difference in our partnership is the amount of time I do not sit on the weekends versus the amount of time he sits," Sara, from the suburbs of Philadelphia, explained. "And naps."

Lockman points to an abundance of research on men's "leisure privilege": Working mothers with preschool-aged children, for example, are 2.5 times more likely to be the one to get up with their kid in the middle of the night. Fathers of infants spend *twice* as much weekend time in "leisure" than mothers of infants.[22] I'm reminded of a friend who, as the father of a newborn, spent at least one day of each fall weekend tailgating and attending a football game — and was indignant that his wife didn't want him doing it on both Saturday *and* Sunday. It's not a question of whether fathers deserve leisure time; it's that many regard that leisure time as a "right" — even as a mother's leisure time dwindles to nothing.

Sometimes the rage accumulates gradually — as you realize that a decision meant to benefit the family is mostly benefitting your partner. Jennifer, who lives in the suburban South, identifies as a queer cis-gendered woman and was married to a straight cis-gendered man for the first four years of parenting. Before they had children, she thought he'd make a good parent — like so many other husbands, he articulated a desire to evenly split the labor of children between them. When they had their first child, her husband was in med school, and Jennifer, who is trained as a lawyer, found a flexible job with a relatively low hourly requirement, which allowed her to take on the majority of the domestic labor. Later, when they struggled to find childcare that fit her hours, she was forced to quit. "It seemed like the right choice for our family," she explained, "even though it meant basically abandoning my legal career."

But the more she gave up in her working life, the more she had to do at home—especially after the birth of their second child: "Expectations of what I did only went up, and contributions from my partner only went down, as he insisted he was too tired to help." He refused to get up, at any point, if one of the children woke up in the middle of the night, insisting he needed a full night's sleep for work.

The guiding logic of this scenario is, in many ways, well-intentioned—and reproduced in homes across the country that would reject the label of "traditional." One parent stays home out of necessity; the other stays with their high-pressure, long-hour job, with the hope that it'll one day pay dividends: "You tend to defer to your spouse and just power through," Jennifer explains, "with the idea that you can one day be more relaxed and comfortable and stable, with the hope that they don't divorce you before that happens."

Jennifer's husband, like many partners of those who work at home, viewed all domestic care as her "job." But as Jennifer points out, it was a job that didn't pay, that required her to be on call twenty-four/seven, and had no breaks. And if she asked for his help, or didn't get something done, the assumption that she just wasn't working hard enough hung there, unspoken, in the air. Was she taking naps while he was at work? Watching too much television? She felt untrusted and unvalued and, most of all, exhausted.

"I saw this dynamic play out in my own marriage, even though I had been the breadwinner of the home for several years, and was the one with better immediate job prospects," Jennifer said. "But I've also seen it play out among my friends, many of whom are still married because they do not know how they could function otherwise." It doesn't matter how mad or tired you feel, after all, when it seems like you have no other options. And it's hard for others to understand why you're so mad and tired when they don't see that your work, in or outside the home, has value.

*   *   *

Economic insecurity makes parents *insecure*. What they do to fight against that insecurity tends to depend on their current class—and, by extension, the level of insecurity they experience. There's a difference between worrying over whether your kid will have enough food for the week, for example, and worrying that your kid can't go to the same expensive college prep summer camp as their friends.

In practice, both strategies are informed by and produce burnout. But it's a particular sort of exhaustion to be poor. It's exhausting to be stigmatized by society, to navigate social programs intended to help that mostly shame. A social worker once told me that he feels that American bureaucracy for aid is intentionally and endlessly tedious as a means to deter those who need it most. All the decisions and multitasking that are already hard to juggle when you're well-nourished and have a safe and consistent place to live become immeasurably more difficult when you don't have those elements in place.

Researchers have found that poverty imposes a "cognitive load" on the poor—there's so much mental energy devoted to finding and maintaining the basics of life that there's little left over to, say, research, save, register, and attend night school, let alone find the energy to do the homework.[23] Paying bills on time is a struggle for people who are middle class and burnt out; think of how much harder it is when you don't have a computer or the extra money for a stamp.

In *Scarcity: Why Having So Little Means So Much,* the economist Sendhil Mullainathan and the psychologist Eldar Shafir break down the ways in which "scarcity captures the mind." As Shafir explained in an interview with *CityLab,* "When your bandwidth is loaded, in the case of the poor, you're just more likely to not notice things, you're more likely to not resist things you ought to resist, you're more likely to forget things, you're going to have less patience, less attention to devote to your children when they come back from school." Poor parents don't "arrive" at burnout. They've never left it.

Lorraine, who's white and identifies as lower class, became a stay-at-home mom when she and her husband couldn't afford childcare. They're getting a deal on rent, but depend heavily on family and food stamps to get by. "I can't afford to take my daughter to toddler classes, and we don't get to go on trips," she says. "I constantly worry about having enough diapers, and there's limited public transportation or walkable areas where I live, and there's many times when I don't have a car to even bring us to the park." All of it makes her feel more burnt out, especially when others in her community make comments about her daughter's normal scrapes and bruises—and connect it to the fact that she sometimes attends a home daycare or the church nursery. It doesn't matter how hard she works to try to parent "right"; others will always shame her for not doing more.

Nana, who identifies as Jewish Israeli and lives in a small suburb, describes "constant fear, stress, anxiety and isolation" as a single parent who's poor. She chose a career path that would allow her to be with her son more, but now finds herself taking on extra work after hours to make ends meet. "Work never ends," she says. "Money is never a sure thing. It makes it much harder to be present for my boy." Lauren is a "financially lower class" full-time college student in the Pacific Northwest, co-parenting her two kids with her husband, who works nights and sleeps during the day. Her burnout intensifies with "the added stress of trying to figure out how bills are getting paid, how to trim the budget, and how far apart ends are going to be in any given month."

And when you're "attempting to be middle class," but also attempting to parent a child with special needs, every task feels exponentially more difficult. "You want to talk about parenting burnout?" Meredeth, who is white and lives outside of Pittsburgh, asked.

"Talk to the parents of special needs kids. We invented parenting burnout."

Meredith describes burnout as the feeling "of having a hundred balls in the air, and knowing you're going to drop some of them, but not knowing which ones and how vital they'll be and the fallout of dropping them." She's constantly trying to figure out how to fit in "one more therapy" for her child in their schedule — but also wondering "Is the therapy worth it? Can we access it? Who must we fight to get it?" Cheryl, who describes herself as white, queer, and neurodivergent, and cares full-time for her disabled children, feels like she's constantly battling the desire to give up, because there's just no way she can possibly "do it right." "What would that mean, anyway?" she asks. "But continuing to try too hard might literally kill me — I might keel over from exhaustion or a heart attack."

Money can help relieve the symptoms of economically exacerbated burnout. But symptom relief is different from a cure. Stephanie, a Latina college professor, blames burnout for the destruction of her marriage. As she gained stability (and a firmly upper middle-class status) she was able to get divorced, and find a therapist, and avoid, in her words "flaming out." But she keeps the anxiety of financial insecurity with her. "Growing up working class means I am always worried about savings, and the fact that I don't think I can help my kids with much beyond college," she said. "And I am still fucking tired and wake up worrying about how to pay for summer camps and braces."

* * *

Upper-middle-class parents like Stephanie aren't worried about covering basic financial expenses. They're worried about downward mobility: If Stephanie's kids don't go to summer camp or get braces, will their chances of maintaining middle-class status go down? It might seem silly, but it's a real and motivating fear: To fall in class status is to reverse the hard-earned upward mobility of your grandparents, your parents, or yourself. It feels abjectly un-American. Which is why so many parents drive themselves deeper into burnout to avoid it.

Take the example of Casey, who lives in the outer suburbs of Philadelphia and identifies as white and middle class. She works as an attorney, and her husband is a nurse. But they have four kids, and recently declared bankruptcy. "If we don't have money, how do we send our kids to camps in the summer and get tutoring for our special needs child?" she asked. "How do we get to birthday parties and keep social plans when we don't have the finances to do so?" What they did, like millions of other people barely holding on to the middle-class lifestyle, was go deeply into debt.

Meredith, a self-described "overeducated white lady," articulates her burnout in terms of rage, "usually over the relentlessness of the job intersecting with the relentlessness of the household," plus the "obnoxious" task of maintaining appearances in her neighborhood. "We have to keep the house well maintained to appease the HOA," she explained, "and if the kids' friends are engaged in X activity, my husband feels guilty if our kids don't join them, so I go along with it so that my husband stops asking about X activity, but then I find myself the only one responsible for where X activity gear is stored and making sure it's clean." And then, she says, "I feel bad about myself for feeling burnout over #richwhiteladyproblems because they are so trivial compared to other people's problems."

Despite their economic security, Meredith says that all of her parenting decisions "come from the place of 'Does this make it more or less likely that my kid will want to live in my basement at thirty?'" In other words: How can they be in a place, both financially and psychologically, of independence? For Alexa, who lives in a small town in northern Idaho, her burnout decreased substantially when her family moved from the East Coast, where "there was a lot more pressure to have the right things and afford private school." In Idaho, they make enough money to work less and pay extra for childcare, including a nanny. "We feel secure," she said, "but saving enough for college still feels very stressful."

That anxiety often plays out in the form of *more* activities. Some middle-class millennials grew up with packed schedules —but those pale in comparison to the way middle-class millennials now feel compelled to schedule their own children, beginning as early as infancy. In *The Playdate: Parents, Children, and the New Expectations of Play,* Tamara R. Mose interviewed parents across New York City about playdates and the unspoken "rules" that guide them. It's not surprising that she found that the primary instigators of playdates aren't kids, but parents—who, despite already packed schedules, always made time for playdates. Not because they took labor off the parents (in many cases, both parents were present for a playdate) but because of "social connectedness," or *class* connectedness, for both the parent and the child.

The transformation from "going to play" to "playdate" formalizes what was once a casual component of a child's life. It moves from child directed ("I'm gonna go play over at Emily's house") to parent appointed, with expectations of parent-guided crafts, snacks, and socialization. And because it's parent guided, it's the parents who decide which other parents are the "right" ones to be socializing with: Almost always, parents of the same class, education level, and parenting style as themselves. In this way, Mose argues, the playdate becomes a primary site of elite social class "reproduction"—even in a place as economically diverse as New York City.

Middle-class parents can be outrageously (if subconsciously) snobby—but their fear of another family's "poor" parenting habits is just another version of that same old class anxiety and instability. When a parent attempts to make connections with the "right" sort of families, what they're really trying to do is build an insurance policy that their kid will maintain those bourgeois connections, habits, and familiarity for the rest of their lives. Within this logic, spending time with the "wrong" kind of family is like exposure to a contagion, threatening to forever infect a child with the disease of downward mobility.

Depending on a parent's place within the economic spectrum, they might expend outsize energy trying to arrange "appropriate" playdates—or conceal that their family might not be appropriate playdate material. Amy, a white mother who lives in Toronto, told me that she *hates* hosting playdates—not because of the kids themselves, but because of what might happen if the other parents know about their class status. "I fear what they will say to their parents because we are renting an apartment and don't own a proper house," she said. "I stress about what to feed them, so that I can appear to adhere to norms around food prep, and I stress that my house isn't clean enough, and that our IKEA furniture is substandard." She always offers to handle all pickups and drop-offs—creating more work for herself—to make sure the other parents don't see their living situation.

In an interview with Malcolm Harris, Mose herself describes the pressure, as a Black mother, to ensure her kids play "the right way": "I always wanted to present as a decent black family because I know of all the stereotypes out there about black families and black children," she said. "So I always wanted to make sure my home was clean, I always wanted to make sure that appropriate food was being offered, and appropriate, meaning organic or fruits and vegetables, not junky food or anything like that."[24] It's labor, in other words, to prove to bourgeois white parents that your kid is worthy to associate with theirs.

Harris compares the playdate to a form of private school, in which "wealthier parents remove their kids from public and sequester them somewhere with a guest list and a cover charge." Which is actually a pretty great way to describe the new bourgeois kid's birthday. When I was growing up, I had a party at the roller-skating rink, and another with the theme of my favorite book (*The Eleventh Hour*). My mom still complains about it. But I was the one directing these parties—and making the invite lists. The contemporary party, especially for young children, is almost laughably transparent in its attempt at class reproduction.

"The birthday party is not necessarily for the child, although many attempt to portray the party as being about the birthday child," Mose writes. Instead, it's a manifestation of "panic": "a need to maintain the mother's identity and role in the community," and to display "economic advantage and thus class advantage."[25] On *Big Little Lies*—a show ostensibly about a murder, but actually about class maintenance—when Renata Klein (Laura Dern) learns that her husband's been arrested for fraud and their assets will be liquidated, she responds by throwing a lavish '70s-themed birthday party for her young daughter. There's no question who the party is for—or what it's meant to communicate.

Big Little Lies is a melodrama, but its plot hinges on only slightly outsize versions of modern parenting anxieties. I talked to a woman named Julie, who describes her family as white and upper-middle class and recently moved from a town near Westchester, New York, where "everyone was just TOO MUCH." A typical mom purchase: sets of Yogibo giant pillows for the kid's playroom (cost: a hundred dollars each). "I just decided that I wouldn't keep up, and would try to do my own thing," she said. "But then of course my son wanted a birthday party at one of those bounce house places. We wound up spending seven hundred dollars plus on a party for twelve kids."

Even parents like Julie who try to resist participating in the "social ritual" of birthdays get drawn in. Little kids, after all, just think they're going to a party—not a thinly veiled demonstration of class insecurity that makes every adult involved quietly hate themselves.

*   *   *

If parenting—like work, and technology—has become this hard, why don't we do anything about it? If it's so clearly a shared societal problem, why do we continue to delude ourselves into thinking it's a personal failure? Take the example of affordable, dependable childcare. It's ridiculously stressful to find. If it's dependable, it's rarely affordable; if it's affordable, it's rarely dependable. The stress of childcare routinely prompts one parent to unwillingly quit a job they love; it prompts other parents to work far more hours than they'd prefer just to cover the costs.

Affordable, universally available childcare—for young children, but also for children who need care in the hours before and after school—would be revelatory. It would lift a profound burden off so many parents, and mothers in particular. We subsidize farmers, we subsidize local business development, we flat-out fund public schooling. So why hasn't it happened?

There seems to be two interlocking, and deeply depressing reasons: Men still don't value domestic labor as labor, and men predominate our legislative bodies and the vast majority of our corporations. They don't treat contemporary parenting—its cost, or the burnout that accompanies it—as a problem, let alone a crisis, because they cannot, or refuse to, empathize with it. Whether or not these legislators identify as conservatives, or "pro-woman," or even "feminist" doesn't matter; what matters is that it has not become a legislative or corporate priority.

And while there are women in politics and the business world who do advocate for these policies, either they do not occupy the positions of power to enforce them, or if they do, they often use their platforms to demonstrate that change isn't needed. Marissa Meyer, formerly the CEO of Yahoo, famously refused to take more than two weeks of maternity leave after giving birth to her first child—a symptom of a work culture that will not accommodate the realities of parenthood, but also a symptom of her willingness to operate by and implicitly strengthen that same culture.

There are exceptions, of course: Patagonia has led the way in establishing subsidized, on-site childcare; at the Gates Foundation, every employee received a full year of parenting leave (which was recently cut to six months, plus $20,000 to pay for childcare costs). But solutions on the corporate level are not enough: As we've seen, the fissuring of the marketplace ensures they'll only extend to a certain class and echelon of worker. Relief from parenting burnout shouldn't be a middle-class privilege. After all, if you offer relief exclusively to the upper-middle class, the fear of "falling" to the lower class will remain. Put differently: You can get rid of the childcare costs, but that doesn't mean you'll get rid of the endless class performance birthday parties or Instagramming perfection.

The causes are systemic. Which is why the solutions have to be holistic. It's straightforward, really: Change the fundamental arrangement in which parenting occurs, and you'll change the way parenting *feels.* Which is why the solution to parenting burnout won't come from books like *Mommy Burnout,* written by a psychologist and family therapist, or *Girl, Stop Apologizing,* by an empowerment expert like Rachel Hollis. Those books address the symptoms of exhaustion (You don't have to be perfect! Ditch the mom guilt!) but avoid the larger, structural causes of that exhaustion. As Lockman very convincingly argues, one of the main ways to set a family up for enduring, equitable distribution of labor is when the non–birth parent takes significant leave, preferably alone.[26] During that time, the labor that would otherwise stay invisible — including, most importantly, the labor of carrying the mental load — becomes visible.

But that takes policy change. You can't fix parenting burnout by making time for Bible study or journaling in the morning, as Jessica Turner suggests in *Fringe Hours,* or by learning how to fight like an adult, as Jancee Dunn argues in *How Not to Hate Your Husband After Kids.* You can't fix it with "self-care," a concept originated by Audre Lorde to describe how to give oneself space to recover from the exhausting battle of fighting systemic oppression, then co-opted by privileged white women to grant permission to escape many of the standards and schedules they've (wittingly or not) helped perpetuate. You can make yourself (temporarily) feel better, but the world will still feel broken.

Parenting is never going to be free of worry, or comparison, or stress. But there can be significantly less of all of those things. To make that happen, we have to admit that it's not enough to have progressive ideals about parenting. Our current iteration of patriarchal capitalism destroys those ideals, no matter how earnest or deeply held, and replaces them with their regressive opposite: dramatically unequal distribution of domestic labor, generalized undervaluing of women's labor, and jobs engineered to favor those unburdened with primary childcare responsibilities.

That doesn't mean that making time for journaling, or going to therapy to work on labor distribution with your partner, or venting with friends won't make you feel better. But it won't make life for other parents — or your kids, when they become parents — easier. I find myself returning to one of the best pieces of advice I've received about how to actually reduce burnout: Think not just about how to reduce your own, but how your own actions are sparking and fanning burnout in others.

That's useful advice for any male partners reading this chapter, but it's useful for everyone, no matter how burnt out you find yourself, and regardless of your status as a parent. If you want to feel less exhausted, less resentful, less filled with unspeakable rage, less ground down to the thinnest, least likable version of yourself, then you have to act, vote, and advocate for solutions that will make life better not just for *you,* or people who look and speak and act like you and have families like yours — but for *everyone.*

CONCLUSION:
BURN IT DOWN

THERE WAS SOMETHING MISSING FROM THAT LAST chapter: me. I'm not a parent and, barring some dramatic life shift, won't be. People have all sorts of reasons for not having kids: They're unable to conceive, they don't particularly like kids, they don't think they'd be good or stable parents, they just don't *want* to. I don't have kids for multiple reasons — all of which can ultimately traced back to burnout and the culture it promotes.

Like an ever-growing number of millennials, I've "delayed" adult milestones: I didn't get a 401k until I was thirty-one. I didn't buy a house until I was thirty-seven, and then only because I moved out of New York. I'm still not married, and don't plan to be. Not because I don't have long-term plans with my partner, but because I just don't see the need. And then there's the kids

—if I got pregnant right now, my pregnancy would be considered "geriatric."

But did I choose to delay these things, or did societal realities make it difficult to do anything *other* than delay them? You can disagree with the decision to go to grad school, but I made it with the agreed-upon understanding that it would culminate in a steady job. I finished my program as quickly as I could, but not quickly enough to graduate before age thirty. I knew of other people who had babies in grad school—*Do it while you have healthcare! You can write your dissertation while the baby sleeps!*—but I was already working all the time, doing the same amount of work while also taking care of a baby seemed nothing short of miraculous.

I graduated and spent the following years chasing jobs around the country with barely a thousand dollars in my savings account—also not the optimal time to have a baby. And then I became a journalist, living in New York, in an apartment barely large enough for a dog, paying a quarter of my salary in student loan payments every month. Meanwhile, my friends started getting pregnant. They talked about strollers (expensive) and birth plans (even more expensive). I barely had enough money saved to cover either. Then they started talking about childcare plans, and how their parents would cover one day, or two. I realized I'd have none of that. They talked about nannies, and nanny shares, and paying double what I had been paid just over a decade before. How could I cover even a portion of those costs, and New York rent, and my student loan payment?

One friend quit the workforce altogether. Another went to a four-day week but was still putting in the same amount of work. There was no place to pump, in private, at work. Even the most ardently feminist of my friends seemed resigned to letting their husband perform far less than the equal amount of labor. I saw how hard they were working, every day, and how the exhaustion accumulated. They loved their kids so much—I loved their kids. I love kids! I was a nanny! They made it work. Why couldn't I?

That phrasing is instructive: They made parenting *work*. More work, endless work, compounding work. Children used to be a labor necessity: a mouth to feed but one that also *ameliorated* the amount of work to be done. But contemporary parenting standards mean that children *become* the work. You must work outside the home to get enough money to pay for their concerted cultivation, but also all the actual labor of concerted cultivation itself. The books I'd need to read, the groups I'd need to join, the stultifying group music classes I'd need to attend, the school choice stress I'd need to resist, the judgment I'd internalize and let expand within me until it devoured me entirely. Work, work, work.

That's why I couldn't see myself doing it: I was already working myself into the ground, spreading myself thin, barely getting by. More work—without support, without accommodation, or understanding—felt like it would disintegrate me entirely.

I know the objections: People make parenting a priority. And if you found yourself in that position, you could figure it out. But my industry, and my specialty within it, was already so precarious. Take away my ability to work all the time and you take away my ability to distinguish myself. Sure, I'd have a baby that I loved. I'd also probably be un- or underemployed.

When people consider having a kid, they often talk about "making the math work" in order to make it possible: They'd stop spending money on this budget item, or enlist a family member to replace an afternoon of care. Or they convince themselves, with various amounts of convenient delusion, that it won't be *that* hard—or that the hard part would only last a short amount of time.

I just could not make the math work. Financially, most of all, but even when I'd moved away from New York and found myself in a more stable financial situation, I couldn't make the math work in a different way. I'd worked so damn hard, over so many years, and had finally landed, with the help of a lot of luck, in a place of tentative security: in my job, in my personal life, with my partner. I'd read enough, and observed enough, to know how, in my particular scenario, children would explode all of that.

Now, I want to be very clear: Children, themselves, aren't social problems. Children are *great*. When I talked to parents about their burnout, I made sure to ask them, too, about what gives them great joy, and the answers were sublime. But the current organization of our society—of school, of work, of the way gender intersects with both—turns children into mini–life bombs. Not them, exactly, so much as the expectations and financial and labor realities that accompany them.

Every day, people decide that the wreckage is worth it. And, to be fair, I had decided, ten years before, that a different sort of wreckage—that of massive student loans—was worth it. And these days, children are much more valuable wrecking balls than a PhD, but the impulses that guide us toward these decisions remain the same: They just feel *right*, like the best possible choice we could make, like something we won't regret. Our hunger to reproduce, like our hunger for knowledge, creates a temporary amnesia, the ability to deny that the harsh lived reality will be that harsh or real for you.

You could call that mindset millennial (*I'm exceptional, and if I just work harder, things will be different for me*) or American, or just biologically human, as our minds trick us into reproducing our species. Our bodies, after all, have been doing something similar for millennia: Otherwise, how would you convince women to go through childbirth, again and again and again? But the history of modern civilization is also the history of women gradually figuring out that they can have the same choices as men: first, to not have as *many* children, and then, today, to not have children at all.

I made the decision not to have children. I understand that some might call it selfish—and that self-indulgence has become the necessary way to frame self-preservation. But if our society continues to make life hostile for parents in general and mothers in particular, it's a decision that more and more millennials will entertain.

In August 2019, NPR ran a piece on millennials titled "Less Sex, Fewer Babies." The piece, like so many of its genre, blames the decline on online dating, more time on the internet, and young men and women prioritizing their careers. Rashmi Venkatesh, who's thirty, married, and has a PhD in science, told NPR that she had envisioned a "fully formed professional life and a fully formed family life." But she simply cannot envision what taking three or four months off for maternity leave would do to her career—or how she'd pay for continued care. That fully formed family life idea "has gone by the wayside."[1]

Stories like Rashmi's—and stories like mine—are increasingly familiar. They're not just anecdotes; they accumulate to make significant statistical change. Between 2017 and 2018 alone, the birth rate dropped two percent. The total number of births hit a thirty-two-year low. These people not having kids—and enduring a "sex drought"? They're millennials. And while increased time on the internet, and dating apps, and career ambitions may be the *direct* cause for less sex and fewer children, the real cause is burnout.

We spend more time on the internet because being on the internet is our job—or because we're so fatigued that the only thing we're up for, during our approximation of leisure time, is social media, or a quick scroll of the news. We don't glom to dating apps because they make dating *better,* but because they make it *optimizable:* a line item we can attend to for five minutes between tasks. The actual number of dates goes down not because people don't know how to interpret online communication, as some suggest, but because actual dating—taking significant time to get to know someone, or multiple someones—deters from the time you could be working. That, or you struggle mightily to convince yourself, after a long day of staring at your computer, that you have the energy to interact with anyone other than your pet on a personal level. We don't have less sex because we're less sexual; we have less sex because we're *exhausted.*

We don't wait or opt against children because we love our careers so much more than we love babies. We just struggle to see how our society, in its current configuration, will allow us to do both without losing ourselves in the process. Women are already second-class citizens. When they become mothers, they only become more so—and have to work even harder to prove otherwise, or live in a way that refuses that fate.

For years, Americans have resigned themselves to burnout. Many of our parents did it in hopes of better, more secure, less burnt-out lives for us—and yet we still do it ourselves, today. We work harder for less, and blame our fatigue and precarity on our own failings instead of society's. But refusal to address burnout has consequences—on the individual, of course, but also on our country as a whole.

This isn't speculation. Just look at Japan, where the fertility rate, as of 2018, was just 1.42. To keep the country's population stable—not even growing, but *stable*—requires a 2.07 birth rate. But year after year, the number of births in Japan decrease. The birth rate in 2018 was the lowest since the country began keeping birth records all the way back in 1899.

In 1995, only 10 percent of Japanese women between the

ages of thirty-five to thirty-nine had never been married. In 2015, nearly a *quarter* of women in that age group were unmarried. Zoom out and it's easy to see why: Once they are married, working women are still expected to perform the vast majority of labor in the homes, and for their children. They spend hours hanging laundry, washing dishes, and cooking, and filling out the never-ending paperwork required for their children's preschools: logs of activities, daily records of activities and meals, sign-offs on every homework assignment. The Japanese version of Pinterest Parenting is the elaborate packed lunch, complete with a theme.

According to one study of government data, Japanese women who work more than forty-nine hours a week still do close to twenty-five hours of housework a week. Their husbands still average less than five. And even if a man wants to contribute more to household duties, the corporate culture of overwork makes it nearly impossible. Workers in all fields are expected to regularly entertain clients and bosses in a way that eclipses American standards.[2] To opt out is, well, not an option—which explains why, in 2018, only 6 percent of Japanese men working in the private sector actually took paternity leave. Of the full year available to working fathers, the average man took just *five days*.[3] As Kumiko Nemoto, a professor of sociology at Kyoto University, told the *New York Times*, "It's so obvious for a lot of women who have jobs that it's very difficult to find a man who is available to be a caretaker in the family."[4]

And burnout prevails: In 2017, employees at a quarter of Japanese companies were working more than eighty *overtime* hours, often unpaid, a month.[5] Workers receive twenty vacation days of leave a year, but 35 percent of them don't use a single day. There's even a Japanese word—*karoshi*—to specifically describe death from overwork. That word came into wide use in the 1980s, as

Japan was on the path to global dominance. But back then, overwork also meant lifetime security: You dedicated yourself to a job that, in turn, dedicated itself to you and your family's long-term care. That's no longer the case, but workers' hours and corporate pressure remain steady.

In recent years, the Japanese government has undergone efforts to stanch what it has come to view as a birth *and* labor crisis threatening the future of the nation as a whole. There have been pro-birth, pro-marriage campaigns, and "Premium Friday" mandates, which force employers to allow all workers to leave at three p.m. on Friday on the last week of the month without deduction of pay, as well as attempts to curb compulsory overtime without pay.[6] In January 2019, the country's environmental minister made headlines after announcing that he planned to take time off after the birth of his child: a whopping two weeks, spread over three months. But many Japanese remain skeptical that any of these changes will produce substantive change. Japanese working mothers no longer have to work until ten p.m., but that doesn't mean that their husbands don't — or that those same women won't be overlooked for promotions or other opportunities in the workplace simply because they couldn't evidence their dedication in the same manner as their male coworkers.

Japan waited until it was at a crisis point — and only then decided to act. But those actions fail to holistically address both the culture of burnout and the gender imbalance that accompanies it. Faced with the prospect of working themselves into the ground on their own — and excelling — or working themselves into the ground while *also* doing all the work for the family as their careers are stymied at every turn, it's no wonder that so many Japanese women are opting out: of marriage, of motherhood, or the idea that womanhood *requires* either.

Japan is unique, people will say. *That won't happen here.* But Japan's ideological compunctions and contradictions are no more or less unique than those of the United States, or any other country's. What's happened in Japan isn't unique, but instructive: a clear signal that when a society ignores, incentivizes, demands, or otherwise standardizes burnout, it compromises itself. The resulting imbalance might not be immediately apparent. But with time, cracks in a nation's most cherished ideological foundations — that hard work is rewarded, that the best succeed, that education is paramount, that *things will work out* — grow and become unwieldy. In America, we've attempted to fill those cracks with the quick fix of *more work*: *more* emails, more kids' activities, more social media posts. We keep going, past the point of exhaustion, because what would happen if we didn't?

But slowly, something has begun to shift. Maybe you broke down, but most likely you didn't. Maybe you got sick of reading too many "life hack" blog posts and want to throw your phone out the window. Maybe you went on vacation and felt nothing. Maybe you realized you were checking Instagram for seemingly no reason at a stoplight. Maybe it's happening right now, as you read this book. Whatever that shift in your own life looks like, the revelation remains the same: *It doesn't have to be this way.*

That's an incredibly liberating thought: that what we've been taught is "just the way things are" doesn't have to be. Just because we've reconciled ourselves to our current reality doesn't mean it's right. Because this is the truth, which becomes no less true if others have had to endure it: We shouldn't have to choose between excelling in work and thriving as individuals. We should feel good about listening to our bodies when they tell us, in every way they know how, that we should *stop*. Parenting shouldn't be a contest. Leisure shouldn't be this scarce. Domestic labor shouldn't even be close to this unequal. We shouldn't be this worried, this terrified, this anxious about *everything*.

What if we don't resign ourselves to working until we or the planet dies? Or refuse to accept that shitty pay is just what we deserve if we do meaningful work? What if we refuse to allow work to seep into every crevice of our lives? The stock market shouldn't be our indication of economic health. Private equity should be banned or highly regulated. The rich shouldn't be nearly this rich and the poor shouldn't be nearly this poor. And we shouldn't excuse any of these inexcusable realities in the name of old, broken myths about who we are and what we stand for—particularly when their endurance only stands to benefit those already in power.

We don't need anarchy, per se, but we do need an acknowledgment of how close we are to collapse—and how ready we are for substantive change. Both tendencies, after all, can be readily exploited. You can draw a crooked line between burnout, and the despair and existential crises that accompany it, and white nationalism, virulent online misogyny, and neofascism. Instead of identifying the real reason for our emotional and financial precarity, millennials have and will turn their eyes and blame where directed. Toward other mothers, toward immigrants, toward people not like us or more scared than us. Desperation drives people to decisions that in the moment make some sort of sense and promise some sort of relief. Just because they're inexcusable doesn't mean they're not explainable.

Burnout has enveloped our current iteration of capitalism. It inflects and infects every interaction; it haunts every decision. It dulls and flattens us; it's so familiar, we forget to be frightened by it. We're only just now beginning to see its long-term effects and treat them seriously. Which means that now, too, is the time to act.

But I don't have a specific list of action items for you. I'm trying, as best as I can, to show, not tell. Every book I read about the economy, or our unwitting addiction to our phones, or the exhaustion of parenting—they all concluded with *solutions*. Some included handy checklists and little boxes of "everyday tips" that could change your day-to-day life; some had extensive, detailed policy solutions. All of those ideas were compelling, and interesting, and deeply unhelpful. Just another way, in the end, for me to fail myself and the world.

Which is why this project, from its original conception as an article to now, has never been about telling you what to do. I can't fix you when it's society that's broken you. Instead, I've tried to provide a lens for you to see yourself and the world around you clearly. So look at your life. At your thoughts about work. About your relationship to your kids. At your fears and your phone and your email account. Look squarely at your fatigue and remind yourself that there's no app, or self-help book, or meal-planning scheme that can lift it. It is a symptom of living as a millennial in the world today. And depending on your race and class and job and debt and immigration status, it is exacerbated even more. But you are not powerless to change it. You can't optimize yourself to beat it, or work harder to make it go away faster. Because you can find and feel solidarity with so many others who feel—if not exactly the same—similarly.

So here's what we *can* do. We can unite in our resistance to the way things are. We can refuse to blame ourselves for wide-scale societal failures, but also understand how fear of losing one's already tenuous standing makes us overly protective of the privileges we do have. We can recognize that it's not enough to try to make things better for our ourselves. We have to make things better for *everyone*. Which is why actual substantive change has to come from the public sector—and we must vote *en masse* to elect politicians who will agitate for it tirelessly.

We don't have to value ourselves and others by the amount of work that we do. We don't have to resent our parents or grandparents for having it easier than us. We don't have to submit to the idea that racism or sexism will be with us forever. We can come to the spectacular and radical understanding that we are each valuable simply because we *are*. We can feel so much less alone, so much less exhausted, so much more *alive*. But there's a lot of work involved in realizing that the way to get there isn't, in fact, working more.

Millennials have been denigrated and mischaracterized, blamed for struggling in situations that set us up to fail. But if we have the endurance and aptitude and wherewithal to work ourselves this deeply into the ground, we also have the strength to fight. We have little savings and less stability. Our anger is barely contained. We're a pile of ashes smoldering, a bad memory of our best selves. Underestimate us at your peril: We have so little left to lose.

ACKNOWLEDGMENTS

Abiding gratitude to the following: Karolina Waclawiak and Rachel Sanders, my editors at BuzzFeed, for ushering the original burnout piece from conception to conclusion, and just generally refining my wild ideas; to the rest of the BuzzFeed Culture team, past and present (Scaachi Koul, Pier Dominguez, Alison Willmore, Bim Adewunmi, Tomi Obaro, Michael Blackmon, Shannon Keating); to my steadfast agent, Allison Hunter, who's been with me from the very beginning, and helped match me with the editorial insight and patience of my editor, Kate Napolitano, who's lit the way through three very different books. Thank you, as well, to the teams at Janklow & Nesbit and HMH, who've facilitated every step of the process and tolerated my own intermittent inability to address my email inbox of shame. To my friends from the pre-burnout days, or at least burnout-in-training days, who keep me grounded in a life far from the internet (Alaina Fuld, Anna Pepper, Beth Randall, Lauren Stratford, Gretchen Fauske, Meghan Frazier, Lauren Hamilton, Keely Rankin, Kate Belchers), and to my favorite text message feminists (Doree Shafrir, Julie Gerstein, Jenna Weiss-Berman). To Jason Williams, who helped me excavate the memories of class and child-rearing in 1980s northern Idaho, and to my fact-checkers, Clementine Ford and Ian Stevenson, whose work is invisible yet truly invaluable. To my long-standing Facebook group—you know who you are—who've helped workshop so many of these ideas, and to the literal thousands of you who responded to surveys and tweets and queries about how burnout became the background of your own lives. This book is what it is because of your testimonies. To my mom, Laura Bracken, a devastating and talented editor who helped tighten every sentence in this book, and to my brother, Charles Petersen, an actual and excellent historian of the twentieth century, who helped call bullshit on my more bombastic claims and reshape and substantiate them. And to my partner, Charlie Warzel, who, in addition to living the story that I tell here, has read every word, and made me, and this book, better on so many levels. You are my person.

NOTES

Author's Note

1. Annie Lowrey, "Millennials Don't Stand a Chance," *Atlantic*, April 13, 2020.

Introduction

1. H. J. Freudenberger, "Staff Burn-Out," *Journal of Social Issues* 30, no. 1 (1974): 159–65.
2. Ibid.
3. "Burn-out an "occupational phenomenon": "International Classification of Diseases." World Health Organization, May 28, 2019.
4. Richard Fry, "Millennials Projected to Overtake Baby Boomers as America's Largest Generation," *Pew Research Center,* March 1, 2018.
5. Erik Klinenberg, *Palaces for the People: How Social Infrastructure Can Help Fight Inequality, Polarization, and the Decline of Civic Life* (New York: Crown, 2018), 10.

6. Kristen Bialik and Richard Fry, "Millennial Life: How Young Adulthood Today Compares with Prior Generations," *Pew Research Center,* February 14, 2019.

7. Tiana Clark, "This Is What Black Burnout Feels Like," BuzzFeed News, January 11, 2019.

8. Tressie McMillan Cottom, "Nearly Six Decades After the Civil Rights Movement, Why Do Black Workers Still Have to Hustle to Get Ahead?" *Time,* February 20, 2020.

9. Judith Scott-Clayton, "What Accounts for Gaps in Student Loan Default, and What Happens After," *Brookings Institute,* June 21, 2018.

1. Our Burnt-Out Parents

1. Hunter Schwartz, "Old Economy Steve Is a New Meme That Will Enrage Millennials Everywhere," BuzzFeed, May 25, 2013.

2. Taylor Lorenz, "'OK Boomer' Marks the End of Friendly Generational Relations," *New York Times,* January 15, 2020.

3. Tom Wolfe, "The 'Me' Decade and the Third Great Awakening," *New York Magazine,* August 23, 1976.

4. Marc Levinson, *An Extraordinary Time: The End of the Postwar Boom and the Return of the Ordinary Economy* (New York: Basic Books, 2016), 5.

5. Elliot Blair Smith and Phil Kuntz, "CEO Pay 1,795-to-1 Multiple of Wages Skirts U.S. Law," *Bloomberg Businessweek*, April 29, 2013.

6. Louis Hyman, *Temp: How American Work, American Business, and the American Dream Became Temporary* (New York: Viking, 2018), 4.

7. Jacob S. Hacker, *The Great Risk Shift: The New Economic Insecurity and the Decline of the American Dream* (New York: Oxford University Press, 2019), xiii.

8. Robert Putnam, *Our Kids: The American Dream in Crisis* (New York: Simon & Schuster, 2015), 1.

9. Levinson, *An Extraordinary Time.*

10. Quoted in Barbara Ehrenreich, *Fear of Falling: The Inner Life of the Middle Class* (New York: Pantheon, 1989), 68–69.

11. Midge Decter, *Liberal Parents, Radical Children* (New York: Coward, McCann & Geohegan, 1975).

12. Ehrenreich, *Fear of Falling.*
13. Ibid.
14. Hacker, *The Great Risk Shift,* 40.
15. Ibid., 27.
16. Joseph C. Sternberg, *The Theft of a Decade: How Baby Boomers Stole the Millennials' Economic Future* (New York: Public Affairs, 2019), 72.
17. "Workplace Flexibility 2010: A Timeline of the Evolution of Retirement in the United States," Georgetown University Law Center; "Employee Benefits Survey," U.S. Bureau of Labor and Statistics.
18. Michael Hiltzik, "Two Rival Experts Agree — 401(k) Plans Haven't Helped You Save Enough for Retirement," *Los Angeles Times,* November 5, 2019.
19. Maurice A. St. Pierre, "Reaganomics and Its Implications for African-American Family Life," *Journal of Black Studies* 21, no. 3 (1991): 325–40.
20. Ehrenreich, *Fear of Falling,* 3.
21. Matthias Doepke and Fabrizio Zilibotti, *Love, Money, and Parenting: How Economics Explains the Way We Raise Our Kids* (Princeton, NJ: Princeton University Press, 2019), 70.
22. Ehrenreich, *Fear of Falling,* 10.
23. Katherine S. Newman, *Falling from Grace: The Experience of Downward Mobility in the American Middle Class* (New York: Free Press, 1988).
24. Ehrenreich, *Fear of Falling,* 210.
25. Dylan Gottlieb, "Yuppies: Young Urban Professionals and the Making of Postindustrial New York" (Unpublished PhD dissertation, Princeton University, May 2020).

2. Growing Mini-Adults

1. Hanna Rosin, "The Overprotected Kid," *Atlantic,* April 2014.
2. Sharon Hays, *The Cultural Contradictions of Motherhood* (New Haven: Yale University Press, 1996).
3. Doepke and Zilibotti, *Love, Money, Parenting,* 14.
4. Newman, *Falling from Grace,* 229.
5. Ibid., 202.

3. College at Any Cost

1. Alexandra Robbins, *The Overachievers: The Secret Lives of Driven Kids* (New York: Hyperion, 2006).
2. "Percentage of the U.S. Population Who Have Completed Four Years of College or More from 1940 to 2018, by Gender," Statista.com
3. "Educational Attainment in the United States: 2018," United States Census Bureau, February 21, 2019.
4. Ellen Ruppel Shell, "College May Not Be Worth It Anymore," *New York Times,* May 16, 2018.
5. W. Norton Grubb and Marvin Lazerson, *The Education Gospel: The Economic Power of Schooling* (Cambridge, MA: Harvard University Press, 2004).
6. Malcolm Harris, *Kids These Days: Human Capital and the Making of Millennials* (New York: Little, Brown and Company, 2017).
7. Ibid.

4. Do What You Love and You'll Still Work
Every Day for the Rest of Your Life

1. Amanda Mull, "America's Job Listings Have Gone Off the Deep End," *Atlantic,* June 13, 2019.
2. Ibid.
3. Miya Tokumitsu, *Do What You Love: And Others Lies About Success and Happiness* (New York: Regan Arts, 2015), 7.
4. Sara Robinson, "Why We Have to Go Back to a 40-Hour Work Week to Keep Our Sanity," *Alternet,* March 13, 2012.
5. Tokumitsu, *Do What You Love,* 7.
6. Ibid., 113.
7. "Great Recession, Great Recovery? Trends from the Current Population Survey," U.S. Bureau of Labor Statistics, April 2018.
8. Christopher Kurz, Geng Li, and Daniel J. Vine, "Are Millennials Different?" *Finance and Economics Discussion Series,* 2018.
9. Tokumitsu, *Do What You Love,* 88.
10. J. Stuart Bunderson and Jeffery A. Thompson, "The Call of the Wild: Zookeepers, Callings, and the Double-Edged Sword of Deeply Meaningful Work," *Administrative Science Quarterly* 54, no. 1 (2009): 32–57.

11. Ellen Ruppell Shell, *The Job: Work and Its Future in a Time of Radical Change* (New York: Currency, 2018).

5. How Work Got So Shitty

1. Guy Standing, *The Precariat: The New Dangerous Class* (New York: Bloomsbury Academic, 2014), 7.
2. Ibid., x.
3. Ibid., 23.
4. Hyman, *Temp*, 7.
5. David Weil, *The Fissured Workplace: Why Work Became So Bad for So Many and What Can Be Done to Improve It* (Cambridge, MA: Harvard University Press, 2014), 50.
6. Ibid., 46.
7. Ibid.
8. Laurel Wamsley, "Denver Post Calls Out Its 'Vulture' Hedge Fund Owners in Searing Editorial," NPR, April 9, 2018.
9. Tara Lachapelle, "Lessons Learned from the Downfall of Toys "R" Us," *Bloomberg Business,* March 9, 2018.
10. Matt Stoller, "Why Private Equity Should Not Exist," *BIG,* July 30, 2019.
11. Abha Bhattarai, "Private Equity's Role in Retail Has Killed 1.3 Million Jobs, Study Says," *Washington Post,* July 24, 2019.
12. Sarah Todd, "The Short but Destructive History of Mass Layoffs," *Quartz,* July 12, 2019.
13. Daisuke Wakabayashi, "Google's Shadow Work Force: Temps Who Outnumber Full-Time Employees," *New York Times,* May 28, 2019.
14. Ibid.
15. Weil, *Fissured Workplace,* 14.
16. "Survey Shows Two in Five Women in Fast-Food Industry Face Sexual Harassment on the Job," National Partnership for Women and Families, October 5, 2016.
17. Weil, *Fissured Workplace,* 7.
18. Samantha Raphelson, "Advocates Push for Stronger Measures to Protect Hotel Workers from Sexual Harassment," NPR, June 29, 2018.
19. "Hands Off, Pants On: Harassment in Chicago's Hospitality Industry," a report by Unite Here Local 1, July 2016.

20. The overturn is currently being appealed and the outcome is unknown at the time of this writing.

21. Weil, *Fissured Workplace*, 8.

22. Hyman, *Temp*, 270.

23. Karen Zouwen Ho, *Liquidated: An Ethnography of Wall Street* (Durham: Duke University Press, 2009), 3.

24. Louis Jacobson, "What Percentage of Americans Own Stocks," *Politifact*, September 18, 2018.

25. Alex Rosenblat, *Uberland: How Algorithms Are Rewriting the Rules of Work* (Oakland: University of California Press, 2018).

26. Zeynep Ton, *The Good Jobs Strategy: How the Smartest Companies Invest in Employees to Lower Costs and Boost Profits* (Boston: Houghton Mifflin Harcourt, 2014), viii.

27. Ibid., 8.

28. Ibid., 10.

6. How Work Stays So Shitty

1. Hyman, *Temp*, 82.

2. Ibid.

3. Ibid.

4. Ho, *Liquidated*, 89.

5. Ibid., 90.

6. Ibid., 56.

7. Ibid, 95.

8. Jodi Kantor and David Streitfeld, "Inside Amazon: Wrestling Big Ideas in a Bruising Workplace," *New York Times*, August 15, 2015.

9. Jonathan Crary, *24/7: Late Capitalism and the End of Sleep* (New York: Verso, 2014), 13.

10. Jia Tolentino, "The Gig Economy Celebrates Working Yourself to Death," *The New Yorker*, March 22, 2017.

11. Sarah Krouse, "The New Ways Your Boss Is Spying on You," *Wall Street Journal*, July 19, 2019.

12. Ibid.

13. Ruppel Shell, *The Job*, 128.

14. Ceylan Yeginsu, "If Workers Slack Off, the Wristband Will Know (and Amazon Has a Patent for It)." *New York Times*, February 1, 2018.

15. Emily Guendelsberger, "I Was a Fast-Food Worker. Let Me Tell You About Burnout," *Vox*, July 15, 2019.

16. "Key Findings from a Survey on Fast Food Worker Safety," Hart Research Associates, March 16, 2015 (http://www.coshnetwork .org/sites/default/files/FastFood_Workplace_Safety_Poll_Memo .pdf).

17. Sarah Kessler, *Gigged: The End of the Job and the Future of Work* (New York: St. Martin's Press, 2018), xii.

18. Rosenblat, *Uberland*, 5; 9.

19. Farhad Manjoo, "The Tech Industry Is Building a Vast Digital Underclass," *New York Times*, July 26, 2019.

20. Kessler, *Gigged*, 9.

21. Ibid., 19.

22. Aaron Smith, "The Gig Economy: Work, Online Selling, and Home Sharing," *Pew Research Center*, November 17, 2016.

23. Kessler, *Gigged*, 103.

24. Ruppel Shell, *The Job*, 62.

25. Alex Rosenblat, "The Network Uber Drivers Built," *Fast Company*, January 9, 2018.

26. Ibid.

27. Eric Johnson, "Full Q&A: DoorDash CEO Tony Xu and COO Christoper Payne on Recode Decode," *Recode*, January 9, 2019.

7. Technology Makes Everything Work

1. Joanna Stern, "Cell Phone Users Check Phones 150x a Day and Other Fun Facts," ABCNews, May 29, 2013; Jonah Engel Bromwich, "Generation X More Addicted to Social Media Than Millennials, Report Finds," *New York Times*, January 27, 2017.

2. Rina Raphael, "Netflix CEO Reed Hastings: Sleep Is Our Competition," *Fast Company*, November 6, 2017.

3. Paul Lewis, "Our Minds Can Be Highjacked," *Guardian*, October 6, 2017.

4. Cal Newport, *Digital Minimalism: Choosing a Focused Life in a Noisy World* (New York: Portfolio/Penguin, 2019).

5. Katherine Miller, "President Trump and America's National Nervous Breakdown," BuzzFeed News, March 26, 2017.

6. Brad Stulberg, "Step Away from the 24-Hour News Cycle," *Outside,* December 1, 2018.

7. Nick Stockton, "Who Cares About My Friends? I'm Missing the News!" *Wired,* September 2017.

8. Rani Molla, "The Productivity Pit: How Slack Is Ruining Work," *Recode,* May 1, 2019.

9. John Herrman, "Slack Wants to Replace Email. Is That What We Really Want?" *New York Times,* July 1, 2019.

10. John Herrman, "Are You Just LARPing Your Job?" *Awl,* April 20, 2015.

8. What Is a Weekend?

1. "American Time Use Survey—2018," Bureau of Labor Statistics, June 19, 2019.

2. Juliet Schor, *The Overworked American: The Unexpected Decline of Leisure* (New York: BasicBooks, 1993), 66.

3. Ibid, 1.

4. Anna Weiner, *Uncanny Valley* (New York: Farrar, Straus and Giroux, 2020).

5. Andrew Barnes, *The Four-Day Week: How the Flexible Work Revolution Can Increase Productivity, Profitability, and Wellbeing, and Help Create a Sustainable Future* (London: Piatkus, 2020), 2.

6. Bill Chappell, "4-Day Workweek Boosted Workers' Productivity By 40%, Microsoft Japan Says," NPR, November 4, 2019.

7. Robert Booth, "Four-Day Week: Trial Finds Lower Stress and Increased Productivity," *Guardian,* February 19, 2019.

8. *Ex Parte Newman*, 9 Cal. 502 (Jan. 1, 1858).

9. Judith Shulevitz, *The Sabbath World: Glimpses of a Different Order of Time* (New York: Random House, 2010).

10. Elizabeth Currid-Halkett, *The Sum of Small Things: A Theory of the Aspirational Class* (Princeton, NJ: Princeton University Press, 2017).

11. Noreen Malone, "The Skimm Brains," *Cut,* October 28, 2018.

12. Kelsey Lawrence, "Why Won't Millennials Join Country Clubs," *CityLab,* July 2, 2018; "New NFPA Report Finds Significant Decline in Volunteer Firefighters," *National Volunteer Fire Council,* April 16,

2019; Linda Poon, "Why Americans Stopped Volunteering," *CityLab,* September 11, 2019.

13. Klinenberg, *Palaces for the People*, 18.

9. The Exhausted Millennial Parent

1. Gretchen Livingston, "About One-Third of U.S. Children Are Living with an Unmarried Parent," *Pew Research*, April 27, 2018.
2. Arlie Russell Hochschild, *The Second Shift* (New York: Penguin Books, 2003), 235.
3. Darcy Lockman, *All the Rage: Mothers, Fathers, and the Myth of Equal Partnership* (New York: Harper, 2019), 16.
4. Table 10: Time Adults Spent in Primary Activities While Providing Childcare as a Secondary Activity by Sex, Age, and Day of Week, Average for the Combined Years 2014–18, Bureau of Labor Statistics, https://www.bls.gov/news.release/atus.t10.htm.
5. Kim Brooks, *Small Animals: Parenthood in the Age of Fear* (New York: Flatiron, 2018).
6. Elizabeth Chmurak, "The Rising Cost of Childcare Is Being Felt Across the Country," *NBC News,* March 8, 2018.
7. Currid-Halkett, *Sum of Small Things*, 84.
8. Ibid.
9. Caitlin Daniel, "A Hidden Cost to Giving Kids Their Vegetables," *New York Times,* February 16, 2016.
10. Conor Friedersdorf, "Working Mom Arrested for Letting Her 9-Year-Old Play Alone in Park," *Atlantic,* July 15, 2014.
11. Lockman, *All the Rage,* 15.
12. Brigid Schulte, *Overwhelmed: Work, Love, and Play When No One Has the Time* (New York: Farrar, Straus and Giroux, 2014), 45.
13. Claire Cane Miller, "The Relentlessness of Modern Parenting," *New York Times,* March 26, 2019.
14. See Emily Matchar, *Homeward Bound: Why Women Are Embracing the New Domesticity* (New York: Simon & Schuster, 2013).
15. Schulte, *Overwhelmed,* 25.
16. Ibid, 29.

17. "Raising Kids and Running a Household: How Working Parents Share the Load," *Pew Research Center,* November 4, 2015.

18. Lockman, *All the Rage,* 25.

19. Claire Cane Miller, "Millennial Men Aren't the Dads They Thought They'd Be," *New York Times,* July 31, 2015.

20. Lockman, *All the Rage,* 90.

21. Ibid, 156.

22. Lockman, *All the Rage,* 33.

23. Anadi Mani, Sendhil Mullainathan, Eldar Shafir, and Jiaying Zhao, "Poverty Impedes Cognitive Function," *Science* 341, no. 6149 (2013): 976–80.

24. Malcolm Harris, "The Privatization of Childhood Play," *Pacific Standard,* June 14, 2017.

25. Tamara R. Mose, *The Playdate: Parents, Children, and the New Expectations of Play* (New York; New York University Press, 2016), 144.

26. Lockman, *All the Rage,* 219.

Conclusion: Burn It Down

1. Sam Sanders, "Less Sex, Fewer Babies: Blame the Internet and Career Priorities," NPR, August 6, 2019.

2. Makiko Inoue and Megan Specia, "Young Worker Clocked 159 Hours of Overtime in a Month. Then She Died." *New York Times,* October 5, 2017.

3. Motoko Rich, "A Japanese Politician Is Taking Paternity Leave. It's a Big Deal," *New York Times,* January 15, 2020.

4. Motoko Rich, "Japanese Working Mothers: Record Responsibilities, Little Help from Dad," *New York Times,* February 2, 2019.

5. Tomoko Otake, "1 in 4 firms in Japan Say Workers Log over 80 Overtime Hours a Month," *Japan Times*, October 7, 2016.

6. Philip Brasor, "Premium Friday Is Not About Taking a Holiday," *Japan Times,* February 25, 2017.

INDEX